THE FILMS OF SAM PECKINPAH

NEIL FULWOOD

D0884870

B T BATSFORD · LONDON

FOR
MICHAEL EATON

First Published 2002

© Neil Fulwood 2002

ISBN 07134 8733 X

A CIP catalogue record for this book is available from the British Library.

Printed in Spain

for the publishers

B T Batsford
64 Brewery Road
London N7 9NY
England
www.batsford.com

A member of the Chrysalis Group plc

CONTENTS

FILMOGRAPHY

TELEVISION

- *The Rifleman* series (1958–59). Story consultant on the first series. The episodes listed are those he wrote, co-wrote or directed: 'The Marshall', 'The Home Ranch', 'The Boarding House', 'The Money Gun', 'The Babysitter'.
- *The Westerner* series (1960). Producer. 'Jeff', School Day', 'Brown', 'Mrs Kennedy', 'Dos Pinos', 'The Courting of Libby', 'The Treasure', 'The Old Man', 'Ghost of a Chance', 'The Line Camp', 'Going Home', 'Hand on the Gun', 'The Painting'.
- *Dick Powell's Zane Grey Theater* (1959). Director. 'Trouble at Treces Cruces' (the pilot episode for *The Westerner*), 'Miss Jenny', 'Lonesome Road'.
- *The Dick Powell Theater* (1962). Director. 'Pericles on 31st Street', 'The Losers'.
- ABC Stage 67 (1966). Director. 'Noon Wine'.
- Bob Hope's Chrysler Theater (1966). Director. 'That Lady is My Wife'.

FILM

- *The Deadly Companions* (1961).
- *Ride the High Country*, a.k.a. *Guns in the Afternoon* (1962).
- *Major Dundee* (1965).
- *The Wild Bunch* (1969).
- *The Ballad of Cable Hogue* (1970).
- *Straw Dogs*, a.k.a. *Sam Peckinpah's Straw Dogs* (1971).
- *Junior Bonner* (1971).
- *The Getaway* (1972).
- *Pat Garrett and Billy the Kid* (1973).
- *Bring Me the Head of Alfredo Garcia* (1974).
- *The Killer Elite* (1975).
- *Cross of Iron* (1977).
- *Convoy* (1978).
- *The Osterman Weekend* (1983).

MUSIC VIDEO

- Julian Lennon, 'Valotte', 'Too Late for Goodbyes' (both 1984).

INTRODUCTION
'BLOODY SAM'

It's an unfair epithet, conjured up by critics who mistakenly thought he was no more than a director with a flair for violence. He was considerably more complex than that. Moralistic but not judgmental, tough but vulnerable, sensitive but stubborn. His sense of artistic integrity flew in the face of commercialism. Pressured to reduce the depth and thematic density of his work by studio executives who answered to the dollar, he stuck to his guns. As a result, he was removed from projects, locked out of post-production, his preferred cuts butchered. Almost every film he made was subject to interference. But damned if he didn't fight for his artistic vision.

Bloody Sam? Bloody-minded Sam, more like.

It's said that life imitates art. His life and art merged from the start. Whatever line might have been drawn between events behind the camera and the vision he forged in front of it, by the end that line had been worn away by booze and cocaine and a life spent living it like he told it.

Sam Peckinpah made films about men. Men who ride together. And he made them in collaboration with men whose loyalty to him was unchallenged. Actors Warren Oates, L Q Jones, Strother Martin, John Davis Chandler, R G Armstrong, Dub Taylor, Ben Johnson and Slim Pickens, cinematographers Lucien Ballard and John Coquillon, composer Jerry Fielding, editors Louis Lombardo, Robert L Wolfe and Roger Spottiswoode. They were his posse and he the last outlaw, a renegade, a desperado, outliving his time even as he cut a swathe through Hollywood, redefining the way that films would be made.

Maverick that he was, star names would be drawn back to him: James Coburn, David Warner and Kris Kristofferson each notch up three appearances in Peckinpah films, Steve McQueen and Ernest Borgnine two apiece. Even actors who only worked with him the once – William Holden, Robert Ryan, Dustin Hoffman, Al Lettieri, Stella Stevens, Susan George – give *tour de force* performances that it can be argued remain unmatched by anything else in their respective filmographies.

Part of Peckinpah's genius was that he could tap into other people's talent. Take Lucien Ballard. Outside of Sam's *oeuvre*, he lensed somewhere in the region of one hundred films, including *The Parent Trap, Hour of the Gun,* the Elvis Presley vehicle *Roustabout,* and *Breakheart Pass.* Undistinguished, all. The best that can be said is that they are nice looking. But on *Ride the High Country, The Wild Bunch* and *The Ballad of Cable Hogue,* his technical ability and eye for composition, allayed with Peckinpah's artistic vision and poet's soul, transcended nice visuals and took cinematography into the realms of art. Coquillon, too: Michael Reeves's *Witchfinder General* [1] was perhaps the only non-Peckinpah project he worked on that demonstrated the clarity of vision of *Straw Dogs, Pat Garrett and Billy the Kid* and *Cross of Iron.*

Cinematographer Lucien Ballard, pictured here with Ernest Borgnine on Ride the High Country – *they would work together again on* The Wild Bunch.

Technical accomplishment and verisimilitude of acting are only part of what sets Peckinpah's films apart. It is their depth and intensity that make them unique. And if what Peckinpah put on screen is breath-taking, the off-camera excesses that made it possible are just as remarkable. The crazed journey into Mexico undertaken by the ramshackle cavalry outfit in *Major Dundee* approximates that made by cast and crew. The horror stories that surrounded the production – arduous location shooting, haemorrhaging budget, demonically driven director – precede accounts of the equally lunatic leadership on Francis Ford Coppola's *Apocalypse Now* and Werner Herzog's *Fitzcarraldo* by more than a decade.

Giving direction to Oates, Jones, Chandler, James Drury and John Anderson, who play the Hammond brothers, the antagonists of *Ride the High Country*, he ordered them to stay apart from the rest of the cast and crew, and to drink and brawl together in order to find the characters' internal dynamic. A decade later, he applied the same technique on *Straw Dogs*, encouraging fights and bouts of wrestling. During shooting, T P McKenna suffered a broken arm, and production was shut down for five days when Peckinpah was hospitalised with pneumonia following a marathon drinking session with Ken Hutchinson which ended with them out at Land's End in the early hours of the morning, in the middle of a storm, singing drunkenly.

Or how about his relationship with Warren Oates? Given an ultimatum by his then wife not to accept a role in *The Wild Bunch* because of the ill-health he'd suffered during his previous collaboration with Peckinpah, *Major Dundee*, Oates made the choice between his marriage and his mentor without hesitation. He went to Mexico with Sam, made one of the greatest movies of all time, and got divorced.

Peckinpah's life away from film-making (such as it was – his need to express himself creatively on the largest possible canvas, the big screen, was overwhelming and all-encompassing; not just a need, but a *raison d'être*) was often troubled and destructive. It is no coincidence that when his heroes are not indulging in what is today referred to, rather wimpily, as 'male bonding', they are contemplating a lonelier perspective: the mistakes they have made, the chances they have passed up, the failure of love. In *Noon Wine*, an adaptation of a story by Katherine Anne Porter which he directed for television while exiled by the studios in the aftermath of *Major Dundee*, the breakdown of a marriage, brought about by a single unpremeditated moment of violence, is charted with chilling perception. The film is heartbreaking in its sense of waste, the ending – an act of suicide – as agonising as anything in *The Wild Bunch* or *Pat Garrett and Billy the Kid*.

Peckinpah's passage through life was marked by a string of twisted and broken relationships. Quizzed on how he came to understand so intuitively the psychology of his characters in *Straw Dogs*, he offhandedly replied that he'd simply been married a few times. If his films are anything to by (and they *are*, for his was a deeply personal vision), his attitude was something along the lines of 'damned if you do, damned if you don't'. His characters are either denied love because of their stubbornness or the transcience of their lifestyle, or experience love only for it to be taken away from them, usually by the intervention of death. Even the pleasant, laconic *Junior Bonner* unfolds against a backstory of parental estrangement.

But then Peckinpah was an intense man. Interviews with potential collaborators were often conducted to the accompaniment of knife-throwing, the door to Sam's office scarred with more notches than Casanova's bedpost. A disagreement with Charlton Heston on *Major Dundee* erupted into near-homicide when the actor, kitted out in full cavalry regalia, drew his regimental sword and charged at Peckinpah! While viewing dailies on *Pat Garrett and Billy the Kid*, Peckinpah was outraged to find that a damaged flange on a camera had rendered a week's worth of footage out of focus; he startled cast and crew by lumbering forward, unzipping, and urinating on the screen.

A man of Peckinpah's genius can be said, for want of a more scientific explanation of where such talent derives, to have been born with an innate sense of creativity, a spark of genius. But his temperament was formed by circumstances.

He was born David Samuel Peckinpah on 21 February 1925, David after his father. In childhood his family took to calling him 'D Sam'. By the time he was a man it was just Sam.

David Peckinpah was a successful lawyer, upstanding citizen and strict disciplinarian. He lived by the law and the Bible. Sam's inability, in early youth, to reconcile this aspect of his father with the man who meretriciously cross-examined witnesses on the stand, building them up to knock them down, goes some way to explaining the polarities that inform the films he would go on to direct. Likewise, while the romantic disillusionment he would so often portray was mirrored in his own turbulent relationships, it has its seeds in his parents' marriage.

His mother, Fern Church, was a highly strung woman whose betrothal to David Peckinpah was something of a second-best, occurring on the rebound from her first suitor, an apparently dubious type. Dubious enough, anyway, for Fern's father, Denver Church, to pay him off and see him out of town rather than accept him as a son-in-law.

Throughout her marriage to David, Fern would respond to threats to her matriarchy by complaining of headaches or nerves. Silence would descend on the house; everyone would walk on eggshells around her. Anyone behaving contrary to this, or daring to answer her back, would have David to deal with. Corporal punishment was part and parcel of Peckinpah's childhood, administered either by the hand or a strip cut from a birch tree.

With Fern's specialist brand of silent tension suffusing the household, it is easy to see why hunting trips into the mountains became such a strong draw for the men folk. They were a quartet: Denver Church, David, Denny (Sam's older brother) and Sam himself. The hunting trips became such a tradition that Sam continued them throughout his adult life. Still, they were a traumatic experience initially. David had seen the development of aestheticism in his son – an appreciation of poetry and art – and he and Denver decided such unmasculine qualities needed ironing out. They took him into the high country, put a rifle in his hands and told him to be a man.

It says a lot about Peckinpah's character that this proving-ground, this wilderness setting for his rite of passage, would be a place to which he would return, year after year.

David Peckinpah and Denver Church set themselves up as role models that Sam and Denny were expected to emulate. Denny conformed, quelling his own artistic aspirations (literary in his case) to follow his father into law. Sam took a different route. It was a journey that led from theatre to television and then to cinema. But before any of that, he made a decision that must have shocked even the machismo-laden David Peckinpah.

Just shy of his eighteenth birthday Sam joined the Marines. At Parris Island, he underwent a harsh training programme that made his father's disciplinary excesses look like a walk in the park. The way Marines were trained during the Second World War was psychologically similar to the Vietnam-era portrayal in Stanley Kubrick's *Full Metal Jacket*. Individuals were broken down, browbeaten, yelled at, punished and humiliated; then they were remoulded as a unit – a lean, effective fighting force. Peckinpah went through hell, but what he learned he would apply on film sets twenty years later. He would demand, expect and settle for no less than everybody's absolute best. He would fire crew members indiscriminately – no warnings, no second chances. But those who were left would follow him without question and give their all.

On completion of training, he was dispatched to China. It was 1945 and the decisive bombings of Nagasaki and Hiroshima had ended the war with Japan. The purpose of the Marines' presence in China was to oversee the disarmament and repatriation of Japanese troops there. Peckinpah saw the aftermath of conflict, gained experience of military procedure, and developed deeply ambivalent political views – all of which he would draw upon in *Cross of Iron*. He also discovered the joys of drinking and womanising. These, too, would be defining factors in his life.

His homecoming in 1946 was marked by a listlessness. His father still expected him to study law and join him and Denny in their practice. But law was conformity, and Sam wanted no part of it. He was looking for something else. He found it in the shape of the woman who would become his first wife, Marie Selland. She was studying acting. As their relationship grew, he enrolled at the same college, initially taking a history course to mollify his parents. He soon dropped out of it, his affinity for the dramatic arts proving too strong to be ignored. Marie was in love with the performing side of it, but Peckinpah's imagination had responded to what happened before the actors stepped up on stage. Preparation, rehearsals, textual analysis of the piece they were performing: Sam Peckinpah had discovered the keystones of directing.

By the time their studies at Fresno State College came to an end, Sam and Marie had married. Marie took work, while Sam continued his studies at USC; here, too, he had the opportunity to adapt and direct plays. With the birth of their first child, Peckinpah was financially compelled to relinquish his academic lifestyle and earn a wage. His temperament made him unsuited to the nine-to-five daily grind, and his artistic impulses were still as strong as ever, so when he was offered the post of director-in-residence at a local theatre, he accepted eagerly.

The workaholic in him began to manifest here. He put in hours above and beyond the requirements of the job. Work consumed him. This, coupled with his drinking and often frightening mood swings, would eventually destroy his marriage. In his capacity as director-in-residence he had his first experience of what might politely be termed 'creative differences'. Peckinpah wanted to direct powerful dramas by William Saroyan and Tennessee Williams. The management wanted nice, safe, inoffensive productions: drawing room comedies, or Rodgers and Hammerstein musicals. The resultant bartering, bickering, compromises and clashes of personality would recur on or behind the scenes of almost every film he made.

Peckinpah directing Cross of Iron*: he drew upon his own military experience.*

Long before cocaine, and while his drinking was still a social activity, Sam Peckinpah's first addiction was to directing. And as with every form of addiction, no matter how much you get, it's never enough. It didn't take long for him to feel constricted by the theatre. Arranging actors on a stage had taught him the value of composition and framing, but the tableaux were static. Adapting, abridging or reconstructing extant texts had given him an understanding of structure and juxtaposition, but the words weren't his. He needed something that was energetic and immediate, a broad visual canvas on which he could express himself. He needed something that *moved*.

He needed the screen.

He came to it in a roundabout manner. Some people get a foot in the door; others get their feet under the table. Peckinpah crept in through the tradesman's entrance. In 1951, still in his mid-twenties, he took a menial job at a Los Angeles TV station. The medium was in its infancy. Ratings and advertising had yet to give the kiss of death to experimentalism. TV stations were by and large independent and willing to go out on a limb: if someone came up with an idea – what the hell! – let's air it and see if takes. Opportunities were rife.

Nonetheless, Sam still had to start out as a stagehand.

Bearing in mind his return to television with *Noon Wine* following the *Dundee* disaster, it is a supreme irony that Peckinpah's small screen breakthrough came as the result of his involvement with feature film production. The movie was *Riot on Cell Block 11*, the director Don Siegel [2]. Sam was hired as 'dialogue director' (read cabin boy to the director). He landed the gig not through contacts at USC, friends in theatrical places or the recommendation of his bosses at the TV station, but because Denny inveigled a politico he was working for into pulling a few strings on his brother's behalf. Consider the outraged depiction of political machinations and behind-the-scenes payoffs in *Pat Garrett and Billy the Kid* and the irony takes on a darker aspect.

Peckinpah directing The Osterman Weekend, *his final film.*

Still, in Don Siegel, Peckinpah found a worthy mentor. Siegel was quick to notice the younger man's talent and encourage it. Decades later, when Peckinpah was once again in exile (this time because of his cocaine habit on *Convoy*) and Siegel reduced to helming the Bette Midler comedy *Jinxed*, Siegel had no qualms about hiring him as second unit director. Between Siegel acting once again as benefactor and Peckinpah pulling himself together and undertaking the assignment in a professional manner, he was allowed one more outing behind the camera, on *The Osterman Weekend*. This might not sound like much, but at least it meant that he got to go out on something other than *Convoy*.

Following *Riot on Cell Block 11*, his hands-on education in film-making progressed by degrees. Siegel hired him in a similar capacity on *Private Hell 36*, before giving him an altogether more tempting assignment redrafting the screenplay for *Invasion of the Body Snatchers*. The Siegel connection also landed him jobs on two Jacques Tourneur films, the westerns *Wichita* (starring Joel McCrea, who would later headline *Ride the High Country*) and *Great Day in the Morning*, as well as *Seven Angry Men*, Charles Marquis Warren's biopic of slavery-abolitionist John Brown.

The rewriting that Peckinpah was permitted to do proved that he had a flair for naturalistic dialogue and an understanding of the structure and dynamics of narrative storytelling. The next step, of course, was to write his own material ... and direct it.

This meant going back to television. Again, Don Siegel played a part. CBS, who were keen to transfer the high ratings of the radio series *Gunsmoke* to television, offered Siegel a chance to come on board. Fearing it would be perceived in the industry as a backward step, he declined, but put in a word for Peckinpah. In the meantime, Charles Marquis Warren had joined the *Gunsmoke* production team. Peckinpah's associations with Siegel and Warren helped, but the quality of his writing spoke for itself. Eleven of his scripts were filmed during *Gunsmoke*'s first two years on air and critics were quick to pick up on his name as a guarantee of hard-edged, gritty drama.

Sometimes too gritty, as it turned out. When *Gunsmoke* debuted on television in 1955, the invidious tentacles of advertising were beginning to curl round the creative freedom of broadcasting – and tighten. Ratings were the bottom line. Big ratings pleased advertisers: more people watching, more products sold. TV stations were becoming reliant on advertisers to sponsor individual shows. Shows that were controversial, cynical or had unhappy endings were likely to be unpopular with audiences. If viewing figures slackened, advertisers would get cold feet and withdraw their support. To keep *Gunsmoke* on the air, its producers bowdlerised the darker, racier scripts (i.e. the more interesting ones). The result: mass appeal to a family audience, consistently high ratings, and mollified money-men.

Commercialism. That was how it had been with the ultra-conservative theatre management of a few years before – and how it would be with all the producers who tampered with his work in the years to come – and the result was a very frustrated Peckinpah.

True, his on-going work on *Gunsmoke* was providing him with a steady income, but it wasn't enough. As much as he tried to imbue each script with his own vision of the Old West, he was hamstrung by the origins of the stories (all were adapted from the erstwhile radio episodes), as well as editorial blue-pencilling prior to filming. He wanted something over which he could exercise more control.

The opportunity came via *Dick Powell's Zane Grey Theater*. Peckinpah had been contributing one-offs to any number of other western anthologies, including *Boots and Saddles, Tales of Wells Fargo* and *Broken Arrow* (of four episodes written for *Broken Arrow*, Peckinpah had the opportunity of directing the last one, 'The Knife Fighter'), but it was with 'The Sharpshooter', written for the *Zane Grey Theater*, that Sam's career in television really took off. In the heyday of television, before pilots were commissioned and/or developed into fully-fledged series on the say-so of executives, a one-off drama could act as an inadvertent pilot if public or industry response were favourable. So it was that viewers were introduced in 'The Sharpshooter' to Lucas McCain, soon-to-be hero of *The Rifleman*.

Peckinpah's hopes for the show – that he could use the character of McCain's son as a device to strip away the myths of the western, a grittier picture emerging as the boy matures and the scales fall from his eyes – were confounded after one series by his producers (although Peckinpah was the creative force behind *The Rifleman*, he had only been contracted as 'story consultant') who inevitably opted for a toned-down, ratings-friendly approach. Friction with his producers was exacerbated when Peckinpah began to direct episodes himself. Setting the pattern for his extravagence as a film-maker, he shot more takes and demanded more camera set-ups than were conventional, pushing the budget beyond what was financially viable.

After he quit the show, he went back to writing screenplays, again for the *Zane Grey Theater*. This time he had Dick Powell's assurance that if one of the scripts caught on, he would be allowed to develop it as a series and act as his own producer. This arrangement resulted, in 1960, in *The Westerner*, starring Brian Keith as Dave Blassingame. The character was Peckinpah's first real anti-hero: a drifter, hard-drinking, scarred by self-doubt; a complex and flawed individual, sometimes driven by purely selfish motives, at other times capable of tenderness, his emotions underpinned by regret. In the opening episode, 'Jeff', he suffers the frustrations of unrequited love, unable to save the eponymous saloon girl from a self-destructive lifestyle to which she has resigned herself. When he rides out of town at the end, he is every inch the loser. In 'School Day', he is wrongly accused of murder and targetted by a lynch mob. In 'Hand on the Gun' and 'The Line Camp', the archetypal dramatic western showdown is turned on its head, with Blassingame powerless to prevent pointless death in the former and complicit in it in the latter. 'Ghost of a Chance' ends with Blassingame leaving the villain of the piece to the vengeful attentions of a group of wronged women, a set-piece Peckinpah would revisit in *Cross of Iron*.

There were thirteen episodes in all, five directed by Peckinpah. A second series was not commissioned. Although it's a damn shame that Peckinpah got only the one stab at it, the show was his chrysalis: he began work on it as a writer and emerged as a confident and technically accomplished director.

Peckinpah's work for television is fascinating to examine for the glimpses it gives of the films that lay ahead. At times *The Rifleman* seems like an extended casting session for the rest of his career. The pilot episode features R G Armstrong and Dennis Hopper. Armstrong would notch up four film appearances for Peckinpah while Hopper, present at the outset, reappears in his last film, *The Osterman Weekend*. An episode called 'The Marshal' again features Armstrong as well as James Drury and Warren Oates, later to reunite as two of the Hammond brothers in *Ride the High Country*. Katy Jurado crops up in 'The Boarding House', fifteen years before her memorable turn as Ma Baker in *Pat Garrett and Billy the Kid*.

The *Westerner* consolidated his posse: Oates and Jurado reappear in 'Jeff' and 'Ghost of a Chance' respectively, while Slim Pickens and Dub Taylor, and (behind the camera) Lucien Ballard, all make their Peckinpah debuts.

Although Brian Keith doesn't feature in Peckinpah's filmography to the extent of these other luminairies, he and Peckinpah established a friendship that led to the unfortunately bittersweet experience of his first movie. Keith must have thought he was doing Peckinpah the favour of a lifetime when, offered a starring role alongside Maureen O'Hara in *The Deadly Companions* (1961), a western produced by Charles B FitzSimons, he accepted on the condition Sam direct it. Maybe it was Keith's insistence on Peckinpah's involvement that stuck in FitzSimons's craw; maybe he had overwhelming ambitions to direct; maybe he was just a control freak with a Hollywood ego. Whatever the reason, Charles FitzSimons was the first in a list spanning two decades of producers who made it their business to meddle with Peckinpah's work. He hovered at the director's elbow from the first day of shooting to the last, overriding his instructions on camera set-ups and dictating how all the major scenes should be staged.

Still, it gave Peckinpah his first taste of the big screen, and despite the second-rate script and less-than-ideal working conditions, his command of the medium was evident. He was soon given another opportunity. On the surface, it didn't seem much of an improvement on *The Deadly Companions*: clichéd script, constrictive budget. But Sam was given the chance to rewrite it. He used this creative freedom to overlay the story with personal touches, flashes of humour and moments of understated pathos. With ageing genre icons Joel McCrea and Randolph Scott on board, *Ride the High Country* (1962) emerged as Peckinpah's first fully realized meditation on what would become his quintessential theme: the effect of changing times on men who belong to a different era, men whose way of life and way of doing things has become outmoded and misunderstood. But men, nonetheless, who would rather go out in a hail of bullets than go along with modernity. When McCrea and Scott face down their nemeses (younger men, superior numbers), the sentiment is clear: 'Let's meet 'em head-on, halfway, just like always.' Their final stand – against youth, against 'progress', against all the mistakes of the past they've been unable to run from – is Sam Peckinpah's first *götterdämmerung*.

The shoot wasn't entirely trouble-free – bad weather meant new locations had to be scouted – and Peckinpah found himself banished in the latter stages of post-production after spending a disproportionate amount of time in the editing suite. Fortunately producer Richard Lyons, under orders from MGM top brass to finish work on the film post haste, was perspicacious enough to maintain contact with Peckinpah clandestinely, implementing his instructions on how to put the finishing touches to it. The frequently intrusive score was beyond Peckinpah's control and proved (no pun intended) to be the only wrong note. Otherwise, *Ride the High Country* is a little gem. Not that Joseph Vogel, then president of MGM, appreciated it. Disconcerted at a surreal wedding scene set in a brothel, he ordered it relegated to supporting feature in a double-bill with histrionic historical drama *The Tartars*. Critical reaction proved him wrong; the film was fêted, the billing eventually reversed. A slew of awards followed: the Silver Leaf in Sweden, the Silver Goddess in Mexico, the Paris critics' award and the Grand Prix in Belgium.

It also brought him to the attention of Charlton Heston and Jerry Bresler. Bresler was a producer working for Columbia. He was the man behind *Diamond Head*, an insipid adaptation of Peter Gilman's novel, but a solid enough hit at the box office for Bresler to cast around for another vehicle for his leading man. What he settled on was a synopsis by Harry Julian Fink (later to make his name as the writer of *Dirty Harry*) called *And Then Came the Tiger*. Behind the lurid title was an epic-in-waiting. It told the story of a disgraced cavalry officer who becomes obsessed with hunting down a vicious indian war-chief. Assigned to guard a prison garrison, he recruits an army of cut-throats, bandits, rustlers and infantrymen from both sides of the civil war, and goes renegade, leading them further into Mexico as he pursues his quarry.

Heston saw the possibilities. Heston watched *Ride the High Country*. Heston knew Peckinpah was the man. Peckinpah was just as enthusiastic: he signed on without hesitation. Fink was greenlighted to write the screenplay proper. Bresler sweet-talked the Columbia money-men: big cavalry epic – big budget. Everyone was excited. Peckinpah started scouting locations.

Things started going wrong a couple of months before shooting was scheduled to start. The script that Fink turned in covered less than half of the action according to his synopsis, and it already ran to 163 pages (or two and three-quarter hours, allowing for the old rule of thumb that a page of script equates to a minute of screen time). Peckinpah was horrified. He petitioned Bresler, who managed postpone commencement of shooting for three months. Oscar Saul was brought in to lick the script into shape; he and Peckinpah worked like men possessed. Their endeavours resulted in something considerably better than Fink's disjointed opus, but it was still far removed from a satisfactory shooting script. Despite Bresler's reservations, Peckinpah was convinced he could pull the film together on set: it would cohere as he shot it.

But before filming could even begin, Columbia got cold feet over the kind of film they had invested in. Cavalry epic? Big budget? Not any more. A bunch of suits in a boardroom decided that it was going to be a moderately budgeted two-hour western. They summoned Bresler and put it on the line: budget and shooting schedule were to be downsized. Bresler kowtowed to his wagemasters.

In cavalier disregard for Bresler's edict, Peckinpah led his company into Mexico and set about making the film as he envisaged it. He went wantonly overbudget and over schedule. Cast and crew members fell ill. Bresler, now siding with the suits against Peckinpah, made a location visit and tried to bully his director into a quicker, more perfunctory method of film-making: few set-ups, less footage shot. No doubt rankled at how much Bresler's behaviour resembled FitzSimons's, Peckinpah rounded on him, threatening that he wouldn't shoot another frame until Bresler removed himself. Heston and his co-star, Richard Harris, stood by Peckinpah: *leave Sam alone or we walk*. Scared at how much more of Columbia's money stood to be lost, Bresler beat a hasty retreat.

A further complication presented itself on set in the alluring shape of young Mexican actress Begonia Palacios, soon to be the second Mrs Peckinpah. As well as the third. And the fourth. All couples fall out; the majority make up again. Sam and Begonia took this pattern of behaviour to something of an extreme: fall out, get divorced, make up, remarry.

With their relationship in its earliest, romantic, idealised stage, Peckinpah returned from filming the now retitled *Major Dundee* (1965) not realising that Bresler and Columbia were ready to take their revenge on him. They waited until he had completed post-production on a two hour forty-one minute cut, then took it out of his hands, hacked it down by nearly a third, had actor Michael Armstrong Jr record a terrible voice-over track, and lumbered it with one of the most atrocious soundtracks ever composed.

When the film premiered, the critics tore it apart like vultures fighting over the newly dead. They made no allowances for Columbia's travesty. The knives were out for

Peckinpah. They stuck it in and broke it off. It was the first time they had turned against him. It wouldn't be the last.

The stigma of *Major Dundee* could have been deflected had Peckinpah been able to bite the bullet on the next project he was offered, *The Cincinnati Kid*, and make the no-brainer that producer Martin Ransohoff wanted. As Richard Luck puts it, 'all Sam had to do was show up on set every day, say "action", "cut" and "print" and by the end of shooting, his career would be back on track' [3]. But if ever there was a man who couldn't bring himself to undertake banal work, no matter the industry kudos or financial rewards that might be had, it was Sam Peckinpah.

The film, as eventually directed by Norman Jewison, tells of a cardsharp (played by Steve McQueen) hustling in New Orleans against a backdrop of the 1930s Depression. The gambling is merely an excuse for the plot, and the film-makers are more interested in McQueen's complicated romantic entanglements with an archetypal 'nice' girl and an equally straight-out-of-Central-Casting vamp (played by Tuesday Weld and Ann-Margret respectively). Peckinpah had no interest in these elements. He focused instead on the social and political elements of the story. Adamant that he wanted to bring the Depression from the background to the foreground, maybe even shoot the film in black-and-white, Ransohoff wasn't having any of this and responded by firing him.

Dundee had been bad enough: the critics had turned against him. Now his standing in the industry was tarnished. 1965 to 1969 were Peckinpah's wilderness years. He wrote scripts. He tried to get backing for adaptations of favourite novels – Max Evans's *The Hi-Lo Country* and *Castaway* by James Gould Cozzens [4]. He tried to re-establish himself. In the end, he went back to television.

The offer came courtesy of Daniel Melnick, an independent TV producer who had managed to interest ABC in a one-off drama based on Katherine Anne Porter's *Noon Wine*, to be screened as part of their *Stage 76* anthology series. Melnick knew from *The Rifleman* and *The Westerner* that Peckinpah was the ideal director. Bresler and Ransohoff mounted a petty little campaign to warn him off, but Melnick was resolute. Peckinpah seized the opportunity. The hour-long film he delivered was a minor masterpiece. Never mind that it was made for the small screen, the artistry and thematic depth are the equal of any of his feature films. His reputation was resurrected; the critics were back on his side again. Nominations from the Writers' Guild and the Directors' Guild followed. Once again, he was in demand.

Typically, though, his return to the big screen with what many would hail as his masterpiece, *The Wild Bunch* (1969), would be arrived at by a tortuous route. Initially, he was offered writing duties on a biopic of Pancho Villa, with producer Ted Richmond's promise that if Yul Brynner, already signed up to play the revolutionary, approved the script, Peckinpah could also direct. Earlier in his career, before *The Westerner*, Peckinpah's contribution to the Marlon Brando project *The Authentic Death of Hendry Jones* (adapted from the novel by Charles Neider) was deep-sixed when Brando decided to have Sam's script rewritten [5]. Now history was repeating itself: Brynner took against the screenplay (which questioned the morality of Villa's crusade) and Peckinpah's services were dispensed with.

The next offer came from Kenneth Hyman, head of production at Seven Arts and the man behind Robert Aldrich's *The Dirty Dozen*. Keen to rush into production *The Diamond Story*, an action thriller intended as a Lee Marvin vehicle (one, he hoped, that would replicate *The Dirty Dozen*'s success), he instructed producer Phil Feldman to liaise with Peckinpah. Hyman wanted Peckinpah to rewrite the script, then direct. Peckinpah was less than impressed with the material, and he and Feldman's attentions turned to the various properties Peckinpah owned: the rights to *The Hi-Lo Country* and *Castaway*, as well as some original scripts. Two in particular stood out: *The Wild Bunch* and *The Ballad of Cable Hogue*.

Right: Peckinpah's masterpiece.

What Peckinpah and Feldman liked about *The Wild Bunch* wasn't so much the script itself (a sketchy affair by Roy Sickner, a former stuntman, and Walon Green) as the possibilities it presented. The story was set against the backdrop of revolutionary Mexico. After being stabbed in the back over *Villa Rides* (Brynner had Sam's script rewritten by Robert Towne, brought director-for-hire Buzz Kulik on board, and the result was a melodramatic pseudo-epic), here was another chance. This time, he'd do it right.

But *The Wild Bunch* might well have been relegated until *The Diamond Story* was completed had it not been for *Butch Cassidy and the Sundance Kid*. William Goldman's script was the talk of Tinseltown. Twentieth Century Fox shelled out nearly half a million for it, and assigned directing duties to George Roy Hill. Feldman realised that, with *The Wild Bunch* already in Peckinpah's hands, he had a shot at producing his own blockbuster: a challenge to *Butch Cassidy* at the box office. If the film was put into production straightaway, they could even get *The Wild Bunch* out first. *The Diamond Story* was abruptly abandoned.

Peckinpah and Feldman worked on *The Wild Bunch* with fervour. Sickner and Green's script was rewritten, something darker and more complex emerging. Locations were scouted, the cast assembled. Lee Marvin was in the frame for the role of Pike Bishop, the Bunch's embittered leader. Hyman wanted Marvin because of their earlier hit with *The Dirty Dozen*; Feldman saw *The Wild Bunch* as a replacement *Diamond Story* and took Marvin's involvement as a given. As it happened, the actor was offered *Paint Your Wagon* (and a paycheque for a cool million). He snapped it up, forsaking the greatest western ever made for one of the worst, and William Holden got the role.

Feldman indulged Peckinpah to the extreme, such was his faith in the project. Multiple camera set-ups captured the film's set-pieces – the violent opening and closing shoot-outs, the train robbery and subsequent pursuit – from a variety of angles. A river bridge was built and spectacularly blown up; the river dammed upstream to compensate for its shallow waters, which would otherwise have proved perilous for the stuntmen who plunged into it. Warner Brothers, who were backing the film, would famously claim, for publicity purposes, that more rounds of blank ammunition were fired during the making of the film than live ones in the entire Mexican Revolution.

Feldman's belief wasn't misplaced. Peckinpah delivered a monumental work. The relationship between the two men was so productive that, with *The Wild Bunch* still being edited, they went into pre-production on their next collaboration, *The Ballad of Cable Hogue*. Things turned sour when Warners began pressing for a much shorter cut of *The Wild Bunch* than Peckinpah had envisioned. With his original cut clocking in at three and three-quarter hours, it was obvious that a more commercial running time would have to be arrived at. Peckinpah anticipated making certain compromises. What he didn't anticipate was Feldman going behind his back. With Peckinpah busy filming *The Ballad of Cable Hogue* (1970), Feldman bowed to pressure from Warner executives and cut ever-larger chunks, including the all-important back story of Deke Thornton's incarceration and Pike Bishop's ill-fated romance, bringing the film in at the two hour mark.

Peckinpah felt betrayed; his antipathy towards Feldman and Warners was very vocal and very public. Consequently, *Cable Hogue* was the last time he and Feldman worked together. Warners didn't understand the film, a part-comedic/part-melodramatic little fable, and released it without a whisper of publicity. Peckinpah's redoubled criticism of his paymasters, as well as the legal action he threatened over their duplicitous editing of *The Wild Bunch*, led to the cancellation of his contract with Warners. As a result, he lost out on the opportunity to direct one of the key films of the 1970s.

Deliverance would have been an ideal film for him. Four city types set off on a canoeing trip, their last chance before redevelopment alters the course of the river. Their backwater idyll turns nasty when they encounter a group of inbred hillbillies whose attitude to outsiders goes way beyond mere resentment. Beset by the forces of nature and the dregs of humanity, their holiday becomes a grim fight for survival. A character piece with terrific action scenes, the wilderness a canvas on which to paint man's most

William Holden in The Wild Bunch.

primitive urge for survival, Sam calling the shots and the whole package wrapped up in Lucien Ballard's expressive cinematography – it would have been something else! Peckinpah's enthusiasm was matched by that of James Dickey. The novelist lobbied for Peckinpah as director.

But with Sam *persona non grata*, directorial duties were assigned elsewhere. Dickey must have been as distraught as Peckinpah: with the wrong director, his novel could easily have been downgraded to a by-the-numbers actioner. Fortunately with the talents of John Boorman, Vilmos Zsigmond (Ballard's heir apparent), a top-notch cast and some memorable banjo riffs, Dickey's dark and complex vision got the big screen treatment it deserved. Still, as Richard Luck opines, 'you can't help thinking about what might have happened had Warren Oates, James Coburn, L Q Jones and John Chandler rowed off into the wilds with Uncle Sam at the tiller' [6].

Instead, Peckinpah's next picture saw him holed up in a farmhouse in rural England, the Appalachian wilds replaced by an isolated Cornish community but the locals just as nasty. Like *Deliverance, Straw Dogs* (1971) has a city dweller out of his natural habitat, a gruelling rape scene (heterosexual as opposed to riverside buggery) and violent catharsis, the implications of which reverberate long after the closing credits.

Peckinpah and Dustin Hoffman on the set of Straw Dogs: *Hoffman tried to have him replaced.*

The film reunited Peckinpah with Daniel Melnick. The producer stuck by him as obstinately as he had on *Noon Wine*. Following Peckinpah's hospitalisation, Dustin Hoffman tried to have him fired, urging Melnick to hire Peter Yates (director of *Bullitt*). Melnick refused to do his star's bidding and ordered that the production be closed down until Sam had recuperated. Repaying Melnick's faith in him, Peckinpah got it together and threw himself energetically into the project. *Straw Dogs* renewed the controversy over Peckinpah's portrayal of violence. Of course, the nay-sayers overlooked the non-occurrence of it in his follow-up, the lyrical and likeable *Junior Bonner* (1971). Like *Cable Hogue*, it was the victim of studio non-comprehension: they didn't get it, so they released it without fanfare or appropriate advertising, and even with the star presence of Steve McQueen it did little at the box office.

It did, however, land Peckinpah his next directing gig. McQueen had co-founded United Artists with Paul Newman, Sidney Poitier and Barbra Streisand. Their intent was to develop projects with more freedom than the existing studio system permitted. McQueen had bought the rights to Jim Thompson's pulp novel *The Getaway*. He and Peckinpah had got on well making *Junior Bonner*. And the rest, to regurgitate an old cliché, is history. *The Getaway* (1972) is one of the highlights of McQueen's *oeuvre*. It might not be top-flight Peckinpah, but it beats the hell out of most films of its ilk. And it did huge box-office. For the first time in his career, Peckinpah's attachment to a project was commercially viable. It all bode well for his next film, a return to the western: *Pat Garrett and Billy the Kid* (1973).

It turned into *Major Dundee* Part II. For Jerry Bresler, substitute James Aubrey. Bresler had been a producer – just one more payrollee beholden to the money-men; Aubrey was a bigger fish altogether. Aubrey was the president of MGM.

And film production was not top of Aubrey's agenda. He was more interested in the development of an MGM hotel/casino operation in Las Vegas and cheerfully undercut the budgets of film after film in order to pump funds into it. He refused to budget *Pat*

Garrett at more than $3 million. His penny-pinching meant that the technician Peckinpah wanted on set in case inclement weather proved detrimental to the cameras was vetoed. This resulted in the aforementioned damaged-flange/urination incident. When word of it reached Aubrey, he forbade Peckinpah to reshoot the footage. With characteristic defiance, Peckinpah reshot every bit of it on the quiet.

Other problems on set paralleled the *Dundee* farrago: sickness struck cast and crew; last-minute script doctoring resulted in weak scenes. Peckinpah's drinking didn't help. It has been said that he was sober for no more than four hours out of any day during filming. It shows: *Pat Garrett* has a washed-out, hazy look to it; characters swig from whisky bottles in every significant scene.

Things got worse in post-production. Aubrey envisaged the film as ninety minutes of gunplay. Wanting to rush-release it, he gave Peckinpah a deadline of less than three months to produce a final cut. Since most of Peckinpah's films started out as an amorphous mass of footage that came to life during editing, a process Sam was used to spending anything up to a year on, this was effectively the kiss of death.

Peckinpah's attempts to compromise, whittling down his hastily assembled three and a half hour rough cut to a movie of just over two hours' duration, were in vain: Aubrey had him barred from the editing room. *Pat Garrett* was eventually released in a 106-minute version that retained only trace elements of Peckinpah's vision. The critics sharpened their axes.

Frequent Peckinpah collaborator Garth Craven was still working on the editing team under Aubrey's draconian rule when he scored a belated victory for his mentor, stealing the preview print and transporting it to Sam's house. Realizing he had forgotten the corresponding soundtrack, he went back the following night and swiped that too. Despite the omnipresent threat of the MGM legal department, Peckinpah was able to arrange a screening some years later at his old *alma mater*, the USC [7].

The effect *Pat Garrett* had on Peckinpah can be gauged by the darkness and perversity of his follow-up, *Bring Me the Head of Alfredo Garcia* (1974). A film that can only have been greenlighted by accident, it was a study in failure, impotence and self-loathing that everyone hated. It died at the box office.

A potential back-on-track blockbuster for Twentieth Century Fox, *The Insurance Company*, fell through when its star, Charles Bronson, refused to work with Peckinpah. Scared that *Alfredo Garcia* would have the same effect as *Major Dundee*, its critical mauling presaging an extended period of unemployment, he took the first thing that came along: *The Killer Elite* (1975). Not that he had any enthusiasm for the script. Staging the whole production tongue-in-cheek, the critics responded to his rubbishing of the material by rubbishing the film itself.

Still, Peckinpah retained enough clout that two major studio productions were offered to him shortly afterwards: the Dino de Laurentiis remake of *King Kong*, and *Superman*. As commercially tempting as they were, they offered no human element; no emotional core. He turned them down [8]. Instead, he responded to an offer from German producer Wolf C Hartwig to direct an adaptation of a novel by Willi Heinrich. *Cross of Iron* (1977) was a grimly realistic war movie, epic in scope but character-driven. Hartwig, a purveyor of pornography, intended it to be his calling card as a respectable producer. He knew nothing of film-making on this scale. His budget quickly drained away. The military hardware he promised Peckinpah failed to materialise (it is one of Peckinpah's many achievements that he managed to make three rusty old tanks look like the entire Russian army). Peckinpah stumped up $90,000 in order to complete the film.

The critics hated it. Orson Welles called it the greatest anti-war film ever made. Welles's assessment was the more accurate.

Again, Peckinpah realized that he needed a mainstream success in order to keep him in the game. Therefore, with great reluctance, he signed up for *Convoy* (1978). A drinker on the scale of Dylan Thomas throughout most of his adult life, Peckinpah had by this time

developed an affinity for cocaine. Throughout most of the shooting (Peckinpah exposed more film on *Convoy* than on any of his other films – including *The Wild Bunch*), he was incapacitated. Scenes were ad-libbed to the point of incoherence. Shooting went over schedule. The budget almost doubled. Pre-production was debilitating. Unable to pare the mass of footage down to anything near a commercially acceptable two hour movie, Peckinpah made no protest when EMI had him removed from the project and appointed their own editing team. After all the battles, all the editing suite lock-outs, all the interference, all the way down the line from *The Deadly Companions*, it was almost unthinkable: Sam Peckinpah just giving up and walking away.

This non-vocal departure could have done wonders for his career, though: EMI hacked *Convoy* down to an audience-friendly length, marketed it as a Sam Peckinpah film (this ploy necessitating a play-down of the director's removal) and it was a box-office smash. There had been no behind-the-scenes skirmishes, no falling out with producers. Even the bloated budget was forgivable now the shekels were rolling in fast. But instead of re-establishing him, *Convoy* was his undoing. Tales of his on set drug abuse strengthened the industry view that he was a spent force. It was common knowledge that James Coburn, on board as second unit director, had called the shots on several key scenes. The Hollywood consensus was unanimous: hire Peckinpah and you'd get a drunkard and a junkie who would push your budget firmly into the red and leave you with a major post-production headache.

For all his worries over *Pat Garrett* and *Alfredo Garcia*, it was *Convoy* that proved to be *Major Dundee* revisited: Peckinpah did not work for another five years. It took Don Siegel and the aforementioned Bette Midler vehicle *Jinxed* for Peckinpah's reputation to regain enough currency for another offer to come his way. *The Osterman Weekend* (1983) didn't give him much to get to grips with: low budget, formulaic material, little scope for directorial flair. But he bit back his frustration and delivered a professional picture, graced with two excellent set-pieces, without going overschedule or overbudget.

It should have made him, if not the golden boy *redux*, then significantly less of a pariah. But two things conspired to bring his career to an end. One was his relapse into cocaine use: editing *The Osterman Weekend* depressed him (the producers, William Panzer and Peter Davis, ended up recutting the film) and he was quick to reacquaint himself with the Columbian marching powder. The other, on 28 December 1984, was the heart attack which killed him.

Sam Peckinpah's last two projects were music videos for Julian Lennon. Had he lived another five or ten years, he might have been reduced to helming promos, MTV fodder or direct-to-video quickies. On the other hand, had the studios recognized him as the artist he was and given him the respect he deserved, the downturn that characterized the last decade of his life might never have come to pass.

But these are speculations. The fact is that Sam Peckinpah lived it like one of his characters. This is what gives his films their extraordinary power: they are populated not by one-dimensional types who preen and posture, defeat the villain and get the girl, but by people who are real. Like their creator, the men who walk or ride through Peckinpah's films (or drive hell-for-leather for the border) are deep, complex and often flawed. Like their creator, they don't necessarily have any liking for the things they do – they just don't have any other choice. Sometimes they just have to live it to lose.

CHAPTER ONE:
REDEFINING THE WESTERN

Six of Peckinpah's fourteen films are westerns. As he had proved with *The Rifleman* and *The Westerner*, it was a genre he could redefine and push back the boundaries of, even as he wholeheartedly embraced its traditions and iconography. All the superficial requirements are in place: indians, Mexicans, outlaws, bounty hunters, gold shipments, train robberies, shoot-outs, bars, brothels and brawling. But these are only on the surface. Peckinpah, at his best (which is to say, when he's not being hamstrung by producers), layers these films with subtext, motivation and character development.

The men who ride the high country, defy landowners and railroad barons, or cross the border into a Mexico scarred by revolution, are driven by remorse, sadness and the hollow feeling of wasted years. The gold or arms shipments they steal are just a means to an end. They take their pleasure in the arms of whores, if at all – sometimes they wait outside, eaten up with guilt, waiting for their comrades to get finished so they can go out there and end it.

Peckinpah's characters often end it – and do so on their terms. Not for romantic or idealistic reasons. Mostly just because it's the only thing left. Nor does Peckinpah make it any easier for his audience. There are no soft option freeze-frames à la *Butch Cassidy and the Sundance Kid*, its bandit heroes cinematically spin-doctored as lovable rogues, caught at their most audacious, preserved in sepia before the bullets can start flying. When Peckinpah uses freeze-frame, as when he uses any film-making technique, the aim is not to make his characters look like idols, but to show them as they are. And that includes the ugly truth of violent death. Sure, they die like men. But they die painfully. And sometimes slowly.

Yet there are moments, on the trail or round a campfire or during a quiet sojourn at a Mexican village, when their lined, leathery faces break into smiles, and their harsh commanding voices give way to laughter. And there are times when their carefully concealed humiliations or their memories of failed relationships cannot be held back any longer and we see the scars on their souls as visibly as those on their skin. Peckinpah's characters are presented in full – flawed, contradictory, anachronisms even as they cling bitterly to the only way of life they know.

Two of these six films – *The Wild Bunch* and *Pat Garrett and Billy the Kid* – are undisputable landmarks and merit individual chapters (Chapters Two and Four respectively). Of the others, three were made before *The Wild Bunch*, and one immediately after. Two are deeply flawed, and two are little gems, works of lyrical and poignant beauty. In varying degrees, they contribute to a rejuvenation, reappraisal and aesthetic reimagining of an all too frequently one-dimensional genre.

'YOU DON'T KNOW ME WELL ENOUGH TO HATE ME': *The Deadly Companions*

Examine the behind-the-scenes circumstances of Peckinpah's weaker output and two constant factors emerge: studio/producer interference, and refusal by same for Sam to rewrite the scripts. His attempt on *The Osterman Weekend* to downplay the convoluted plotting of Robert Ludlum's novel was vetoed by producers, who wanted nothing more than a spy thriller with a couple of solid action scenes. This led to his much-quoted complaint (which probably got him crossed off Ludlum's Christmas card list) that the source material was a 'fifth-rate piece of shit' and it was all he could do to try to inject some life into the proceedings.

The Osterman Weekend was his last film and there is an awful sense of history repeating itself, of a career punctuated by comprised working conditions coming full circle. Twenty-three years earlier, on his first film, he'd come up against the same problem.

Written by A S Fleischman, the screenplay for *The Deadly Companions* was an exercise in cornball dialogue, cardboard characterizations and improbable plot developments. How much of this is due to Fleischman and how much to the uncredited co-scripting of the producer, Charles B FitzSimons, is open to debate.

Nonetheless, even stripped down to its bare bones, the basic story of *The Deadly Companions* is still risible. It starts with Yellowleg (Brian Keith) tracking down his arch-enemy Turk (Chill Wills), a man who tried to scalp him years earlier. Yellowleg still bears the scars on his head and never removes his hat in company. Far from instigating a dramatic showdown with Turk, Yellowleg finds him on the verge of being hanged for cheating at cards.

Improbable Plot Development No. 1: Yellowleg saves Turk's life and joins forces with him and his partner, a brash gunslinger named Billy. The three of them set off to rob a bank at Gila City.

Coincidentally, another outfit are also interested in making an unscheduled withdrawal from said premises. Shots are exchanged. His aim affected by an old war wound (if clichés were products, that one would have a trademark symbol next to it), Yellowleg ends up shooting a young boy. The lad, a victim of the Standard-Hollywood-Wrong-Place-At-The-Wrong-Time-Formula, is the son of local saloon girl Kit (Maureen O'Hara).

In expiation, Yellowleg offers to accompany Kit on her odyssey across the desert to the town of Serengo. It is here that Kit's husband is buried; she wants her son laid to rest next to him.

Improbable Plot Development No. 2: Yellowleg has Turk and Billy ride along with them. Not a smart move. Billy tries to rape Kit. Yellowleg intervenes. Turk and Billy take their leave. Left alone in indian territory, Yellowleg and Kit witness a stagecoach under attack by a group of braves. Closer investigation shows that the stage is empty and the indians are whooping it up in a bizarre mixture of celebration and re-enactment. While they sleep off their revelry, Yellowleg steals a horse from one of them. For the remainder of the journey, the brave stalks them, intent on getting his steed back.

Despite this, Yellowleg and Kit make it to Serengo. En route – cue Improbable Plot Development No. 3 – a romantic attachment has evolved between them. This is threatened, however, by the return of Turk and Billy. Due to some hamfisted editing by FitzSimons, who barred Peckinpah from post-production, the climactic gunfight is a confusing affair. It appears to be Turk who fires the bullet that kills Billy, which doesn't make a lot of sense. It's far more logical for Yellowleg to blow him halfway to hell. What *really* doesn't make sense is that Yellowleg, who now has more reason than ever to take Turk out of the equation, desists from scalping him at the behest of Kit. Turk's life spared, Yellowleg and Kit ride off (quite literally) into the sunset and everyone lives happily ever after – presumably.

So, quite apart from the questionable matter of a woman coming to feel love for the man who, accidentally or not, was the instrument of her son's death, we are asked to believe that a man who has spent seven years on the trail of the SOB who tried to hack

Maureen O'Hara as Kit in The Deadly Companions.

the top of his head off would (a) hold back from killing him not once but twice, (b) actually enter into partnership with said SOB, and (c) let said SOB and his equally dubious partner ride along as part of an ad-hoc funeral cortège.

Hmmm.

As Peckinpah later acknowledged, the film was built on gimmickry. The death of the child is simply an excuse to send Yellowleg and Kit out into the desert together – and a distastefully cynical one at that. Yellowleg himself is no less a gimmick. His name derives from the sergeant's stripe he wears on his trouser leg. The scarred-head/ refusal-to-take-hat-off business is a stand-in for characterization. Likewise Turk. The name, short for turkey, is based on his feathered costume. He and Billy are all-purpose villains straight out of Central Casting.

Kit is potentially the most interesting character. Robbed of her only child, all that she is left with is the need to reunite him in death with his father, and in doing so prove to the sanctimonious citizens of Gila that she was legally married. She stands at an intersection of pride, shame and grief. A character so traumatically afflicted could, in an intelligent screenplay, be used to examine a whole range of emotions, her journey across the barren wastes developed as a metaphor for the human condition. Sadly, forbidden to either rewrite the script or give direction to O'Hara (FitzSimons, who was her brother, undertook to direct her himself), there was little Peckinpah could do.

Nor was he given much opportunity to probe Yellowleg's psyche. Revenge as a double-edged sword is something Peckinpah would return to in later films, but here his only chance to explore the theme is in a scene where Yellowleg recounts the story of an acquaintance who spends five years hunting an adversary. The pursuit over, the foe dispatched, all he is left with is an emptiness; he has lived for the killing of one man and now that man is dead, what does he have left? The third-person monologue provides a framework for Yellowleg to voice his own doubts. It is tantalizing to imagine how masterful this scene might have been if Peckinpah had been able to strip it down, psychologically reconstruct it and present it in dialogue rich with saddle-creased poetry. As it is, the only hint we are given of Yellowleg's self-loathing is when (in the one memorable line in the film) he answers Kit back during an argument declaring: 'You don't know me well enough to hate me'.

Indeed, it is tempting to re-imagine the film as it might have been had the director been given total control. As it is, all that Peckinpah felt he deserved credit for was holding off the panoply of gimmicks as best he could so that they weren't too intrusive. A pragmatic point of view, but perhaps he was being slightly unfair to himself. Hitchcock once said that to make a great film, one needs three things: a great script, a great script and a great script. What FitzSimons gave him was a dud. Worse, he compromised Peckinpah's performance on set. At the risk of hagiography, it could be said that the deficiencies of *The Deadly Companions* are entirely the fault of FitzSimons, while its occasional flashes of brilliance are the work – against all the odds – of Sam Peckinpah.

His achievements, with the script out of reach, are technical ones. The film was shot in colour and CinemaScope, and proves he was able to make the transition from television to the big screen with confidence. His eye for detail and composition are already evident. His staging of scenes to emphasize a certain point of view (a technique honed to perfection in *The Wild Bunch*, particularly in the scene where they ride into Agua Verde for the first time) has its precursor in the stagecoach sequence. The shifting perspective as Yellowleg, initially convinced he's witnessing a vicious attack, gets close enough to realize the indians are larking around, is cleverly done, subverting the mounting tension and delivering a surreal punchline.

Still, for all that Peckinpah was able to steal these directorial flourishes from under FitzSimons's nose, *The Deadly Companions* offers little to indicate the quantum leap he would make with his next feature.

'A LITTLE OLD-TIME ACTIVITY': *Ride the High Country*

Guns in the Afternoon was a cluttered 145-page screenplay by N B Stone when it came into the hands of Sam Peckinpah. It was sentimental, had inauthentic dialogue and relied on genre clichés. Nonetheless, in its tale of two former lawmen joining forces to safeguard a shipment of gold, only for one to doublecross the other, Peckinpah saw enough of the thematic concerns that he'd tried to develop in his Television shows to want to direct it.

This time he was allowed to do what he liked with the script. He left the basic narrative unchanged, rewrote virtually all of the dialogue (giving us such lines to treasure as 'smellin' bad enough to choke a dog off a gut wagon' and 'you damned dry-gulchin' Southern trash'), and re-envisaged the little matter of which protagonist dies at the end. Oh, and he changed the title.

What he achieved was masterful, a low budget picture which MGM treated like a B-movie but which had a quality of acting, cinematography, intelligence and moral complexity that made it stand head and shoulders above most of the A-pictures of the day. It elevated the western to art and established an intellectual blueprint for Peckinpah's career as a film-maker.

As wonderful as it must have been to discover the movie in 1962, to have borne witness to Peckinpah's first fully realized artistic statement, *Ride the High Country* is inspirational to watch in retrospect, so prominent are the precedents it sets for his later work.

Foremost is the simplicity of narrative, free of the gimmicks that blighted *The Deadly Companions*, allowing room for character motivation and development. The story starts with the ageing Steve Judd (Joel McCrea), once a sheriff, agreeing to a contract with a bank to collect deposits of gold from claims staked at the nearby mining town of Coarsegold and deliver them safely back to town. Recent outbreaks of violence and robbery have left six miners dead and the bank are eager to hire someone of sound reputation to protect their interests.

Arriving in town to finalize the contract, Judd encounters an old friend, Gil Westrum (Randolph Scott), a man who once served as his deputy. Westrum is now running a stall at a carnival for loose change and free drinks, trading on the hyperbolised reputation of his past exploits. His sidekick, Heck Longtree, runs rigged camel races and isn't opposed to brawling and womanising. Learning of Judd's mission, they agree to ride with him but plot behind his back to steal the gold.

Westrum is uneasy about betraying his old friend and tries, on the trail, to win him over to the idea of appropriating the funds for themselves. His oblique approach is lost on Judd, whose moral rectitude becomes apparent when they stop for lodgings at a farm owned by Joshua Knudsen (R G Armstrong) – Judd and Knudsen debate religion around the dinner table, matching each other biblical quote for biblical quote.

Knudsen's only companion, his wife having passed away, is his daughter Elsa (Mariette Hartley), to whom Heck takes a fancy. Elsa confides in him that she has agreed to marry one of the miners in Coarsegold, Billy Hammond, but is unable to leave the farm because of her father's possessiveness. This is demonstrated when he catches them talking in the yard, exiles Heck to the barn, and drags Elsa inside where they argue and he ends up striking her.

Back on the trail next day, they are joined by Elsa. She has run away and asks them to take her with them to Coarsegold. Judd and Westrum are all for giving her a pistol and leaving her to make her own way, but when Heck – all false sincerity and ulterior motives – offers to stay and take care of her, they relent and let her ride with them. Making camp, Heck tries it on with Elsa, but she spurns him.

The following day they arrive at Coarsegold and while Judd and Westrum begin collecting deposits of gold, Heck takes Elsa to the Hammonds's camp. Billy, while a handsome dude, is less than civilized – and his brothers are plain white trash. They ridicule Heck and he rides miserably off to rejoin his companions.

Against her better judgement, Elsa goes through with the wedding. The ceremony takes place in Kate's Place, a bar-cum-brothel, and is presided over by Judge Tolliver, a pitiful inebriate. Billy drags Elsa into a back room to consummate the marriage, but knocks himself out when he falls over. The other Hammond brothers crowd into the room, intent on finishing the job for him. Judd and Heck intercede and Elsa leaves with them.

The matter is put before a miner's court, the Hammonds pointing out that she and Billy were legally married. Westrum intimidates Tolliver, forcing him to testify that he doesn't have a licence to perform marriages. He does, but Westrum makes doubly sure by taking the licence from him at gunpoint. To the Hammonds's fury, the decision goes against them, and when Judd, Westrum and Heck leave for the journey back, Elsa is with them.

Convinced now of Judd's integrity, Westrum decides to steal the gold and make his getaway under the cover of night. Judd prefigures him. Heck surrenders his gun. Westrum, challenged by his old friend to draw, unbuckles his gunbelt and lets it drop to the ground. Judd announces his decision to turn them in when they get back.

Presently, they are intercepted by the Hammonds, who have discovered the ruse and given Tolliver a beating. When Judd refuses to hand over Elsa, a gunfight ensues. Driven into the mountains by the Hammonds's onslaught, the situation is only resolved when Heck, whom Judd trusts enough to allow him to arm himself, shoots one of the brothers and takes his rifle. He unleashes a fusillade on the others and they retreat.

Asked by Judd to turn over his weaponry, Heck proves himself the faster draw. But he doesn't take the opportunity, instead apologizing to Judd as he hands the gun over. Westrum berates him and plots to escape later that night. He is successful, and backtracks

Heck proves himself the faster draw in Ride the High Country.

to where the dead Hammond brother's horse is still tethered. He takes his pistol, as well, and gallops off.

Judd and Heck continue to Knudsen's farm where they see Knudsen kneeling by his wife's grave. They have approached the farmhouse and are crossing the yard before they realize Knudsen is dead and the Hammonds have sprung an ambush. Sheltering in a ditch, first Heck then Judd are wounded.

As the shots ring out, a cut to the high country above the farm reveals that Westrum, far from fleeing in the opposite direction, has been following them. He comes charging down, gun blazing. The Hammonds shoot his horse from under him, but he makes it unscathed to the shelter of the ditch. He and Judd challenge the Hammonds to meet them halfway. The two old-timers walk out to face the three remaining brothers. In the exchange of shots, the Hammonds go down, but Judd sustains another wound, this one fatal. Westrum promises to 'take care of things'. Reconciled, his friend forgiven, Judd takes one last look at the mountains behind him then sinks back to the ground.

It's almost too easy to describe how explicitly *Ride the High Country* prefigures later Peckinpah films [1] – but it still makes for an interesting list. Let's start with visual elements. Leitmotifs are scattered throughout the opening scene: Judd rides into town, an old man, his hair grey, but still cutting an imposing figure in the saddle (cf. William Holden in *The Wild Bunch*, James Coburn in *Pat Garrett and Billy the Kid*); a police officer in a uniform that makes him look more like Dixon of Dock Green than a marshall tries, ineffectually, to be assertive with Judd (authority figures are scornfully depicted in *The Wild Bunch, Cross of Iron* and *Convoy*); an automobile proves intrusive and threatening as Judd, dismounting, crosses the street (Mapache's car is used to drag Angel around in *The Wild Bunch*, Cable is run over by Hildy's car in *The Ballad of Cable Hogue*); a mother drags her children away from the spectacle of a gyrating belly dancer (children doing, or bearing witness to acts that corrupt their innocence is revisited in virtually every Peckinpah film – specific examples are cited in successive chapters).

At Coarsegold, characters get roaring drunk and dally with prostitutes (cf. *The Wild Bunch, The Ballad of Cable Hogue, Pat Garrett and Billy the Kid*); at Knudsen's farm, the image of chickens pecking desultorily away is used to precede an outburst of violence (cf. *Pat Garrett and Billy the Kid, Cross of Iron*). That the climactic gunfight takes place not in the high country of the title but a farmyard, is an effective metaphor for the territory, once wild in the protagonists' youth, now being tamed and fenced off (cf. *Pat Garrett and Billy the Kid*).

Heck waxing lyrical about going to San Francisco, angling to persuade Elsa to go with him, is prescient of Hildy's determination to make a new start in that selfsame city in *Cable Hogue*. Judd's backstory of love and loss (a relationship that, had it worked out, would have saved him from becoming such an isolated figure in later life) is taken to its logical conclusion (love unattained because of death) in the tragedy that befalls Aurora in *The Wild Bunch*. Judd's uncertainty about a younger man ('he'll do,' he says of Heck in a barely suppressed tone of doubt, 'he'll do just fine') foreshadows Pike's ambivalence about 'Crazy' Lee.

Other bits of dialogue strike a chord: the vehement oath 'peckerwood' (elevated to dimestore poetry when preceded by 'you goddamn two-bit redneck' in *The Wild Bunch*); a Hammond brother's exhortation to 'start the ball' as they square off with Judd and Westrum (cf. Lyle to Tector Gorch in *The Wild Bunch* when ambushed by Mapache's men).

Aside from these obvious examples, *Ride the High Country* is a blueprint in theme and subtext. Men outliving their times, technological innovations having made them anachronisms; the value of comradeship and the ease with which it is betrayed; guilt, regret and redemption; religion and law as questionable values; flawed men doing bad things because there's no other option. With only a few exceptions, you can pick any film that has the words 'directed by Sam Peckinpah' in the credits and find any and all of these obsessions swirling in the very celluloid, like the demons that drove their creator.

The polarities in Peckinpah's personality owed to his father. The rectitude with which he quoted the Bible had always seemed to Sam at odds with his courtroom performances. Right and wrong, so clearly demarcated in the Bible, merged into a pervasive grey area that occupied the space between the dock and the witness box. In Steve Judd, Peckinpah had the ideal canvas to investigate these complexities.

Judd is an older man. His formative years are rooted in a time that is becoming lost. So too Peckinpah's father and grandfather were, for him, a connection to the past – or at least to the mythic imaginings of it that he so yearned for. Judd is a former lawman, now riding the range doing whatever job he can find that dovetails with his own sense of personal integrity. Similarly, David Peckinpah and Denver Church were stern authority figures who believed in a stoically masculine ethos. As the film progresses, Judd's self-respect seems more like self-righteousness. Consider his exchange with Elsa, just before they return to her father's farm.

> Elsa: My father says there's only right and wrong, good and evil. Nothing in
>   between. It isn't that simple, is it?
> Judd: No, it isn't. It should be, but it isn't.
> Elsa: What's going to happen to him [Heck]?
> Judd: I'll testify for him. They shouldn't be too harsh.
> Elsa: Will you testify for Mr Westrum?
> Judd: No, I won't.
> Elsa: Why?
> Judd: Because he was my friend.

What Westrum refers to as Steve's 'iron-bound code of ethics' is a form of sheer bloody-mindedness that seems to overwhelm all other concepts. If friendship can be remoulded in this fashion to suit Judd's sacrosanct concept of justice, then materialism doesn't even come close.

> Westrum: Partner, you know what's on the back of a poor man when he dies? The clothes of pride. And they're not a bit warmer to him dead than they were when he was alive. Is that all you want, Steve?
> Judd: All I want is to enter my house justified.

Integrity is one thing, but this mentality leaves Judd rather too resemblant of Knudsen for comfort.

Knudsen, if anything, has an even more severe approach to personal relationships. Whereas Judd personifies law and order at its most inflexible, Knudsen represents the Old Testament at its grimmest and most unforgiving. Two biblical quotes are displayed at the Knudsen property. The more palatable is hung up indoors:

> When pride cometh then cometh shame
> but with the lowly is wisdom.

A sentiment obviously tailored for the moral improvement of the self. Even Westrum is inspired to tell Heck 'there's a lot of truth in those words'.

The other, challenging the bounds of propriety, gives the truer measure of Joshua Knudsen. It is carved on his wife's headstone and reads thus:

> Therefore, O harlot, hear the word of the Lord!
> I will judge thee as women that break wedlock
> and shed blood are judged. I will give thee blood
> in fury and in jealousy

This aspect of Knudsen's fundamentalist religious beliefs is brought even more disturbingly into focus in his treatment of Elsa after he catches her with Heck in the yard. Even though what passes between them is little more than an amiable conversation by moonlight, Knudsen drags her inside, ranting that 'the likes o' him don't stop at talking'. When she protests, he deals her an open-handed blow that knocks her to the floor.

And yet Knudsen's overriding imperative is to protect his daughter. It is just his methods of doing so that are questionable. But then, both Knudsen and Elsa are characters in whom ambiguities are writ large. True, Knudsen is a zealot, but his death at the hands of the Hammonds proves that his prejudices against the denizens of Coarsegold are well founded. On the other hand, Elsa – who is ostensibly the character the audience should most sympathize with; ill-done-to, a veritable prisoner in her own home – is the catalyst, in her unswayable determination to run away to Coarsegold and get married, for the deaths of her father and Steve Judd.

Peckinpah brings a similar degree of non-judgemental ambivalence to his depiction of the Hammonds. Macho assholes they may be, abusing women and starting fights with men at the drop of hat – and brawling amongst themselves when there's no-one else around – but their behaviour represents a white-trash thesis on fraternity. The gee-whizz pride with which Billy introduces his brothers to Elsa, ascribing specific attributes to each in turn, shows that the Hammonds respect each other's individuality even as they function as a unit [2]. Their code is demonstrated at the gunfight. Huddled in Knudsen's farmhouse, they are challenged by Westrum: 'Are you too chicken-gutted to finish this thing out in the open?' When Elder (John Anderson) suggests they 'catch 'em when they raise up', Billy rounds on him: 'Ain't you got no sense of family honour?' Elder desists from arguing the point and falls in behind his brother.

Heck attempts to take liberties with Elsa in Ride the High Country.

Just as multi layered is the relationship between Judd and Westrum. Conventionally, Westrum should be the minor villain of the piece who comes back to the fold when faced with a greater enemy in the shape of the Hammonds. Likewise, Judd should be the charismatic hero with all the cool dialogue. Which is how it was in The High Country According To N B Stone. Reimagined by Peckinpah, however, Judd is an ambivalent figure, upstanding but aloof. It is Westrum, laconic and witty, who is the more likeable.

From his first scene, sporting false whiskers and trading on a fictionalised version of the past, it doesn't take a Pinkerton agent to see he's a charlatan, a huckster. But it is this genial amorality which endears us to him. His repertoire of one-liners only wins us over the faster. At table in the Knudsen kitchen, as Judd and his host conduct an allegorical quick-draw competition, spitting out chapter and verse the way a Peacemaker spits bullets, it's Westrum who gets the last word. 'You cook a lovely ham hog, Miss Knudsen,' he compliments Elsa, 'just lovely. Appetite, chapter one.'

Hauling Heck off Elsa when he gets a little too fervent with her out on the trail, Judd responds to the youth's show of anger by decking him with one punch. Then he rounds – verbally – on Westrum. 'When I questioned you about that boy, I should have gone a bit deeper into the subject of character,' he pontificates. Westrum is oblivious to the criticism. 'Good fight,' he deadpans; 'I enjoyed it.' Shortly afterwards, when Elsa tells him 'you got just what you deserved', Heck bristles at the sight of Westrum smirking at him from across the campfire. 'You got something to say?' he demands. 'No,' Westrum replies affably, 'I think she about covered everything.'

For all his joshing, Westrum would seem the more logical choice as mentor to Heck – he's certainly the kind of guy Heck will end up as in middle-age – but slowly his role in the formation of Heck's character is superseded by Judd. The fight, abrupt as it may be, is the turning point. It puts Judd and Westrum on an equal footing in their influence on Heck [3]. Westrum helps him up and dusts him off.

Heck: That old man is about half rough.
Westrum: You learned a lesson, didn't you?
Heck: I surely did.
Westrum: Got room for another?
Heck: Let her fly.

And poor Heck goes sprawling on his ass again. From here on in, his cockiness wears off. When he delivers Elsa to the Hammonds at Coarsegold, a more human side becomes apparent. He sees immediately that she doesn't realize what she's getting herself into. For the first time in his life, Heck starts to care about someone, to fear for them, to want to protect them. As his stands outside Kate's Place, a picture of anguish, listening to the rowdy wedding celebrations from within, it is Judd not Westrum who joins him. 'No use standing here tormenting yourself, son,' he says. 'Come on, I'll buy you a drink.'

Westrum's conduct, on the other hand, grows harsher. The signs of regeneration in Heck that Judd responds to are seen by Westrum as weakness. When Heck voices his uncertainty about going through with the robbery, Westrum leaves him with no way out.

Westrum: Tonight we move.
Heck: I don't know.
Westrum: You don't know what?
Heck: I started out thinking he [Judd] was an old moss bag, but I changed my mind. Kinda hate to turn against him.
Westrum: Are you with me or not? ... The thing for you to remember is that we made a deal.
Heck: Yes, sir.

Judd has now become the sympathetic father figure, Westrum his bullying alter ego. This is further evidenced when Heck and Judd intercede at Kate's Place. Heck goes in, fists balled, and for his troubles takes as many blows as he gives. Judd follows him in, slowly, with determination, gun already drawn. His jaw is set in a rigid line. The law man of old is back – and back in control. Even as Heck picks himself up off the floor, it's Judd that Elsa runs to, clutching his arm like a child clinging to a protective parent. Later, however, when Judd has subdued Westrum and it is within his power to be merciful and forgiving, the full strength of his ramrod concept of the law comes to the fore and, with the exception of Knudsen, he becomes perhaps the least magnanimous character in the film. The roles have shifted again, and our perceptions with them.

Ride the High Country is a ninety minute western that MGM saw as little more than a B-picture. Complex, isn't it?

Through all the layers of character and motivation, and paralleling the development of Heck as a man, runs the central theme of the film: men growing old. From *The Wild Bunch* on, this would be refined into the more *götterdämmerung*-like theme of men outliving their times. That Peckinpah fashioned such an aesthetically valid statement of intent with only his second film is an achievement. What is quite remarkable is that he was thirty-seven when he made it.

Every frame of *Ride the High Country* is stamped with affinity and sympathy for older men, as well as a readiness to show them as still able to cut it with gun or fist. They talk about the past continually, much to Heck's contempt. But there is never sentiment or nostalgia. Sure, the times might have been better, but there were prices to be paid. Bedded down in Knudsen's barn, Heck's attentions towards Elsa prompt Westrum to mention a former girlfriend of Judd's, Sarah Truesdale. Judd's reaction is predictably unemotive, so it is left to Westrum to find the words. And he certainly does find them, soliloquising like it was he who had carried the torch: 'The way she smiles. [The] look in her eyes where you're talking to her, the kind of look that makes you feel you've said something real important ... I guess losing Sarah is what you might call a hazard of our profession.'

Judd and Westrum, reminiscing about the old days in Ride the High Country.

The scene is beautifully understated. It opens a small chink in Judd's defences, making us wonder what else he's been holding inside and for how long. It also begs the question of how lonely and isolated Westrum's life has been, that he can assume the disenchantments of his friend's life with such ease, slipping into Judd's festering, unexpressed regrets as if he were pulling on an old and patchy item of clothing. This metaphor is an obvious one, since Peckinpah uses it in the shape of Judd's footwear. His worn-down boots are used first for comic effect, Judd deflecting Westrum's comment on their state with a rare display of humour: 'Juan Fernandez made those ... special order – I had a hell of a time getting him to put that hole in there. A fine craftsman, Juan, but he never did understand the principle of ventilation.' Later, though, voicing the first thing that comes to mind in an attempt to change the subject when Westrum mentions Sarah, he ruminates about getting them fixed at the next town.

Likewise, while the sight of genre icons McCrea and Scott parading around a barn in their longjohns or bathing their feet in a stream might raise a smile, the moment when Westrum asks Judd to untie him (the implication is that he suffering from arthritis), is all too real. This mirrors a much earlier scene, that of Judd's interview with the bank officials. Two dour men, father and son, one old and one middle-aged: not only do they have the gall to tell him they 'expected a much younger man' ('I used to be,' Judd replies bitterly; 'we all used to be'), but go on to disabuse his entire way of life by declaring 'the days of the forty-niners are past and the days of the steady businessman have arrived'. After all this, embarrassed to put on his spectacles in front of them, he withdraws to the washroom to read the contract. The critics who berate Peckinpah's later films for violent content conveniently forget moments like these, where humour and pathos combine to give a sharper insight into his characters' humanity.

The conditions under which Judd and Westrum have conducted their working lives are memorably enumerated in a scene whose narrative purpose (Westrum's continued attempts to gauge if Judd has any inclination towards getting in on the robbery himself) is all but jettisoned by Peckinpah in his search for the heart and soul of his characters:

> Judd: Just to pass the time one day, I sort of calculated what it was worth gettin'
> shot at. I figured about a hundred dollars a shot.
> Westrum: You'd have earned quite a sum by now.
> Judd: Gettin' hit. I figure that's worth anywhere from a thousand on up.
> Westrum: That's three thousand I know you've got coming.
> Judd: Four brings it up to date.

Four bullets taken in the course of his career! And that's not the full story. Judd goes on to describe the more prosaic setbacks: 'all those fights and bush-whackings ... that time in Lincoln County, five weeks in the hospital and six months out of work.' And yet this is what they look fondly back on when all they have up ahead are more nights of not sleeping so good.

In David Lynch's *The Straight Story* – a film whose concerns and iconography are subtly Peckinpahesque – Alvin Straight (Richard Farnsworth) opines that 'the worst part of being old is remembering when you were young'. Of course, Alvin Straight is older than any of Peckinpah's protagonists, but if Steve Judd or Pike Bishop or Pat Garrett had lived another decade or so ...

Judd and Westrum, while remembering what it was like to be young, are still not so old that they can't have one last crack at recapturing it. Westrum professes to having 'an overwhelming hankering for a little old-time activity' when he offers his services to Judd (who has been too proud to ask for his assistance outright). Judd, on the other hand, aligns age with proof of one's character. Of Heck's boyish tendency to talk big and ogle at girls, he remarks, 'He can't have too much behind him ... No pride, no self-respect. Plenty of gall, but no sand.'

By the time they have set in motion the events at Coarsegold, and through the disintegration and renewal of their partnership on the trail afterwards, the lives of all three will have changed: Heck has some of the gall knocked out of him and develops a little sand; Westrum takes on some of his friend's sense of self-respect and accountability; and Judd, in his dying words, heals the rifts of the recent past, demonstrating his humanity even as he maintains his integrity.

'That mining town is a sinkhole of depravity,' Knudsen says of Coarsegold; 'a place of shame and sin.' Offering grace at dinner, he asks the Lord to forgive Judd and co. their mercenary desires. Judd tries to reason with him, arguing that they are transporting gold, not trafficking in it. (Westrum strikes a truer if more cynical note when he assures Heck, out of earshot of Knudsen, 'the Lord's bounty may not be for sale, but the Devil's is – if you pay the price.')

Knudsen's words will come back to haunt them when they reach the town – if it can be called a town, that is. As they ride in, the sight that greets them prompts another burst of sarcasm from Westrum:

> Westrum: Lovely place. A beauty spot of nature. A garden of Eden for the sore
> in heart and short of cash.
> Judd: We didn't come here to enjoy the scenery.

Just as well. Coarsegold consists of a main street of ragged tents, each equipped with a wood stove belching smoke through an outlet in the canvas. Badly written signs announce individual claims. Piles of firewood and overturned wheelbarrows provide decor. Snow, trodden down into a dirty sludge, covers everything. At the head of this appalling vista, huge peals of vulgar laughter emanating from its obese proprietress, stands the only proper building: Kate's Place.

The place is bad. The people are worse. A group of young women laugh at Judd, Westrum and Heck as they ride past, one of them tossing out a bucket of what could be slops or something decidedly worse. They are lucky not to be splattered by the effluent. Equally filthy is the Hammonds's little home-from-home, to which Heck escorts Elsa. We see the youngest of the clan first, shaving in a broken mirror. He appears backward, perhaps inbred. But he is a class act – and a model of hygiene – compared to the others. Okay, so Billy has the chiselled good looks, but underneath that handsome exterior beats the heart of a twenty-two carat gold bastard. Instead of expressing gratitude to Heck for bringing to him his bride-to-be, Billy accuses him of getting it on with her. Elsa placates him: 'Mr Longtree was a perfect gentleman.'

'Why?' Billy sneers. 'What's wrong with him?'

Heck reins in his horse and trots defeatedly away. With the pettiness of young children, the Hammonds pelt him with stones [4]. Elsa, half pityingly, bites back her laughter. The act shows her up as the deluded innocent her father has created – in allaying herself with Billy, she knows not what she does. She perceives the Hammonds's behaviour as humorous only because it is the opposite of her father's demeanour. It is not till later – hauled into the back room of a whorehouse, her virtue threatened by all four of them – that she learns the truth.

Before he instructs Heck to take her to the Hammonds's tent, Judd tells Elsa, 'It's not too late, you can change your mind.' But the girl is headstrong. 'I came to Coarsegold to be married,' she insists, 'and that's what I'm going to be – married.'

Marry in haste, repent at leisure, the old adage has it. Elsa begins to repent of it no sooner than the marriage ceremony begins. The Hammonds ride up to Kate's Place singing raucously. The tune is 'When the Roll is Called Up Yonder We'll Be There', the last verse portentously rewritten to include the line 'for to tie the knot that binds them till they die'. The man doing the tying of said knot is a shambolic drunk. Kate is quite simply the bridesmaid from hell – corpulent, distastefully dressed, braying with unwholesome laughter. That she takes it upon herself to outfit three of her whores as flower girls is one of her least questionable acts. It gives some measure of Coarsegold that Kate's girls are the only inhabitants who come across in anything remotely approaching a positive light.

This is indeed the vision of Hell that Knudsen warns of – and which, tragically, comes thundering out of Coarsegold and into his own backyard. But his vision is preconception, not perception. Knudsen and Judd, the two characters in the film most defined by the fortitude of their convictions, both die of the same cause: a nasty dose of the Hammonds. Knudsen dies because he shirks the world, Judd because he stands up to it. Knudsen dies alone, Judd standing side by side with his old friend.

> Westrum: Partner, whaddya think?
> Judd: Let's meet 'em head on, halfway, just like always.
> Westrum: My sentiments exactly.

And so they rise up to face their antagonists, the mountains behind them as they stride out for one last bout of old-time activity. The shots ring out; the Hammonds go down. Judd, too, sinks into the dust. 'How did we figure, a thousand dollars a shot?' he asks. Westrum nods.

'Those boys sure made me a lot of money.'

Heck and Elsa make their way over, concerned. Judd waves them away. 'I don't want them to see this,' he says; 'I'll go it alone.'

All this is rhetorical. The price of each shot is reckoned in human terms, not dollars and cents. As for going it alone, Judd takes with him into the hereafter the reaffirmation of his friendship with Westrum:

> Westrum: Don't worry about anything. I'll take care of it. Just like you would.
> Judd: Hell, I know that. I always did. You just forgot it for a while, that's all. So long, partner.
> Westrum: I'll see you later.

Westrum leads Heck and Elsa away. Judd looks back over his shoulder, gazing on the snow-capped peaks. Then his lifeless body slumps forward and out of the frame. The mountains remain in focus. Against their timeless splendour, Peckinpah measures the stature of one man's life.

'DOING WHAT YOU'VE GOT TO DO' : *Major Dundee*

Transferred to a godforsaken little garrison in New Mexico as a result of disciplinary proceedings, Major Amos Dundee (Charlton Heston) arrives in time to witness the aftermath of the latest raid by Apache war chief Sierra Charriba. Affronted by the wholesale murder of men and women and the kidnap of children, Dundee undertakes to hunt Charriba down.

Joining him in his completely unofficial mission are indian scout Samuel Potts (James Coburn), the hardy Sergeant Gomez (Mario Adorf) and the annoyingly over-enthusiastic Lieutenant Graham (Jim Hutton). The latter acquires armaments from a munitions train bound for another fort entirely. A convicted rustler is released from the garrison's jail to outfit the regiment with horses. Not that it's much of a regiment. Tim Ryan (Michael Anderson Jr), the youthful bugler who is the only survivor of Charriba's attack, signs up; so does Reverend Dahlstrom (R G Armstrong), keen to do the vengeance-is-mine act on the Lord's behalf. But with enlisted men thin on the ground, and the Negro guards who volunteer swelling the ranks by only half a dozen, Dundee is forced to consider the incarcerated men: thieves, cut-throats and Confederate prisoners. Marshalling them in the parade ground, he offers them quarter pay and a pardon when it's all over. Speaking up for his fellow internees, Captain Benjamin Tyreen (Richard Harris), expatriate Irishman, Confederate, and one-time friend of the Major, invites him to go to hell. Tyreen is still sore about Dundee giving evidence against him following a duelling incident. Dundee, provoked by Tyreen's incitement against him of his would-be army, offers him revised terms: volunteer or be hanged.

Tyreen and his Confederates volunteer.

The regiment ride out of the garrison under Dundee's command – Tyreen acting as his second-in-command – and the long trek into Mexico begins. Tempers are frayed from the start: the Confederates sing 'Dixie' as they ride, the Union boys angrily responding with 'The Battle Hymn of the American Republic'; Dundee and Tyreen are at each other's throats; one of Tyreen's men baits the guards with racist insults. This particular incident is resolved when Dahlstrom steps in and gives the Confederate a righteous kicking.

Their first taste of action finds them hopelessly unprepared. Charriba's men spring an ambush during a river crossing. There are casualties, and essential supplies (including the Major's 'medicinal brandy') are lost. They head for the nearest village to recuperate and replenish their provisions. It turns out to be under the command of French troops, who are battling the Juristas in nearby territories. Spokeswoman for the villagers Teresa Santiago (Senta Berger), a German-born nurse who is the widow of the mayor, tells Dundee that they have nothing to offer: under the auspices of the French, depletion and hunger are rife. Using a small bore howitzer, Dundee opens fire on the French garrison. Surrender is immediate. Dundee redistributes the supplies liberated from the fort to the

Major Dundee surveys the aftermath of the disastrous river crossing.

villagers, then orders an evening of drunkenness and celebration. Young Ryan gets taken in hand by local beauty Linda (Begonia Palacios) and made a man of. Tyreen takes a fancy to Teresa, but Dundee wins her over first.

Under cover of darkness, the French prisoners escape and make their way to Durango, which is occupied by their fellow countrymen. This is what Dundee was planning all along. He dispatches a small decoy unit to lead them on a wild goose chase. Meanwhile, he and the rest of his regiment continue their pursuit of Charriba. They are presently re-joined by the decoy unit, and it would seem a simple matter now of taking care of the unfinished business with Charriba, before going home.

The situation turns nasty with the desertion of O W Hadley (Warren Oates), one of Tyreen's men. Dundee wastes valuable time having him tracked down. When Gomez brings him back, he also brings news of French reprisals against the village. Teresa and Linda, who have been lucky to escape with their lives, accompany him. Dundee resumes his courtship of Teresa, but not before he makes Hadley answer for his cowardice. Hadley's story of going back for a woman and having every intention of returning is patently false, but Dundee's sentence of death by firing squad is delivered so ruthlessly that it divides the regiment. Tyreen's men are in favour of filling the Major full of lead. Tyreen acts in true 'Lawrence of Arabia' style, performing the execution himself. He then swears to Dundee that he'll kill him once Charriba has been dealt with.

Not that the death threat seems to worry him: he's soon getting amorous with Teresa down by the river. Her charms, however, render him a little slow at reacting when a couple of Charriba's scouts take pot shots at him. Tyreen and Gomez arrive in time to despatch the indians with a few well-aimed rounds, but an arrow in the leg leaves Dundee in agony. They smuggle him into Durango and manage to arrange medical treatment. He orders them back to the regiment, saying he'll rejoin them.

Teresa makes her way to Durango, full of concern, only to find him with a whore. He pleads with her, but she leaves. Later, he gets drunk and passes out in a seedy bar. Tyreen and Gomez come looking for him. They get him sobered up; he brawls with Tyreen; they leave in a hail of gunfire from irate French soldiers.

Rejoining the regiment, they make their last push in search of Charriba. The Apaches, having converged behind them during their enforced encampment, begin stalking *them*. Come nightfall, Dundee's men bed down. Outwitting the minimal and ineffectually placed sentries, Charriba's men make their attack. But Dundee's lowered defences are a bluff: his men rise up and lay waste to their antagonists. Charriba is shot by Ryan.

The objective achieved, Tyreen has a score to settle with Dundee. But even as they square up to each other, Potts alerts them that a platoon of French lancers are approaching at full pelt. The Frenchmen take their positions along the banks of the Rio Grande, effectively cutting off Dundee's return to American soil. Again using the howitzer, Dundee fires on them, provoking a bloody confrontation. Despite heavy losses, Dundee's regiment prevails. Dundee and Tyreen, side by side in a river red with European blood, look set to resume their duel, until French reinforcements appear on the opposite shore. In an unprecedented *volte face*, Tyreen rides into their midst, sword drawn, sacrificing himself so that Dundee and his men can cross the river and make it home.

The critical tendency to regard *Major Dundee* as a backwards step is certainly accurate in relation to the backstage betrayals that saw the studio rip the heart out of Peckinpah's original two hour forty minute cut, but what of the film that remains? Objective analysis is difficult: the film is laden with a heartbreaking sense of 'what if'. While Sam Leavitt's cinematography is by no means bad, it is tempting to re-imagine the film as shot by Lucien Ballard. One also wishes Jerry Fielding had written the score; as it is, the film opens with an appalling song, 'The Major Dundee March' (vocals courtesy of an untuneful outfit calling themselves Mitch Miller's Sing Along Gang), the basic motif of which the rest of the orchestration is based on. The music was the studio's choice; its inclusion was as painful to Sam as any of the cutting or re-editing. The blame, too, can be laid at Columbia's door for the clunky voice-over, a device which papers over the gaping holes in the narrative with the dull prose of Ryan's diary entries.

At the time of release, Peckinpah stated that his original cut 'ran beautifully', an assertion that would seem to be born out by Richard Harris's claim that the full version of *Major Dundee* was the best film he had ever starred in. Five years down the line, with *The Wild Bunch* in the bag and *The Ballad of Cable Hogue* under way, he was still bemoaning *Dundee*'s fate, describing it (in its original incarnation) as the finest film he had made. Fighting talk, especially in view of his achievements on *The Wild Bunch*. Columbia took the bait and threw down the gauntlet: come and re-edit the film. But Peckinpah backed off. He was too busy, he said, on *Cable Hogue*. As David Weddle observes, '*Dundee* was more useful as a lost masterpiece than a rediscovered failure' [5]. Peckinpah's thinking is easy to fathom – a legitimate grudge about the desecration of a major work would give him ammunition against any future interference – but in declining Columbia's offer, he shot himself in the foot. Not only would his tale of woe count for nothing in the face of future battles with producers, but passing up the chance to restore *Major Dundee* counts as two own-goals: (i) he deprived his audience of, if not a masterpiece, then certainly a damn good movie, and (ii) he allowed his critics to reassert that the shortcomings of *Dundee* were his, not Columbia's.

As it stands, *Major Dundee* is never less than entertaining, but unfortunately it begins to disintegrate in its last three-quarters of an hour. The music and voice-over irritate from the start, but it's the tension-weakening romantic subplot that really damages the film. Dundee is introduced as an embittered man, full of hate that his superiors have removed him from the arena of conflict and made him little more than a jailer. Charriba's outrage adds indignation; the presence of Tyreen makes it even more personal; that the makeshift army he assembles are reprobates, far below par to the type of professional soldiers he is used to commanding, just adds salt to the wound. It is therefore reasonable to expect that when he finally confronts Charriba, his fury will know no bounds.

Not so. Well into the second hour, when things should be picking up speed, an exciting finale in sight, he goes and falls in love. Men in love – those whose ardour is requited, anyway – tend not to be dangerous, on-the-edge, or up for a damned good ruck with a marauding war-chief; they tend instead to be somewhat lyrical and non violent. The resultant deceleration of the film's pace is bad enough, but it also necessitates pushing into the background terrific characters such as Dahlstrom, Aesop (leader of the 'coloureds' who volunteers for no other reason than boredom with guard duty) and Wiley (the inebriate mule packer brought memorably to life by Slim Pickens), so that a rather bland heroine can take centre stage. Brickbats are often aimed at Senta Berger's performance as Teresa, and though an actress of limited expressiveness in any role, she's no worse here than in any of her other appearances. She's simply given stultifying dull material to work with. The potential for her development as a Mexican Florence Nightingale, her dedication to healing and non-violence in contrast to the undisguised violence of Dundee's soul, exists but is not developed. For all that Dundee's wounding provides an ironic coda to it, their consummation is risible, not least because it is preceded by Hadley's execution, Dundee's heartlessness in this scene being directly at odds with Teresa's humanitarian ethics.

A better indication of the ephemerality of romantic liaisons for the fighting man can be found in Ryan's dalliance with Linda. When he reports for roll call the next morning – monstrously late, smug as hell, the young lady still on his arm – Dundee tears him off a strip. Ryan takes Linda in his arms, passionately kisses her goodbye, and falls in with the rest of the men, who whoop and holler their approval. (Peckinpah compounds Ryan's sexual rite of passage by having the young man take his first shave in the next scene.)

Of course, once a romantic element has been introduced into a western, it soon has to be removed or sidelined so it doesn't intrude upon the requisite climactic gunplay. The Ryan/Linda relationship is dealt with by having the young man 'put it in the saddle' and ride off with his *compadres* (although Peckinpah does have a heart, and reunites them later). The Dundee/Teresa relationship is a different matter, and is curtailed as arbitrarily as it began.

The film has already suffered a slowing of pace, the intensity of earlier scenes mellowing to the point of soporific. When Teresa bursts in on Dundee with his whore, there is another change in tone: an abrupt lurch into psychological portraiture. Dundee, who exhibits no interest in women before he meets Teresa, suddenly degrades himself in a cheap room, then drinks himself into a stupor of self-loathing. When Tyreen and Gomez find him, the implication is that they don't just rescue him from imminent discovery by the French forces stationed in Durango [6], but save him from himself.

With hindsight, Peckinpah's intent is discernible: there is a comparable scene in *The Wild Bunch* where Pike Bishop visits a young prostitute, the resultant sense of guilt and shame pushing him towards self-destruction. The scene is more fully realized in *The Wild Bunch*, however, since Pike's psychology has been explored throughout the film. *Major Dundee* contains no foregoing moments of insight into its anti-hero's character, no suggestion as to why he would risk sabotaging his relationship with Teresa. The most probable reason would be to drive her away from him so that he can resume his single-minded pursuit of Charriba – but this doesn't explain his subsequent descent into drunken abandonment. Just as sudden, and equally unconvincing, is his recovery; he

Dundee's men open fire on Charriba's forces in Major Dundee.

re-establishes command of the men as if nothing had happened, and engineers a well-thought-out piece of military strategy to trap and swiftly defeat Charriba's army. Again, *The Wild Bunch* succeeds where *Major Dundee* fails: Pike's self-loathing is expurgated through catharsis; Dundee's confrontation, however, is logically planned and professionally executed. There is no sense of a man driven by his past, his regrets, or his demons. He's simply a soldier doing what he does best. And since his campaign against Charriba owes to a desire to be a leader of men again, instead of a jailer, his morose indulgence in drinking and whoring – which serve only to prolong his enforced absence from his men – makes even less sense.

Essentially, Peckinpah's brief journey into Dundee's heart of darkness is not preceded by anything relative to it, nor does it influence the denouement. A better insight into Dundee's character is given in Hadley's execution scene. Hadley, shackled, is on horseback as Gomez brings him back to camp; he proceeds to spin his cock-and-bull story in denial of the charge of desertion. Dundee hears him out, then speaks to Gomez: 'Sergeant, I don't want to look up at him.' Gomez, mounted next to Hadley, kicks him from the saddle. As he continues to embellish his story, Hadley literally crawls in front of Dundee. Again, the Major listens impassively. Then he demolishes Hadley's account: he couldn't have gone back for a girl because the town had been routed by the French by then (although it never seems to occur to Dundee that he was the cause); he had no intention of returning immediately afterwards because he stole three days' supplies.

Realizing he can't hoodwink his way out, Hadley tries grovelling. He beseeches Tyreen not to let Dundee kill him. Tyreen, although in no less doubt about Hadley's guilt, speaks up for him:

Tyreen: Major, hand him over to us. I'll deal with him. I'm not going to let you
    kill him.

Dundee: You used to be a soldier. Do you know what you're saying?

Tyreen: I know what I'm saying. I'm saying if you kill that boy that's the
    beginning of it and not the end.

Dundee: You're wearing out, Ben. You were like a rock once and now you're
    crumbling like old chalk.

This is who Dundee really is: a strict, unemotional, my-word-is-law military officer. And he does what military officers do: lead men, fight campaigns, and punish transgressors. He is single minded. His refusal to deviate from the standard procedure of punishing desertion by execution almost tears his regiment apart. When Tyreen regretfully tells Hadley that he's obliged to let Dundee pass sentence ('you should have remembered you belong to the Major and not to me'), the Confederates step forward, guns at the ready, and it's all that Tyreen can do to make them hold their positions. Hadley's valediction – 'Hell, Major, you're just doing what you've got to do, but damn your soul to hell for it – and God bless Robert E Lee!' – looks set to gain him instant martyrdom and tip the stand-off into actual violence. It is left to Tyreen to prevent Dundee's campaign from disintegrating then and there: he carries out the sentence himself. Tyreen's gun roars even as Hadley invokes the name of Lee.

Just as Dundee's lack of emotion in this scene renders nonsensical the 'troubled soul' business in Durango, Tyreen's vow that he will kill Dundee after Charriba is defeated is delivered with such cold hatred that his suicidal gallop into the midst of enemy forces at the end of the film (result: Dundee's continued existence) is inexplicable.

It is easy, in discussing a flawed film, to speak of glimpses of a director's genius. To do so with *Major Dundee* would be a disservice. In Hadley's execution, Peckinpah's genius is more than glimpsed – it's stamped across the screen. There are enough scenes of equal brilliance – Dundee's address to the prisoners; the Confederates trying to out-sing their Union opponents (a stand-off wittily subverted when the regiment's politically unaffiliated criminal element strike up with 'Clementine'); the racist incident that results in the retributive beating doled out by Dahlstrom; the ambush crossing the river; the charge of the French lancers – to make *Major Dundee*, even in the version Columbia released, a better film that it is generally remembered as.

Nor can Columbia's editorial butchery disguise the first-rate cast: Heston and Harris are excellent; Oates, Chandler and Armstrong reunite from *Ride the High Country*; Coburn (not the obvious choice for a one-armed indian scout, but turning in a fine piece of characterization nonetheless) makes his Peckinpah debut, along with L Q Jones, Ben Johnson, Dub Taylor, Aurora Clavel and Slim Pickens (who gets the splendid opening line 'If you want an injun-fightin', mule-packin', whisky-drinkin' volunteer, sir, well by God you've got one!'). Even Senta Berger would reappear in *Cross of Iron*.

Major Dundee is also watchable as an exercise in Spot The Try-out For *The Wild Bunch*: the scenes at Teresa's village prefigure those at Angel's, the protagonists discovering their humanity as they learn of the villagers' tribulations; reprisals effected by the French are resemblant of Mapache's tyranny; as mentioned, Dundee and Pike reach their personal nadir in the company of whores; both films feature crossings into Mexico for unorthodox purposes.

All told, it is frustrating that Peckinpah never accepted Columbia's offer to re-edit *Major Dundee*, since it leaves unanswered two questions that might have gone some way to critically restoring the film's reputation: would its weaker elements – the interlude in Durango particularly – be strengthened by the reinstatement of deleted material? And would the romantic subplot, which occupies too much of the second half, be so intrusive coming, say, earlier than the half way mark in a two hour forty-one minute film?

'YOUR DIM REFLECTION, LORD': *The Ballad of Cable Hogue*

Perhaps the most unusual treatment of the western in Peckinpah's filmography is *The Ballad of Cable Hogue*. Hell, it's probably his single most unusual film, not least because it trades cordite for comedy. At the time of its release in 1970, comedy westerns were already established as part of box office repertoire, Elliot Silverstein's *Cat Ballou* (1965) and Burt Kennedy's *Support Your Local Sheriff* (1968) having proved hugely popular, the former even netting an Oscar for its star, Lee Marvin.

Peckinpah's oddity, however, is more than just slapstick amongst the sagebrush. It's about revenge, God, water, friendship, love, loss of same, the re-attainment thereof (almost!), and – inevitably – the unstoppable force of changing times. It's also frequently hilarious.

From the synopsis, though, it doesn't sound so funny:

Cable Hogue (Jason Robards), a saddletramp and one of life's losers, is stuck in the desert with his partners in crime, Bowen and Taggart (Strother Martin and L Q Jones). Down to one canteen, they rob him of same (it contains enough water for two of them to get out of the desert, but not three) and leave him to die. Swearing vengeance, he begins a long trek across the inhospitable sands. He keeps up a one-way dialogue with God, alternately pleading with and berating the Almighty. After four days, plagued by a sandstorm and ready to admit defeat, he finds water.

Reinvigorated, he continues his odyssey, finally encountering a stagecoach. He learns from the driver (Slim Pickens) that he is midway between the towns of Gila and Dead Dog, a route that is troubling in that there is nowhere to stop and water the horses. Declining a ride into Dead Dog, Hogue returns to the well and erects a sign charging ten cents a drink. When the first drifter who happens along displays an indisposition to make with the coinage, reaching instead for his gun, Hogue shoots him.

His second customer, a self-proclaimed reverend named Joshua Sloane (David Warner), is forthcoming with payment and not only gets to drink from the well, but gradually becomes friends with Hogue. Joshua spouts biblical rhetoric continually – in one of his aureate discourses, he suggests naming the spot Cable Springs – but proves to be an incorrigible lecher. He also reminds Hogue of the concept of land registry.

Hogue borrows Joshua's horse and hightails it into Dead Dog to stake his claim. He tries to interest the stagecoach office in financial involvement with what he now sees as a way station. His approach is less than subtle and the manager (R G Armstrong) throws him out. He fares better at the bank, where the manager, impressed by his straight talking, agrees to a loan. He immediately makes an outlay on Hildy (Stella Stevens), the town whore with whom he becomes instantly smitten.

Joshua helps him turn the way station into a successful business. On their forays into town, Joshua pursues a young woman to the aggravation of her considerably older husband, while Hogue tries to persuade Hildy to join him in the desert. She initially refuses, saying that what she really wants to do is go to San Francisco and find a wealthy husband. Later, run out of town by a moral majority, she indulges Hogue in a romantic interlude. She is still intent on San Francisco, but intimates that she wants him to go with her. Hogue stubbornly insists on staying in the desert, convinced that one day Bowen and Taggart will pass that way again and he can take his revenge.

Disconsolate at this aspect of his persona, first Hildy then Joshua leaves. The stagecoach continues to make its regular stop and the way station is no less successful for there being only Hogue to run it. Soon enough, Bowen and Taggart alight from the stage. Hogue puts on a hospitable front, advocating that he owes his good fortune to them. He mentions that he's so busy he doesn't know how he'll find time to get to the bank with all the money he's earning. Inviting them to stop by again, he sees them off cheerily when the stagecoach continues its journey.

The temptation is too great for his former partners and they sneak back to rob him. They joke about stealing his water as well. Finding nothing in the way station itself, they

Cable Hogue becomes acquainted with Hildy.

search the grounds. Bowen is perturbed by the rattlesnake Hogue keeps in a cage. Taggart, meanwhile, finds a patch of ground covered with a tarpaulin, over which sand has been piled to disguise it. The two set about digging. Once they're entrenched, Hogue returns, firing off a warning shot. They can't return fire unless they emerge from shelter (presenting an easy target). Hogue taunts them that he has water and they don't. He further plays on their nerves by throwing rattlesnakes into the pit.

They break cover. Hogue gets the drop on them. Taggart, convinced that Hogue's too yellow to pull the trigger (he had his chance once before but squandered it), makes his play. He doesn't know that Hogue has already shot one man for attempting to violate his water rights.

Taggart pays for this misconception with his life. Hogue hesitates from killing Bowen, though, and instead tells him to bury Taggart. He is still undecided about Bowen's fate when Hildy returns from her travels, dressed in fine clothes and chauffeur-driven in an automobile. She tells him she is going to New Orleans. Hogue decides to quit the desert and go with her. With astounding magnanimity, he turns the way station over to Bowen and collects his belongings. Throwing his luggage in the car, he accidentally disengages the handbrake and it starts careering down a slope. Hogue saves Bowen, hurling him out of the way. When he tries to stop the vehicle's progress, it runs over him.

Joshua returns, driving a motorcycle, as Hogue lays dying. For the first time, he takes on the demeanour of a true man of God, delivering a moving and unsentimental eulogy.

If, ostensibly, this does not resemble the plot of a comedy, then what is it? As a western, it satisfies a cursory visual checklist (dusty plains, stagecoaches, a town whose chief institutions are a bank, a saloon and a brothel) – and as a Peckinpah western, it offers us familiar faces from *Ride the High Country, Major Dundee* and *The Wild Bunch* – but, damn it, you can count the number of shots fired on the fingers of one hand. As an allegory for men out of time trying to hold back the forces of progress and technology, it's decidedly heavy-handed. As a work of satire (taking a sideswipe at notions of society, commerce and religion), it's detracted from by large doses of slapstick and pratfalls. In fact, with all the speeded-up footage and laddish close-ups of Hildy's cleavage, it's more Benny Hill than Boot Hill [7].

Yet, strangely, it *does* manage to function, with varying degrees of effectiveness, as all of the above. Maybe the best way to appreciate *The Ballad of Cable Hogue* is to take its title literally. A ballad, in the literary sense, is a long narrative poem, often describing an occurrence or turn of events that is outlandish or larger than life. Good examples of this are in the poems of Robert Service (most notably 'The Shooting of Dan McGrew') and Banjo Paterson, whose perennial favourite 'The Man from Snowy River' was the inspiration behind the 1982 Kirk Douglas starrer of the same title.

Considered thus, *Cable Hogue* emerges as a shaggy dog story, its coincidences – Bowen and Taggart showing up just *after* Hildy's departure; Hildy returning *before* Hogue can change his mind about sparing Bowen; Joshua reappearing as Hogue lays dying, just in time to give him absolution – not just forgivable, but part of its charm.

And the film *is* charming. It's everything conventional wisdom would have us believe a Peckinpah movie is *not*. Slow motion ballets of death are notable by their absence. Nothing unpleasant happens to the heroine (even her eviction from Dead Dog at the hands of the good townsfolk happens off screen). Such rewards as the hero gets are the result of running a legitimate business and not acquired by robbery.

Even the treatment of religion is handled differently. It says something that Peckinpah casts David Warner as Sloane when none other than R G Armstrong (the puritanical Knudsen in *Ride the High Country*, the vengeful Reverend Dahlstrom in *Major Dundee* and, as we shall see, the downright fanatical Ollinger in *Pat Garrett and Billy the Kid*) is biding his time further down the credits list. With Armstrong in the role, Joshua might well have been expected to handle snakes and decry women as harlots. As it is, he runs from the former [8] and tries every trick in the book to have his wicked way with the latter. His attempted seduction of a young woman grieving for her brother – Joshua having misread the circumstances and assumed it is her husband who has passed on – is, while nowhere near subtle, a splendid bit of comedy. Elsewhere, the embryonic friendship between Hogue and Joshua, rather than being built on Joshua's priesthood, is almost scuppered because of it.

> Hogue: There's a preacher out in my diggings. He'll tell you. You wouldn't doubt
>   a man of the gospel, would you?
> Bank manager: Of course. That's the first man I'd doubt.
> Hogue: Well, I'll be damned. Looks like I came to the right place after all.

The banker's seed of doubt blossoms not long afterwards. Hogue, making an investment in Hildy's services, is interrupted just as he is beginning to enjoy himself by a stentorian preacher pronouncing righteousness in a revival tent across the street.

> Preacher: God's pure and natural elements are being threatened by the Devil ...
>   The Devil seeks to destroy you with machines! ... Inventions are the work of
>   Satan (9).
> Hogue: I gotta go. That pious son of a bitch could have sold me out.
> Hildy: Hogue, Hogue, come here.
> Hogue: Nah, lost it. No good.

The friendship between Hogue and Joshua develops as they build the way station in The Ballad of Cable Hogue.

One of the most delightful aspects of *The Ballad of Cable Hogue* is that all its themes are dealt with through wry banter and throwaway lines.

Concerning the nature of revenge:

> Joshua: Vengeance is mine saith the Lord.
> Hogue: Well, that's fair enough with me – just as long as he don't take too long and I can watch.

Concerning water rights:

> Joshua: You are a Good Samaritan to offer help and water to a needy traveller.
> Hogue: Hallelujah, brother! That's ten cents a hit ...
> Joshua: Cast thy bread upon the waters and let this man of God have his just needs ...
> Hogue: Ten cents, you pious bastard, or I'll bury you.

Concerning one's right to bear arms:

> Drifter: Give me that rifle.
> Hogue: I'll give you what's in it.

'Ten cents, you pious bastard, or I'll bury you': water rights according to Cable Hogue.

There are as many moments that engage the heart as there are that tickle the funny bone. When Hildy joins Hogue in the desert, his comic attempts at housekeeping are quickly replaced by scenes of tenderness. Wearing a diaphanous nightgown, Hildy beckons Hogue to join her, but all he can do is stand there looking at her. 'You've seen it before,' she says laughingly. 'Lady,' he breathes, 'nobody's ever seen you before.'

Hogue's admission of how he feels about her is as lyrical as it is faltering – which gives some indication of how good Robards's performance is – and provides an insight into the mindset of a loner: 'Sometimes out here alone at night, sometimes I wonder what the hell I'm doing out here ... [but] in town I'd be nothing. I don't like being nothing. I've been that before. Out here, I've got a good start.'

Hogue's relationship with Hildy is – inevitably – compared to the one that he shares with Joshua. There is a beautifully simple moment that puts everything effortlessly into perspective. Hogue and Hildy, bickering as the date of Hildy's departure for San Francisco draws near, find their domestic situation further complicated by Joshua, who is seeking sanctuary from a Dead Dog resident whose wife he has recently 'converted'. Pushed to the limit, Hildy throws them both out. All that happens onscreen is that they crawl into their bedrolls and bid each other goodnight. What is left unsaid draws on one of the most fundamental aspects of the western. From the earliest celluloid expositions of cowboys riding the plains to the cumulative artistic mastery of Clint Eastwood's *Unforgiven*, the one staple of the genre has been the campfire scene. How typical of Peckinpah that when he does

Bowen and Taggart double-cross Hogue in The Ballad of Cable Hogue.

it in *The Ballad of Cable Hogue* (in order to show how understated and intrinsically more strong are the bonds of friendship between men than the romantic connections between men and women), he opts to leave out the fire.

Indeed, it is Joshua who tries to put into words what Hogue goes through when Hildy leaves: 'It doesn't matter how much or how little you've wandered around, how many women you've been with, every once in a while one of them cuts right through, right straight into you.'

Hogue, understandably, wants to know what one can do about it.

'I suppose, maybe, when you die you get over it.'

The Ballad of Cable Hogue is at its most successful when pathos and humour are combined, nowhere more notably than in its opening and closing sequences. Essentially, Peckinpah puts Hogue in the same predicament, albeit through a different set of circumstances, as he was at the outset: stuck in the desert and looking death in the face.

When the film opens, Hogue is staring it out with a lizard. He has a knife in his hand. 'Sorry, old timer,' he tells the reptile, 'but you're only part poison and I'm hungry for meat. Thirsty, too.'

The lizard accepts this stoically. Its dignity is ill rewarded seconds later as a shot rings out and it goes the way of most animals in Peckinpah's films – i.e. straight to its maker.

Bowen and Taggart double-act their way over (Peckinpah deliberately casts the same actors who played T C and Coffer, the bickering bounty hunters in *The Wild Bunch*). Hogue's horse is nearby, his rifle on the saddle. He keeps Bowen and Taggart talking, berating them for decimating the only food for miles around ('you peckerwoods just raised hell with our supper'). All the time, he edges closer to the rifle. He seizes his chance – only to blow it seconds later. His dubious partners act all wounded and sheepish, convincing him they were only joking. Undone by his good nature, and his reluctance to commit violence, Hogue allows Bowen to get close enough to wrest the gun from him. He and Taggart then take Hogue's canteen and his horse and go on their merry way. 'Old Cable is yeller, old Cable is white,' they sing, in ragged harmony, 'old Cable is dying but that's all right.'

For Cable it's less than all right. He declaims a stream of invective and promises retribution at their retreating backs – 'I'll get out, don't you worry none about that, just worry about *when* I get out' – then begins walking himself. A panoramic long shot – so damn long it could almost be a point of view from God's perspective – reveals the extent of Hogue's isolation. He is alone, betrayed by his partners and without supplies. It would take a miracle to save him. The theme song, which accompanies a split-screen montage [10] depicting Hogue's ordeal in the wilderness (a truncated version of the thirty days and thirty nights), seems inappropriately optimistic.

> Tomorrow is the song I sing,
> Yesterday don't mean a thing.
> I'll make today my next day's dawn
> And I'll still be here grinning when the sun goes down.

After a couple of verses in like manner – 'tomorrow,' the vocalist assures us, 'ragmen can be kings' – full screen is reinstated: Hogue in close-up, clothes dusty, face beaten by the sun, his lips parched. 'Ain't had no water since yesterday, Lord,' he opines. 'Gettin' a little thirsty. Just thought I'd mention it. Amen.'

The music resumes, the orchestration louder, jauntier [11]. Hogue's stumbling progress continues. His second address to the Almighty is not quite so perfunctory. Some of the brusqueness that will define his character (he isn't so hesitant on the trigger next time round) has begun to emerge. 'Yesterday I told you I was thirsty,' he grumbles, 'and I thought you might turn up some water. Now, if I've sinned, you just send me a drop or two and I won't do it no more – whatever in the hell it was I did.' He then pauses, remembers who he's talking to, and this time he lifts his eyes to the firmament. A harder man he is no doubt becoming, but he never entirely loses his humanity. 'I mean that, Lord,' he adds, and there is genuine humility in his voice.

In the time it takes for the song to conclude, the tone has changed again. Four days have passed and the H_2O has not been forthcoming. The same defiance he displayed to the disappearing figures of Taggart and Bowen is back in force. 'If you don't think I put in my suffering time, you ought to try going dry for a spell,' he rages. 'If I don't get some soon, I ain't goin' to have no chance to repent. Careful now, you're about to get my dander up!'

Throughout, Robards's acting has combined humour and grittiness. Now he takes the character into his most abject moment of desperation. If threatening God not to get him mad is more redolent of Hogue's last stand than the road to Damascus, his next words are those of acceptance; no piety, just a willingness to give himself over to the inevitable: 'Lord, you call it. I'm just plain done in. Amen.'

At this point he is not simply on his knees – he's on his back. God – for we must assume that His is the great, uncredited, unseen cameo – is merciful. Hogue is given water where there was none.

By the end, he is back where he started: alone in the desert. It is tempting to say that he has returned to the same place, but the truth is he has never moved from it. The desert is a fitting metaphor for Hogue's soul: empty yet teeming with small details and idiosyncracies; a wasteland that is strangely beautiful, suddenly fertile when it seems most barren. If you wanted to get existential about it, you could make a case for Cable Hogue as a fleabitten T E Lawrence, transformed and ultimately defined by what he finds in the sands – and what he finds out about himself.

Earlier scenes are recast: Bowen and Taggart, first seen stealing his water and his horse, come back to steal his money; the lizard, its mortal coil shuffled off with the help of the aforesaid, is replaced by rattlesnakes – and this time it's the animal life that comes out tops. The same test of character is levied upon Hogue – and this time he acts. Decisively.

But some things don't change. Hogue faces just as heartbreaking a prospect of solitude as he did when Bowen and Taggart abandon him. The only difference is that now he has all the water he needs. But with the discovery of that water has come friendship, love and material success. In sacrificing items one and two, and using item three as bait, so that his thirst for revenge (if such turn of phrase isn't labouring the point too much) can be satisfied, Hogue has all but thrown away his humanity. After all, first time round he was, if not communing, then at the very least *communicating* with God. Now all he can do is sit, rifle slung across his knees, and think melancholy thoughts about Hildy while Bowen buries his former partner.

Peckinpah often described his films as morality plays. *Cable Hogue* fits the profile succinctly. His orchestration of the finale requires as great a suspension of disbelief as anything produced for the theatre, and indeed resembles a play in that it regroups all of its major characters (and therefore its main themes) in the same spatially compressed location. The desert has become Peckinpah's stage with the way station as a painted backdrop. Hogue is centre stage: around him gather Bowen, the redeemed sinner standing in for the lost friend; then Hildy, the muse and (overlooking the fact that she's a prostitute) romantic ideal [12]; the stagecoach drivers (a Greek chorus with Suth'n accents); and finally Joshua, the farcical lecher reinvented as a true man of God.

For if Hogue found God in the desert, couldn't the Almighty have also stumbled across Joshua? And, seeing that Hogue had been neglecting Him, sent the errant preacher back to settle the reckoning? Perhaps Hogue sees it this way; facing his self-styled 'last reckoning' with the same lack of sentiment as before ('no trouble, just dying') he tells Joshua 'it's about time you earned your keep'.

> Hogue: Preach me a funeral sermon. A good one. Don't make me out no saint, but don't put me down too deep.
> Joshua: You mean now?
> Hogue: Yeah. It's not so much the dying that you hate, it's not knowing what they're going to say about you.

As with so many of Peckinpah's alter egos, Cable Hogue expresses something fundamental, an idea we've all probably entertained but never vocalized, and he does so with a sense of poetry that belies its simplicity. If only we knew what would be said about us when we are gone. Wouldn't it ease our passing, to know that someone had understood the measure of our life?

Many critics have admitted to having difficulty with the ending. Some would maintain that it doesn't work, that it deflates the film. Not so. What it does puncture (quite wilfully) is Hogue's long-anticipated showdown with Bowen and Taggart. The scene is pivotal, but not climactic. In killing Taggart, the debt is repaid. In sparing Bowen, Hogue steps back from the abyss; the worst excesses of his personality have been curbed. He resolves to leave for San Francisco, to find Hildy. Fate brings her back to him. Pure coincidence, to be sure, but for Hogue to leave the desert would be unfaithful to the landscape of the film – and he'd only die just as arbitrarily somewhere else. (Let's face it, how prosaic is the motorcycle accident which ends Lawrence's life?)

The car puts in its terrible appearance ('ugly lookin' damn thing, ain't it?' Pickens says, speaking for his director) just as Hogue seems to be getting back everything he thought he'd lost. That the stagecoach is present as well, provides a literal side-by-side comparison of the old and the new, technology muscling in alongside tradition. The quickly dispensed-with showdown (the antithesis of the drawn-out, sweaty close-ups of Sergio Leone) emphasizes the fact that *this* is the most dangerous element of the story: progress.

When Bowen tells Hildy's chauffeur to park it 'on the rise', he drives it up on to the hillock in reverse. Subtextually, this suggests retrogression: with transport no longer reliant on horses (which have to be rested and watered), the way station will soon be a thing of the past, a ramshackle empty building beside an unused waterhole. There is also a sneaky implication that Bowen – albeit inadvertently – has just effected his second betrayal of Hogue (if only he'd ordered the chauffeur to park it on level ground ...). Finally, as it growls its way backwards, it startles the horses, another visualization of modern machines upsetting the old way of doing things.

Right: On the set of The Ballad of Cable Hogue*: Peckinpah was serious even when he made a comedy.*

521

If subtext and symbolism seem to seep through the very sands, it should also be remarked that the humour quotient is well up. In Peckinpah's films, the protagonists are just as likely to buy it as the villains ... if not more so. Time after time, they bite the dust, one main character (*Ride the High Country, Major Dundee, The Killer Elite*) or both (*Pat Garrett and Billy the Kid*); sometimes just about everybody (*The Wild Bunch, Bring Me the Head of Alfredo Garcia, Cross of Iron* – don't let the freeze-frame fool you: they're all going down); either that, or they may as well be dead for all they've been through and what it's cost them (*Straw Dogs*). All of these films show death for the wasteful, regrettable thing it is, something to be despised even though it's sometimes the only option.

In *Cable Hogue*, Peckinpah treats death with no less significance, but uses dramatically different tactics – first he laughs at it, then detracts from it by instilling the life just taken with dignity, assuring us that Hogue will not be forgotten. When Joshua delivers the eulogy, it veers wonderfully between realism and rhetoric, interspersed with laconic comments from Hogue himself.

> Joshua: We are gathered here in the sight of the Lord to lay to rest –
> All: Cable Hogue!
> Hogue: Amen to that.
> Joshua: Most funeral orations, Lord, lie about a man ... whitewash him with a really wide brush. But you know, Lord, and I know that it just is not true ... Cable Hogue was born into this world, nobody knows when or where. He came stumbling out of the wilderness like a prophet of old.
> Hogue: Sounds right, is right.
> Joshua: Out of the barren wastes he carved himself a one-man kingdom.
> Hogue: Well, I don't know about that.
> Joshua: Some said he was ruthless.
> Hogue: Who said that?
> Joshua: More than one, Hogue. But you could do worse, Lord, than to take to your bosom Cable Hogue. He wasn't really a good man. He wasn't a bad man. But, Lord, he was a *man*.
> Hildy: Amen to that.

These homilies are punctuated by laughter. Hogue even tips Hildy a wink. As the oration continues, Joshua's unbroken delivery seguing from Hogue's bedside to his graveside, the tone changes from good hearted to heartfelt.

> Joshua: When Cable Hogue died, there wasn't an animal in the desert he didn't know. There wasn't a star in the firmament he hadn't named. There wasn't a man he was afraid of ... In some ways he was your dim reflection, Lord, and I feel he is worthy of your consideration ... Take him, Lord, but knowing Cable, I suggest you do not take him lightly. Amen.

When the mourners leave – by stagecoach, car or motorcycle – they leave us with the sense that they are not mourning his passing but celebrating the fact that he was around in the first place. It's hard to see how else the film could have been brought to conclusion: it *has* to begin and end in the desert, redemption bestowed in death, the full range of emotions having been travelled. For Hogue to live, it would certainly have diluted Peckinpah's predominant theme of times and traditions changing for the worse. It would have implied that God lets people off the hook. It would have attached no price to absolution.

It doesn't work that way. Peckinpah knew that better than anyone. And even when he was making a comedy, it didn't change the fact that the man was serious.

CHAPTER TWO
THE WILD BUNCH

Complicated men offer complicated observations and perceptions. Simple men see things in a simplistic light and communicate them in simple terms. Sam Peckinpah was a complex man who, by his own admission, was often unable to determine where he stood on various issues; a complex man who nonetheless sought to explore his idiosyncracies in essentially simple stories. Nowhere is this aspect of his personality – unsure, probing, questioning, looking at everything from a multiplicity of angles – more inherently crucial to any of his films, or as nakedly portrayed in its aesthetic, as in *The Wild Bunch*.

And if the suggestion of the inherent and the explicit being equally informed by the same dichotomy of the artist's psychology isn't ironic enough, then consider Peckinpah's own view of his masterpiece: 'I wasn't trying to make an epic, I was trying to tell a simple story about bad men in changing times. *The Wild Bunch* is simply about what happens when killers go to Mexico. The strange thing is that you feel a great sense of loss when these killers reach the end of the line' [1].

Indeed, one appreciates why Peckinpah would want to distance his film from the concept of the 'epic' as understood by fans of mainstream movies: pomp, splendour, glittering costumes, the proverbial cast of thousands – these things were not for him. It is telling, the way he refutes this genre of film-making. The use of the phrase 'simple story' indicates that narrative complexity is less important to him than characterization; it is subtext and character motivation that gives the film depth. His identification of his protagonists, however, labels them inescapably as anti-heroes and the mention of a journey – a final one, an odyssey to 'the end of the line' – conjures something of the Homeric. Something – dare we say? – epic.

The sense of ambivalence increases as we watch the film. Its protagonists are most certainly killers, capable of using women as shields during gunfights and willing to execute (and be executed by) their own kind if the circumstances demand it. They fight amongst themselves and take their pleasure from whores. Their very profession is theft. And yet they demonstrate moments of cameraderie that are rich in loyalty and laughter, moments of humanity that destroy any stereotypical expectations the audience might be harbouring, moments of regret and remorse that are amongst the most profound and affecting captured on film, and – finally – they stand together in the face of insurmountable odds, despite the inevitable and ultimate price.

The range of emotions and contradictions, the sense of contrast and comparison between characters as well as between individual scenes, arises not only from imagery and thematic concerns, but from the characters' motivations.

Returning briefly to Peckinpah's epithet, it must be acknowledged that, in terms of its narrative, *The Wild Bunch* does tell an essentially simple story. And there can be no doubt that Peckinpah was quintessentially a storyteller, albeit one whose tales are resonant with depth and detail.

The Bunch in military disguise.

Plotwise, *The Wild Bunch* goes like this.

In 1913, a group of outlaws led by Pike Bishop (William Holden) and his right-hand-man Dutch (Ernest Borgnine) ride into the town of Starbuck disguised as soldiers. They hold up a railroad office and steal the payroll. They are ambushed by a group of bounty hunters in the pay of railroad boss Pat Harrigan and led, reluctantly, by Pike's former partner Deke Thornton (Robert Ryan) who has been given the choice of hunting them down or going back to prison. Massacre ensues. Six of the bunch escape alive, but one of them, blinded and unable to ride, is soon put out of his misery – at his own request. The five who remain – Pike, Dutch, the brothers Lyle and Tector Gorch (Warren Oates and Ben Johnson), and Angel (Jaime Sanchez), a young, idealistic Mexican – join the oldest gang member, Sykes (Edmond O'Brien), at a prearranged rendezvous where they discover that far from getting away with the payroll, all they have carried back with them is sacks of washers.

Realizing they were set up, and concerned that Thornton and his posse will be following, they ride for Mexico. During an interlude at Angel's village, they learn of the atrocities inflicted there by the self-styled revolutionary General Mapache (Emilio Fernandez). Two particular incidents, the death of his father and his rejection by Teresa, the girl he is in love with, inflame Angel's desire for revenge.

Leaving the village, the Bunch ride to Agua Verde, the town Mapache is using as his headquarters. Witnessing Teresa's willing prostitution of herself to Mapache, Angel shoots and kills her. Pike and Dutch manage to defuse the situation. They attract the

attention of Commander Frederick Muhr 'of the Imperial German army' who is acting
as Mapache's advisor. The Bunch enter into a trustless alliance with them, agreeing to
steal munitions from a troop train on the general's behalf. Mapache begrudgingly
releases Angel in order that they can function as a team.

Angel convinces Pike to let him have a case of rifles and ammunition so that he can arm
his people. Pike agrees, the robbery is executed and the Bunch make their escape from both
Thornton's band of bounty hunters and the outraged US troops. Outwitting Mapache's
second-in-command, Herrera, who tries to rob them of the guns, they trade with the
General on their terms: the weaponry for their payment in gold, a few cases at a time.

When Dutch and Angel conduct the final transaction with Mapache, the General,
realizing he is a case of rifles short, accuses Angel of theft. The young man is brought
down from his horse before he can flee the settlement, leaving Dutch to ride out alone.
Attempting to leave Agua Verde, despite Dutch's protests, Pike and the Bunch are forced
to turn back after seeing Sykes shot at and wounded by the bounty hunters. They return,
unaware that the old man has been found by Angel's compatriots.

Forced to watch Angel being dragged around the square behind Mapache's newly
acquired motor car, Pike tries to buy him back. The General refuses. Herrera warns them
not to upset his mood. The diversions of drink and women prove futile and the four
remaining outlaws – Pike, Dutch, Tector and Lyle – strap on their pistols, load their
shotguns and confront Mapache. For an instant, it seems he is going to release their
comrade; instead, he cuts his throat. Massacre ensues.

By the time Thornton and the bounty hunters enter Agua Verde, Mapache's forces have been destroyed and the Bunch are dead. Thornton refuses to ride back with the posse and convey the news to Harrigan. Sitting in glum contemplation at the town gates, he is joined presently by Sykes, who is now riding with the newly armed men from Angel's village. They have encountered and summarily finished off the bounty hunters. Sykes invites Thornton to ride with them and Pike's erstwhile friend and partner in crime agrees.

A fairly straightforward narrative then, and instantly recognizable in its generic content (outlaws, bandits, train robbery) and geographic settings (Texas, Mexico). But nonetheless, this is a western that is like no other.

The Wild Bunch dares to be different right from the start. Peckinpah uses the opening credits to set out his stall. In a sequence that runs almost six minutes, the Bunch are introduced to us in military guise. They ride into town along the diminishing perspective of a set of railroad lines, passing by a group of giggling children. Some of the children look ethnic; Mexican. One of the Bunch – Angel – will soon be revealed as a Mexican. Pike and Dutch – grizzled, middle-aged men – glance at them as they pass, looking away again as they continue to ride into town. It is as the Bunch are shown receding from this tableau that Peckinpah's camera reveals the childrens' activity: armed with sticks, they are prodding scorpions further and further into a swarming colony of red ants. A series of close-ups show their juvenile delight. The soundtrack alternates between sombre bass notes and sharp regimental drumming.

The ants overrun the scorpions, a dismaying image of creatures usually regarded as dangerous being defeated by much smaller beings whose supremacy is only due to superior numbers – an image that will be revisited in explicit terms at the end of the movie. At this point, a voice is heard, warning an unseen audience 'Do not drink wine or strong drink ... lest ye shall die.' Peckinpah cuts away, a few words into this homily, taking us into the centre of the town and revealing our dime store moralist as an old man addressing the predominantly female constituency of the local Temperance Union. The Bunch pass by and ride slowly along the main street, the evils of drink still being decried even as the soundtrack music resumes.

They dismount across the street from the South Texas R.R. [Rail Road] Administration Offices. 'It's all quiet, sir,' one of them says. Pike nods. 'Let's fall in,' he orders; 'follow me.' At this point, they could still be taken for genuine soldiers (although the exchange is also indicative how professionally Pike plans and executes his robberies), and the following vignette plays nicely on this supposition. Crossing to their target, Pike inadvertently bumps into an old woman carrying an armful of parcels. There is a split second pause, as if Pike is considering her expendability, then he stoops to retrieve the dropped packages. 'I beg your pardon, ma'am,' he says, playing the gentleman officer perfectly. 'Allow me, ma'am,' Dutch joins in enthusiastically, taking them from him. Pike offers her his arm and they continue crossing the street.

An overhead shot captures the incident, almost as if the director were stepping back for the first time to take a detached, if somewhat wry, look at his characters.

Not so.

The very next shot shows us the true point of view: that of Thornton, Harrigan and a motley conglomerate of hired killers, from a nearby rooftop. In effect, Peckinpah takes the gentlest image so far in the movie and casts over it the shadow of violence.

Overhead shots of the Bunch entering the Administration Office heighten expectations of approaching conflict. Inside, the manager is reprimanding a young clerk. His authority is spectacularly undermined as Pike grabs him and throws him against the wall. The other employees, and a few members of the public waiting to be served, are similarly herded.

Throughout, images freeze frame at crucial moments, the rich colour of Lucien Ballard's magnificent cinematography replaced by a glum sepia, like an old photograph or newspaper cutting. It is as the Bunch reveal their true nature – not soldiers but criminals, not heroes but robbers – and Pike delivers in grim close up the first of many classic lines –

*Pike Bishop, the hardened
professional criminal.*

'If they move, kill 'em!' – that the final freeze-frame occurs, a last melancholy bass note
sounding as the credit 'directed by Sam Peckinpah' appears on screen.

   Already, in these first few minutes, we are presented with questions of identity and
nationality, images of death and religion, juxtapositions of youth and middle age, and
given the first hint of the relationship between Pike and Thornton. And in a manner
which forces us to look at these things from myriad points of view.

   But this is not just a sophisticated piece of attention grabbing, something that looks
cool while the necessary business of credits is dealt with: it establishes, instead, a
texture to the film-making, a depth of artistic and technical control to which Peckinpah
remains true throughout the film entire. Viewed in context of the ensuing ambush,
bloody shoot-out and desparate escape, it also introduces motifs which lend this
extended set-piece the feel of a 'mini movie' – a self-contained film in its own right.
Religion reappears in the pious hymn 'Shall We Gather at the River?', sung as the
Temperance Union manoeuvre themselves into the thick of things; children are again
present, clinging to each other as bodies fall around them; 'good' Christian women are
used as shields or trampled by horses; Pike continues to bark terse exhortations: 'Come
on, you lazy bastards!', 'Let's go!'. In a brilliant encapsulating image – the erstwhile

group of children bringing their macabre game to a fiery end, burning both ants and scorpions alike – Peckinpah draws to a conclusion this first section of the film ... then dissolves to a coda which shows humanity in an even worse light: T C and Coffer (L Q Jones and Strother Martin) – two of the less competent bounty hunters – squabbling over the corpses that litter the main street, arguing as to who killed whom, before being grudgingly reunited in mutual greed, stripping the dead of their boots and guns. The cruelty of childhood is reinforced as the town's children – with a callousness not dissimilar to their ant-incinerating counterparts on the wrong side of the (railroad) tracks – run through the streets, their fingers cocked into imaginary guns, shouting 'Bang! Bang! Bang! Bang!'

The shoot-out itself is an extension of the editing techniques used in the credit sequence, but with slow motion in place of freeze-frames. It is at once exquisite and excruciating, imbued with a balletic grace even as it demonstrates the painful, protracted nature of violent death. This crosscutting of slow motion footage with normal speed film – its inherent quality for disorientation and emotional confusion accentuated by the continual alternation of points of view and the juxtaposition of different but simultaneously occurring incidents, some of which constitute cause and effect – is the visual lightning-rod by which Peckinpah is able to incite in his audience such drastically contradictory responses.

The Bunch, their numbers already depleted, make good their escape. What follows is concerned with motivation, psychology and personal conflict between characters, a no less heady brew than what has preceded, the violence instead conducted verbally or by the intrusion of memory, its attendants regret and self-loathing.

But Peckinpah has one bit of viscera to attend to first.

Falling from his horse, one – unnamed – member of the Bunch blubbers to Pike that he can't see but he can ride ... before admitting that he can't, in fact, do either. 'Finish it, Mr Bishop,' he pleads. Pike's gun roars before the second syllable of his surname can be properly enunciated, as if he can't bear to hear it spoken. This is the point at which Pike begins to emerge as a man – flawed, remorseful, and driven by an unresolved conflict within – but nonetheless a man, not neatly categorized as an outlaw.

Here, too, religion is revisited and themes of honour and loyalty introduced (the latter, with typical irony, done at the expense of harmony in the Bunch's interrelationships):

> Pike: You boys wanna move on or stay here and give him a decent burial?
> Tector: He was a good man and I think we ought to bury him.
> Pike: He's dead! And he's got a lot of good men back there to keep him company.
> Lyle: Too damn many!
> Dutch: Well I think the boys are right. I'd like to say a few words for the dear dead departed. [Sarcastically] And maybe a few hymns 'd be in order. Followed by a church supper – with a choir!
> Lyle: You crazy bastard.

It is interesting that Tector and Lyle should be so concerned with observing the proper formalities. As later scenes will show, these are men whose favourite pastimes are drinking and whoring. The exchange is, however, merely the first of several verbal stand-offs the brothers will provoke. When the rendezvous is made, the Bunch eager to divide up the loot, the twosome sound off against Pike's democratic philosophy of equal shares, asserting that Sykes doesn't deserve so much for just tending to some horses; nor does Angel. 'He's just startin' out,' Lyle says, 'and this is mine and Tector's openin' for a new territory.' Elsewhere, their behaviour towards Sykes is contemptuous and threatening; their juvenile comments on Teresa's choice of Mapache for a lover (Tector: 'She ain't your woman no more'; Lyle: 'Look at her lickin' the inside of that general's ear') pre-empt Angel's shooting of her; and their mocking response to the toast Muhr proposes when they agree to rob the munitions train leaves the Bunch just a short step away from serious confrontation.

This is only one aspect of the internal tensions within the Bunch: Pike and Angel are brought into disagreement when the latter becomes obsessed with revenge. Finally, even Pike and Dutch come to loggerheads over Thornton. Peckinpah's understanding of the male psyche comes across strongly in a scene where Pike defends his former partner even as he and the bounty hunters close in, while Dutch evinces a palpable sense of frustration that his place in Pike's estimation is forever secondary to Thornton.

> Dutch: Damn that Deke Thornton to hell!
> Pike: What would you do in his place? He gave his word.
> Dutch: Gave his word to a railroad!
> Pike: It's his *word*!
> Dutch: That ain't what counts – it's who you give it *to*! [2]

Ultimately, all of these tensions are resolved – not through talking, bringing differences into the open, or sharing feelings (we are, after all, talking about *men*) – but through the Bunch pulling together at crucial moments, standing as one, facing off whomever (bounty hunters, US troops, Mexicans – it all adds up to the same us versus them divide) and – in the final analysis – all differences forgotten and all debts paid, they are resolved through death.

But to return to the share out at the rendezvous, the scene is as skilfully constructed and as self-contained as that which has preceded it. The initial conflict, introduced by Lyle and Tector, is dealt with quickly. Pike suggests that if they are unhappy with equal shares, 'Why in the hell don't you just take all of it?', Tector and Lyle exchange nervous glances. 'Well, why don't you answer me, you damn yellow-livered trash?' Pike demands.

Lyle becomes placatory: 'Pike, you don't know – '

'I don't know a damn thing,' Pike snaps, 'except I either lead this Bunch or end it right now!'

The brothers Gorch seem unwilling to put him to the test, and back off. The sacks of money are opened and tempers immediately flare up again. They haven't salvaged a single dime from the railroad offices: each sack is filled with washers (or, to quote the educationally challenged Lyle, 'silver rings'). They have been well and truly set up. Sykes doesn't help the mood by cackling at the pointlessness of their endeavours – Lyle comes close to striking him – and Angel, perhaps unwisely, taunts the brothers: 'You can have my share.'

Suddenly, it's guns drawn and thieves falling out – twenty-five years before *Reservoir Dogs*. But the tension ebbs to a sense of melancholy, which in turn gives out to laughter and wisecracks as Pike reflects wryly that he should have followed Lyle and Tector's lead and spent his money running whores instead of stealing horses and uniforms. Lyle boasts that 'me and Tector was gettin' our bell ropes pulled by two – *two*, mind you – Hondo whores'. Dutch roars with laughter: 'While Pike was dreaming of washers, you were matching whores in tandem.' Lyle looks bemused by the expression. 'That's one behind t'other,' his brother explains.

By now the Bunch are in hysterics, even Pike seeing the funny side. As an example of how men behave around each other, the scene is eloquently realized – and it provides a perfect counterpoint to the elegiac tone of the scenes which probe Pike's psychology.

During the course of the film, Pike Bishop makes three mistakes – two of them shown in flashback. Each is attributable to carelessness and each costs him dearly: the incarceration of Thornton, and the lives of Angel and of a woman with whom he was in love. That his usual professional approach – a mixture of pragmatism and steely resolve that is capable of tipping over into ruthlessness – is subject to these lapses is a failing that gives him cause for bitterness and remorse.

Just how ruthless Pike can be is illustrated by his marshalling, deployment and treatment of his own men. The shooting of the blinded member is a case in point, and his

'Silver rings': the Bunch realize that the money sacks contain washers.

frequent homily 'Come on you lazy bastards' pretty much sums up his attitude in general. But genuinely shocking is an incident from the opening robbery/ambush sequence: the way he uses 'Crazy' Lee. The youth – younger even than Angel – is the gang member to whom Pike delivers his iconic 'if they move, kill 'em' line. When rifles are spotted on the roofs of neighbouring properties and the Bunch realize they'll have to shoot their way out of the Administration Office – and, indeed, out of Starbuck itself – Pike tells 'Crazy' Lee: 'Hold 'em as long as you can after the shootin' starts.'

'I'll hold 'em till hell freezes over or you say otherwise, Mr Bishop,' he hollers, full of youthful enthusiasm – the kind of enthusiasm that is dangerous in volatile situations. The look on Pike's face tells us he has already singled the lad out as a liability. There is no misapprehension about 'Crazy' Lee leaving Starbuck other than in a coffin.

Ensuing scenes of him terrorizing the hostages – forcing them to take up the chorus of 'Shall We Gather at the River?' and (in an image that prefigures Mapache's attentions towards Teresa) licking the ear of a prim-looking woman after she calls him trash – vindicate Pike's decision. This is a supremely stupid young man, too excited by the power a gun in his hand gives him over those who are unarmed to realize he has been abandoned. Even when he glances out the window, the gunshots over and his comrades nowhere to be seen, he is more concerned with the hostages' attempted escape – he fires his pump-action shotgun repeatedly after them, exclaiming that 'feathers flew like a turkey' – than his own.

As it happens, it's nothing he need worry about. Harrigan and Thornton burst in, 'Crazy' Lee spinning to take aim at them. Three bounty hunters outside fire through the uprights of the porch surrounding the building. 'Crazy' Lee falls to the floor, gasping in adolescent defiance, 'How'd you like to kiss my sister's black cat's ass?' Then, just to make his point, he rolls over, grimacing, and takes all three of them out. Harrigan fires three shots into him, his mouth twisting into a line of grim satisfaction. In a subsequent scene, Thornton lambasts him:

> Thornton: Tell me, Mr Harrigan, how does it feel, gettin' paid for it? Gettin' paid to sit back and hire your killings, with the law's arms around you? How does it feel to be so goddamn right?
> Harrigan: Good.
> Thornton: You dirty son of a bitch!

The next (and last) time 'Crazy' Lee is mentioned comes as a coda to Tector and Lyle's second dissension in the ranks. Crossing the desert to the Mexican border and Angel's village, *en route* for Agua Verde, the Bunch plummet from their horses as they thunder down a steep incline. Tector blames Sykes for incorrectly harnessing the saddles and airs the view that they'd be better off without him. (That's 'without' in the mortal sense.) Pike's response is unequivocal: 'We're gonna stick together, just like it used to be. When you side with a man, you stay with him and if you can't do that you're like some animal. You're finished. *We're* finished. All of us!'

A laudable sentiment – and his desire to instill it in his men is the sign of a true leader. But it's more than that: it is the code Pike has tried to live by but failed; it is the key to his driven personality. Unfortunately, it is left sounding rather hollow when he falls from the saddle trying to remount and lands on his bad leg. Tector and Lyle are quick to mock. Remounting, he reins in his horse and rides silently away. Sykes joins him, airing a vote of thanks for Pike's intervention, as well as effecting a demonstration of solidarity. During their conversation, the old man asks how 'Crazy' Lee acquitted himself:

> Sykes: Back there in Starbuck, how'd my boy do?
> Pike: Your boy? Crazy Lee?
> Sykes: Yeah, Cl ... My daughter's boy. Not too bright but a good boy.
> Pike: Why didn't you tell me he was your grandson?
> Sykes: You had enough things on your mind. Besides, he had to pull his own weight, just like the rest of us. I just wanted to make sure he didn't let you down, run when things got hot.
> Pike (slowly): No, he did fine. Just fine.

It is not mere coincidence that Peckinpah chooses 'Crazy' Lee's death and the revelation that he is related to Sykes to bookend the incidents at the rendezvous and the crucial sequence that follows – a sequence that incorporates the film's first flashback, reveals the deeper layers of Pike's character and reaffirms the connection between him and Thornton. The cumulative effect is to give Pike one more thing to brood over and torture himself with.

From the laughter and unity with which the rendezvous scene closes, quips about washers and Hondo whores still ringing in our ears, Peckinpah cuts to the solitary figure of Thornton, sitting away from his campfire-huddled posse. Coffer approaches him and, in a rare instance of respect, asks what kind of man Pike is. Thornton's reply is direct: 'The best. He never got caught.'

Sykes and Pike Bishop: men growing old.

Peckinpah segues back to the Bunch, likewise preparing to bed down for the night, Pike's face replacing Thornton's in close-up. He and Dutch ruminate on the failings of the day and the vagaries of the future:

> Pike: This was going to be my last. I'd like to make one good score and back off.
> Dutch: Back off to what?

It's a question that Pike has no answer for, and the conversation turns to the necessity of another job. Pike suggests robbing the payroll of any of the garrisons along the border. Dutch is unsure.

> Pike: I didn't say it was gonna be easy, but it can be done.
> Dutch: They'll be waiting for us.
> Pike: I wouldn't have it any other way.

Immediately he says this, Peckinpah introduces the flashback: Pike and Thornton taking it easy in an upmarket bordello. Judging from Pike's assertion that they've got 'more money than we can spend and not a care in the world', they are nicely in profit from a successful heist. Pike is in shirt sleeves and enjoying the ministrations of two girls (cf. the brothers Gorch), while Thornton, fully dressed, is eager to make a move:

> Thornton: We've overstayed our welcome.
> Pike: What the hell's the matter with you? ... They're not gonna look for us in their own back yard.
> Thornton: How can you be so damn sure?
> Pike: Being sure is my business.

This line echoes repeatedly as a heavy knocking comes at the door and one of the whores opens it. Framed in the doorway, a Pinkerton agent aims and fires, wounding Thornton. Pike makes a run for it as two other agents enter the room, outpacing them. Thornton's antagonist handcuffs him, asking of the others as they return from their half-hearted pursuit, 'Did you get him?'

'No,' comes the reply, 'the bastard got away.'

The scene is brief but shot through with a grim clarity, just as bad memories always are. Yet despite the brevity, Peckinpah cuts back to Pike and Thornton – both slightly distanced from their respective Bunches – at several points during the flashback. This serves to reinforce the connection between the two men and to push a sliver of self-loathing further into Pike's conscience: in being wrong about being sure – in not living up to his reputation as 'the best' – Pike has put Thornton in a situation where he has to ride against his friend or go back to prison. It might be labouring a point to label Thornton's agreement with Harrigan a 'deal with the devil', but the concept is mirrored later in the film when the Bunch strike a deal with Mapache, out of necessity rather than choice. Moreover, in running out on Thornton, Pike has broken the code he holds sacrosanct – the code he repeatedly forces on the Bunch.

Wouldn't have it any other way? Really, Mr Bishop?

An isolated Deke Thornton: his alliance with Harrigan a result of Pike's complacency.

The nature of Pike's second mistake, the flashback coming approximately halfway through the film, is similarly explored in the context of the scenes which frame it. Having celebrated their deal with Mapache in an evening of laughter and drunken cavorting, Tector and Lyle indulging their predilection for running whores in tandem while the others enjoy the pleasures of a steam room, the Bunch ride out to intercept the munitions train. The foregoing scenes show them with their individual personalities very much to the fore. The ensuing robbery will show them functioning collectively. It is in the period of statis between that Peckinpah takes us further towards the centre of Pike's loneliness and sadness.

Dutch, having noticed Pike massaging the scarred flesh of his bad leg in the steam room, asks how he came to receive the wound. The provenance is recounted in voice-over as well as visually in the flashback:

> Pike: I had a woman I wanted to marry ... She had a husband. If I'd had any sense I'd have killed him. He wasn't around and I got careless. One night he walked in on us. Got her with the first shot, got me here with the second. Then the damn coward turned and ran.
> Dutch: Ever catch up with him?
> Pike: No, but there isn't a day or an hour goes by that I don't think about it.

These words are imparted with understandable bitterness, but are made poignant by the fact that we see both sides of Pike and Aurora's relationship – the brittleness (Aurora giving him a good hard slap for being late – 'two days!') as well as the tender intimacy – before, in one rueful act, all the varied facets and possibilities of a romantic union are taken from them.

Pike, not one for displays of sentiment, chooses to take the subject no further. There is a train to be robbed and an oleaginous Mexican to deal with after that. He brings the topic of conversation back to the here are now. 'This is our last go around, Dutch,' he says. 'This time we do it right.'

And indeed, the robbery is executed with military precision – a fact that is beautifully accentuated in the shots of US troops, most of them greenhorn recruits, slumbering, oblivious to what is happening even as the Bunch uncouple the passenger carriages from the munitions wagons and make off with the front half of the train. Afterwards, it is the same degree of guile and professionalism that ensures their escape (dynamiting a river bridge to foil their pursuers), and gives them the upper hand over Herrera and his division of Mapache's men. Nothing other than stoic solidarity would allow six men, surrounded and vastly outnumbered, to rig up their own wagon with dynamite and light the fuse rather than accede to a show of force. Just as when Pike tells 'Crazy' Lee 'if they move, kill 'em', it is clear that he means it. Herrera, certainly, is convinced and orders his men to stand down. With the same granite-faced impassivity, Pike cuts the fuse.

Throughout, there is margin for error – and Peckinpah heightens the tension by having Dutch *almost* jolted from the train during the robbery (Angel is quick to assist him); the Bunch entire *almost* blown to smithereens along with the bridge when a back wheel of their wagon drops through rotted timber; and bloodshed *almost* occur when one of Herrera's men panics and looses off a single shot (Herrera has him executed) – but it is only after they outwit Herrera and the delivery of a case of rifles is made to Angel's comrades that Pike makes his third mistake.

As mentioned earlier, it is his decision to send Angel with Dutch to complete the transaction with Mapache that leads to Angel's capture, torture and eventual brutal demise – a mistake that comes complete with the dark irony that it was Angel's actions which instigated the Bunch's dealings with Mapache. Pike is given less time to brood over it than with Thornton's imprisonment or Aurora's death, but nonetheless it is the horrific maltreatment of Angel that pushes Pike over the edge. It is worth noting, too, that here more than anywhere else, Dutch acts as the personification of Pike's conscience – mostly as expiation of his own guilt at leaving Angel to the not-so-tender mercies of Mapache [3]. It weighs so heavily on him that he eschews Pike and the Gorch brothers' decision to visit some cheap whores and sits outside the brothel, squinting into the distance, waiting for Pike to give the order.

Pike, having taken his pleasure but not looking very happy, is left with nothing but to confront himself. His face a portrait of self-disgust, he watches the girl he has been with: she is more concerned with washing his sweat off her than tending to the cries of her young child. Seconds later, he will walk in on Tector and Lyle and snarl, 'Let's go!' (Lyle blinks in slow realization of what Pike means, then, still looking rather dazed, replies, 'Why not?')

But for now, Pike broods malevolently. Here is a reminder both of the family he could have had with Aurora, and the futility of bringing children into a world changing beyond what he is prepared to accept. It is no wonder, analyzing the scene in his seminal book *The Western Films: A Reconsideration*, that Paul Seydor lapses from the academic to a parlance more suited to one of Peckinpah's characters: 'in that squalid room ... Pike makes a discovery that he is quite unprepared for and that comes too late for payment by any price less dear than his life: no matter how, a man alone ain't got no bloody fucking chance' [4].

With its tortured anti-hero, doomed Ophelia figures (Teresa and Aurora), old men and wise fools (Sykes and, as shall be shown at Angel's village, Don Jose), Rosencrantz and Guildenstern-style double-act (T C and Coffer), and sacrificial idealist (Angel) – and with its themes of guilt, betrayal and revenge, as well as the redemptive catharsis of its denouement – *The Wild Bunch* can justifiably be considered in Shakespearian terms. If *Major Dundee* is, to quote R G Armstrong, '*Moby Dick* on horseback,' then Peckinpah's chronicle of Pike Bishop and his Bunch is Jacobean tragedy goes to Mexico.

To further the analogy, the film also lends itself to the three-act structure (in two – mind you, two – different ways).

Narratively – Act One: ambush, escape, rendezvous, flight to Mexico (specifically, Angel's Village); Act Two: alliance with Mapache, train robbery, Herrera's treachery, Mapache's betrayal; Act Three: the Bunch's last stand.

Or (the narrative parameters accordingly altered) geographically – Act One: Starbuck; Act Two: Angel's village; Act Three: Agua Verde.

The spell at Angel's village is short lived but immensely important: before the Bunch confront the forces of change and their personal demons at Agua Verde, it is here that they are given their humanity. Peckinpah sets up their arrival in an almost clichéd fashion – 'Any disrespect to my family or to my people,' Angel announces, 'and I will kill you' – before puncturing the mood as the Gorch brothers enquire if Angel has a sister: they'd be proud to make her acquaintance. Likewise his mother. Laughter rings out at the punchline: 'That goes for your grandma too, sonny.'

Unconventionally, it is not the attitude of Pike and his fellow Americans that is questioned here, but Angel's. As Angel rails at the death of his father and the loss of his girl, Don Jose – the village elder – tells Pike that the young Mexican's view of Teresa is unrealistically romantic. Rather unflatteringly, he likens Teresa to a mango, 'ripe and waiting'.

'Angel dreams of romance,' Pike muses, 'while Mapache eats the mango.'

None of this is any consolation to Angel, nor is Don Jose's assurance that his father 'died like a man'. In fact in only inflames him further. Eventually, Pike puts it on the line: 'Either you learn to live with it, or we leave you here.'

On the surface, this is the Pike of 'if they move, kill 'em', but, when not contending with Angel's fiery personality, he and Don Jose are left to share a conversation in which they are pinpointed as old men, looking at a world they find increasingly difficult to understand, bemoaning the loss of the old ways. 'In Mexico, *señor*, these are the days of sadness,' Don Jose says, underlining the human cost of Mapache's revolution.

And yet in some ways, the village – particularly in the bucolic compositions of Lucien Ballad's cinematography – symbolizes the pastoral ideal, somewhere a man of Pike's age and world-weariness can feel at home. This feeling seems to rub off on the others, with Lyle and Tector taking a surprisingly innocent, almost childlike, interest in one of the

Angel, anguished at Mapache's attack on his village.

village girls. None of the lechery of their Hondo reminiscences or their forthcoming Agua Verde cavortings is evident: they – and the girl – are simply happy.

'Now that,' says Pike, nodding to them, 'I find hard to believe.'

'Not so hard,' Don Jose reflects, in what is perhaps the film's key line of dialogue: 'we all dream of being a child again, even the worst of us. Perhaps the worst most of all.'

There is acceptance in the words – the old man knows they are outlaws, but does not judge them. Perhaps, had circumstances been different, the Bunch could have found a home here; could have found some kind of respite. But Thornton is pursuing them and they need to decide on another job. Reluctantly, they leave the village and continue their journey to Agua Verde, to one last good score, to the end of the line.

In a film full of mirrored scenes (and, as we shall see in the bloody finale, a scene with a mirror), Agua Verde is the flip side to Angel's village. But it also presents a reversal and – in the climactic massacre – a reprisal of Starbuck. When the Bunch enter Starbuck they are outfitted in uniforms while Thornton and the bounty hunters are clad in more traditional western garb; at Agua Verde, it is Mapache's troops who are uniformed, while the Bunch wear similar clothes to Thornton's mob. Further similarities become apparent when the bloodshed starts.

The village idyll is displaced by constant reminders of changing times: there is the presence of German officers; technological advancement is symbolized in Mapache's newly acquired motor car. Later, when the Bunch present him with a Gatling gun taken from the train, and Muhr insists 'it must be mounted on a tripod', it is easy to start thinking of armoured cars and tanks, particularly when Sykes has already appraised the automobile and made mention of the development of the aeroplane:

The Wild Bunch:
iconography in motion.

Sykes: I hear they got one of those things up north that can fly.
Tector: No, that was a balloon, you damned old fool.
Pike: No, the old man's right. They've got motors, wings, go sixty miles in less
     than an hour. Gonna use 'em in the war, they say.

The imminence of war makes the Germans' presence all the more scabrous, and raises questions of nationality. The Bunch will soon inform Muhr that there is no love lost between them and their government, but nonetheless a comparison between Americans and Germans exists as surely as does a comparison between the bloated, corrupt revolutionary Mexican (Mapache) and the fiery, idealistic young man from a humble village (Angel). That Peckinpah uses Agua Verde as the arena for both sets of comparisons is testament to his refusal to see mankind in black and white – for him, things are never that easy.

And it's not just national politics that come under the microscope – sexual politics are also examined. The rivalry between Angel and Mapache – not so much over Teresa as, perversely, over her death – sets up the film's denouement, Angel's desire to take revenge for his father finding fulfillment as the Bunch avenge his murder.

One could almost describe Angel's death as martyrdom. The analogy is made when the Bunch challenge Mapache. Tector and Lyle following, Pike leaves the brothel; Dutch is waiting outside. They share a meaningful look, then – amazingly – both men smile. From where their horses are tethered, they take shotguns and ammunition. To the accompaniment of a militaristic drumming that recalls the opening credits, they walk through Agua Verde, four dangerous men with a renewed sense of purpose. Their progress through the streets – the camera framing them tightly, then moving back to watch them cut a determined path through crowds of soldiers and townsfolk, then moving in again so that they fill the screen – is iconography in motion. They come to the courtyard to confront Mapache.

Mapache: Ah, *los gringos otra vez*. What do you want?
Pike: We want Angel.
Mapache: You want Angel, no? All right. I am going to give it to you.

The use of 'it' instead of 'he' becomes distressingly clear. Mapache hauls the beaten and bloodied Angel to his feet, steadying him as he stumbles. Taking out a knife, he cuts Angel's bonds. Angel struggles to stay upright, his arms held out in a horrible parody of crucifixion. Mapache finishes the job by cutting his throat.

This is not the only juxtaposition of religious imagery with the bad death of a young person: earlier, while Pike and the Bunch pour over a map, explaining for the benefit of the German officers how they intend to execute the train robbery, they are interrupted by a funeral cortège of old women bearing Teresa's body.

Maybe Pike has this in mind a few seconds later.

As Angel's body falls, four guns roar: Pike, Dutch, Tector and Lyle send Mapache to his maker. He pivots, gouts of blood erupting from his body as each shot hits home. There is absolute silence, the tension palpable. The Mexicans are motionless, as if paralyzed by disbelief; some of them even have their hands raised. It seems, for one moment, as if the Bunch could walk out of the courtyard and live. But this is tragedy; and, just as with Shakespeare, it takes only one act to pass the point beyond which the remaining characters – those for whom the stage of this final act has been set – can turn back. And if the shot that sets Peckinpah's visceral ballet of apocalypse in motion is fired by Pike, it is Dutch who provides the overture.

Dutch: the man who calls into question Pike's defence of Thornton; who is forced to turn his back on Angel in order to leave Mapache's settlement alive; who smiles at the thought of confronting Mapache; who, near the start of the film, responds to Pike's statement that he wouldn't have it any other way with the affirmation, 'Pike, I wouldn't have it any other way either.'

It is Dutch, now, who sniggers delightedly, grinning at Pike as if to remind him of this exchange; as if daring him to prove that all his talk of starting it together and finishing together isn't just talk.

Pike proves it. He spots Muhr lurking in an archway near the now properly mounted Gatling gun. He takes aim, slowly and deliberately, and drops the German with one shot.

What follows is five minutes of violent action, unflinchingly directed. The editing and intensity up the ante on even the battle at Starbuck. Herrera reaches for his pistol and is the next to die. The General's troops begin to return fire; a heavy wooden table is overturned to provide cover: women and children huddle terrified behind it. Firing at random, the Bunch make for the Gatling gun, positioned in one of a colonnade of archways fronting the building that houses Mapache's women. As the Bunch seek cover here, many of these women run out; Lyle, firing blindly, shoots one of them. (Soon, Dutch will resort to using a woman as a shield, her body riddled with bullets as he advances on his antagonists.) The surviving German officer, Muhr's adjutant, attempts to utilize the Gatling gun but is shot by Tector.

During the dispute with Herrera, when Pike threatens self-destruction by dynamite, it is Tector who is ready with the Gatling gun, then mounted on a wagon: 'Start the ball,' his brother tells him. Now, liberating the weapon so that it can be turned on the Mexicans, he does just that. Another reference to the robbery – when Dutch, helping to offload the munitions onto the wagon, exclaims, 'Hey, we got grenades!' – comes in a subsequent shot where, crouched behind a low wall, he tosses said incendiary devices into the enemy's ranks.

Swathes of Mapache's men are cut down or immolated, but any notion of the Bunch's advanced weaponry evening out the odds against the revolutionaries' superiority in numbers is quickly dispelled. Pike is the first to take a bullet. As he bursts into one of the rooms, a young woman, her back firmly against the wall, watches him – not with fear but anticipation. Pike glances around: something is wrong. He sees his reflection in the

The Gorch brothers dying in a hail of bullets.

mirrored door of a wardrobe and fires. In *Pat Garrett and Billy the Kid*, this image is revisited, but as a symbolic act; here it is purely instinctual, the angle shifting so that it is the woman's reflection we see as the glass shatters. His instincts are proved right: a soldier falls dead from behind it.

But – as thrice before – Pike makes a simple but critical mistake. He turns his back on the woman. Outside, Tector and Lyle are being overwhelmed, the Gatling gun pivotting wildly as bullets ricochet around them, one of them winging Lyle. Pike, reloading, starts to edge into the fray again, concerned by their screams. The woman produces a gun from behind her back and takes aim as carefully as Pike did with Muhr.

'Bitch!' he grunts as the bullet strikes him. He spins round and blasts her with his shotgun, throwing it away from him in disgust even as her body crumples.

Stumbling along the colonnade, he throws over a table (this visual motif from the beginning of the battle suggesting that the end is soon to come) and he and Dutch shelter behind it. Dutch, we see, is badly wounded, the front of his shirt mottled with blood. Pike snarls his trademark exhortation for the last time: 'Come on you lazy bastard!' But even as he says it, his expression turns to horror at the almost simultaneous deaths of Tector and Lyle. Dragging himself over to the Gatling gun, he returns fire, his toll easily reaching double figures by the time his arc of bullets cuts across the box of remaining grenades and the resulting explosion rouses Dutch. Peering from behind the table, Dutch mouths the last line of dialogue any of the Bunch are to voice: 'Give 'em hell, Pike!'

Again, a manful homily presages death. A young boy, shown in an earlier scene to hero-worship Mapache [5], aims a rifle that looks almost too cumbersome for him to handle. But, as he pokes the barrel through a set of railings (parallel lines that echo the railroad tracks on the outskirts of Starbuck by which children presided over the death of ants and scorpions) and lines up his shot, it is clear that he knows exactly how to handle it.

It is the darkest, least palatable irony of the film: Pike Bishop – who is described by Thornton as a *man*, and whose lectures to the Bunch revolve around the importance of manly behaviour – is killed by shots in the back from a woman and a child.

Dutch is the last to die, the violence turning to poignance – and the sense of catharsis to one of repulsion – as he is shot down making his way to where his friend has fallen. The camera frames him in tight composition looking over at Pike, ravaged and bloodied, before his eyes finally close.

The end of the line for Pike, Dutch, Tector and Lyle. The end of the line for Mapache and Muhr and the dirty business of political motivations. But – as indicated by the occasional cuts away from the battle, to Thornton watching the proceedings through binoculars from a vantage point outside Agua Verde – there are still matters to be resolved.

From the outset, *The Wild Bunch*'s characters communicate – in terse and muscular language – an elegy for changing times and a reliance on a certain code: 'Those days are closing fast', 'We started it together, we'll end it together.' And, once the air is clear of gunsmoke and the cost in human lives can be reckoned, Peckinpah stages his final scenes in reconciliation of these themes.

Buzzards are already settling as Thornton leads his posse into the courtyard. His face creased with weariness, he goes over to the Gatling gun and looks down at the bodies of the men he has been chasing. There is sadness in his eyes, but nothing judgemental. He reaches out to Pike and takes the pistol from his holster, the act as much a final image of connection as it is a valediction. His reverie, though, is disturbed by the inevitable juvenility of T C and Coffer. They are ready to 'load up' (i.e. take the bodies back to Harrigan as proof of the Bunch's demise) and, like children, instead of keeping silent in the face of this corpse-littered aftermath, they mock what they do not understand. 'You ain't so damn much now are you, Mr Pike?' Coffer jeers.

Thornton, disgusted, walks away.

They find him sitting outside the town wall, his posture reminiscent of that of Dutch as he waits for Pike, Tector and Lyle to get done with their whores. 'You ain't comin'?' asks Coffer.

Thornton doesn't want to waste words on him. 'No,' he says.

As they ride off, T C asks about Sykes. Coffer announces that they'll 'pick him up on the way'. They disappear into the distance, voices raised in a rough chorus of 'Polly wolly doodle all the day', idiotically oblivious to what awaits them.

Thornton doesn't budge as the survivors leave Agua Verde, an exodus of men, women and children, many wounded or crippled, all poverty-striken. He grimaces as shots resound on the soundtrack of his memory. He is still sitting there as Sykes rides up, accompanied by men from Angel's village – the men to whom the Bunch gave rifles:

> Sykes: Didn't expect to find you here.
> Thornton: Why not? I sent 'em back. That's all I said I'd do.
> Sykes: They didn't get very far.
> Thornton: I figured.

The implication is clear: T C, Coffer and their fellow mercenaries are now buzzard-bait in some nearby canyon. Fittingly, the last few survivors file past at this point, one of them carrying the Gatling gun.

Sykes: What are your plans?

Thornton: Drift around down here. Try to stay out of jail.

Sykes: Well, me and the boys here, we got some work to do. You wanna come along? Ain't like it used to be, but it'll do.

And for all that this line is as elegiac as Don Jose's remark about childhood is poetic, Thornton's response is laughter – rueful, certainly, but there is something in it that suggests the old ways have not quite been lived out.

In choosing to defy Harrigan and renounce the company of the bounty hunters (a wise decision, considering), Thornton has paid his debt. He accepts Sykes's offer and this newly formed outfit – this, as it were, replacement Bunch – ride off to whatever their own destiny is, sure to carry with them the legend of the four men who took on an army at Agua Verde.

Sykes, too, seals the union with laughter. And it is laughter that fills the soundtrack as the masterpiece ends: the laughter of Pike and Dutch and Angel and the Gorch brothers. Images of them at key moments – moments of unity – are superimposed on the closing frames.

In showing us the Bunch as ageing men, refusing to change even as social, technological and global affairs are reshaping the world around them, Peckinpah demythologizes the Old West. Yet in their deaths, he reminds us where the myths came from in the first place.

CHAPTER THREE
RELOCATING THE WESTERN

The three films Peckinpah made between *The Wild Bunch* and *Pat Garrett and Billy the Kid* were his first features not to be westerns. Together with *Bring Me the Head of Alfredo Garcia*, made immediately after *Pat Garrett*, they form an interesting and thematically diverse quartet.

Junior Bonner sees a return to the lyrical tone of *The Ballad of Cable Hogue*, while *The Getaway* heralds a move into action thrillers, a genre Peckinpah would return to in *The Killer Elite* and *The Osterman Weekend*.

Straw Dogs and *Bring Me the Head of Alfredo Garcia* are darker films altogether, the former a psychological drama featuring a scene so contentious that it is still banned on video; the latter one of the least shown, and easily the least understood, of Peckinpah's entire output.

What they have in common is subtextual in some and explicit in others, sometimes a matter of iconography and sometimes of narrative structure. From a Cornish farmhouse besieged by psychotic locals to a nightmare ride across an hallucinatory Mexico with a severed head as a travelling companion, by way of rodeo riders going home and crooks on the run from vengeful associates, all are so firmly rooted in Peckinpah's vision of the Old West that, despite being updated and relocated, they are westerns at heart.

Paradoxically, what also connects these films is the very thing that differentiates them from the actual westerns. Their protagonists are loners. True, Peckinpah explores a relationship in each case, be it marital and fractious (David and Amy in *Straw Dogs*, Doc and Carol in *The Getaway*), familial and dysfunctional (*Junior Bonner*) or naive and destined to end badly (Bennie and Elita in *Bring Me the Head of Alfredo Garcia*), but unlike the positive aspects of companionship explored in *Ride the High Country* and *The Wild Bunch*, the effect is to pinpoint his characters at their most isolated.

'HEAVEN AND EARTH ARE RUTHLESS': *Straw Dogs*

Tolstoy once said that the best way to begin a story was to thrust one's readers directly into the drama. Which is pretty much how Peckinpah likes to start. *Straw Dogs* opens with the return of Amy Sumner (Susan George) to the Cornish village of her birth. She's glamorous and drives a sleek, white sports car, suggesting that the boundaries of her world have expanded far beyond the reach of the locals. In tow is her bookish, bespectacled husband David (Dustin Hoffman). (How they ever became a couple is something Peckinpah wisely leaves unexplained.) He's an American college professor, looking to the solitude that a village life offers so that he can complete his research on astrophysics (or as he blandly puts it, 'possible structures of solar interiors').

Witnessing their arrival are village idiot Henry Niles (David Warner) – who has been taking an unwholesome interest in the local children, particularly the microskirted teenage temptress Janice Hedden (Sally Thomsett) – and Amy's old boyfriend Charlie Venner (Del Henney). Venner offers to help with the renovation already being carried out on Trencher's Farm, the isolated property the Sumners have taken residence in, and David accepts. Venner's friend Phil Riddaway (Donald Webster) tags along.

The two locals currently undertaking the work, Chris Cawsey (Jim Norton) and Norman Scutt (Ken Hutchinson), are vexed at Venner's interference. Scutt, who can't keep his eyes off Amy, is jealous that Venner once had her. It isn't long, however, before they band together in mutual contempt of David.

Work progresses slowly, the incessant hammering, sniggering and cracking of jokes at David's expense providing a nervous backdrop to the gradual breakdown of David and Amy's marriage. David responds to Amy's accusations (that he isn't a man, that he's only come to England so he can run away from problems he faced in the US) by withdrawing deeper into his research. Amy resorts to schoolgirl spite, obliterating one of his formulas from the blackboard.

Frustrated, but unwilling to stand up to his wife, David drives into the village to the pub. His first sight, on parking the car, is of Henry Niles being struck about the face by his brother John as a warning to stay away from the children. In the pub, David is greeted with hostile silence. The impasse is broken when neighbourhood dignitary Major Scott (T P McKenna) arrives. He tells David that the vicar, the Reverend Hood (Colin Welland), is intending to drop by Trencher's Farm, and offers to drive back with him.

The atmosphere between David and Amy is palpable, but conversation turns to the upcoming church social and the couple promise to attend. Later, the guests having departed, it seems that things might be resolved between them. The moment is lost when David, opening the wardrobe to hang up his clothes, discovers their cat, hanged. He can't bring himself to tell Amy, and closes the door again. Perplexed at his sudden change of mood, she looks in the wardrobe herself. Angry at him for letting her find out this way, she demands that he challenge the locals the following day.

He muffs the intended confrontation, instead inviting them into the house for a drink and asking them to set the antique man trap he has acquired as an *objet d'art*. While they help him mount it above the fireplace, Amy makes a big show of entering the room with a tray containing several glasses of beer and a saucer of milk. Venner and his cronies evade the issue by asking David to accompany them on a hunting trip the following day.

This is simply a ruse to abandon David on the moors (they give him a shotgun and tell him to wait quietly while they flush a brace of birds in his direction) so that Venner can pay a house call – on Amy. Admitting him, she confronts him about the cat. He reacts by forcing himself on her. She protests at first, but her resistance meets with a fist to the face and a flurry of slaps.

While David stands alone in the wilds, his gun loaded but of absolutely no use to him, Venner brutally rapes his wife. Whether through conflicting emotions, numbed insensation or fear of another beating, Amy capitulates. But her ordeal is far from over. No sooner has Venner finished than Scutt barges in, shotgun trained on him. Venner co-operatively holds Amy down while Scutt takes his turn.

By the time David returns from the moor, Venner and Scutt are gone. Amy is unable to tell him about the incident. They edge towards another argument. Amy insists that he fire Venner and his cronies. He reluctantly agrees.

The next evening, Amy's attempt to put on a brave face for the church social is defeated by the leering presence of her rapists. Reverend Hood stages a feeble magic show. The abrasive shrieks of laughter from the children seem to make mockery of her ordeal. Janice, noticing Amy's discomfort, uses the opportunity to make advances towards David. Concerned for his wife, he brushes her aside without a thought. Peeved, she switches her attentions to Henry Niles. As inexperienced as he is with girls, he does not hesitate to accept her offer to go for a walk, alone.

David and his antagonist Venner in a bizarre stand-off with Scutt; Amy looks on.

Janice's younger brother sees them leave; the word soon gets round. Her father, Tom Hedden (Peter Vaughan), makes it his first priority to give Henry a beating. Venner, Scutt, Cawsey and Riddaway volunteer for lynch mob duty – and they go looking for Henry [1].

Led into an outhouse by Janice, who is making a good job of seducing him, Henry's excitement turns to fear when he hears men approaching outside. Janice begins to call out to them, not realizing what they will do to Henry. He restrains her. Not knowing his own strength, he inadvertently kills her.

Meanwhile, David and Amy have left the event, a heavy fog descending as they drive home. Henry, running for his life, blunders out in front of them. David knocks him down. Knowing nothing of Henry's history of psychiatric problems, or the search for Janice, David's only concern is to get Henry back to Trencher's Farm with them, where they can ring for help.

Unable to raise the doctor or get through to the police, David leaves a message for Major Scott, then, in desperation, tries the pub. The landlord promises, should he see the doctor, that he'll inform him of the situation. Eager to get Hedden and his volatile mob out of the pub, no sooner does he hang up than he passes the information on to them. Hedden grabs his shotgun and they set off for Trencher's Farm.

When David refuses to hand Henry over, they lay siege. Bricks take out the windows. Cawsey, a rat-catcher by trade, lets a few of his furry friends loose in the house to frighten Amy. Major Scott's arrival seems fortuitous, but when he orders Hedden to give him the gun, he gets both barrels – point blank. Amy pleads with her husband to let them take Henry, but David knows that, as witnesses to Scott's killing, the mob have no intention of letting them live. Responding to appeals from Venner ('open the door and let us have Niles, I won't let them hurt you – please, love'), Amy switches allegiance. David finally does what she's wanted him to do all along – stand up, be a man – and the results horrify her: he gives her a Venner-like slapping around, threatening to break her neck if she doesn't do as he tells her, then arms himself with a variety of weapons and prepares to defend his property. He turns out to be very capable, very capable indeed.

Disarming Hedden, he turns the shotgun on Riddaway. It's empty. Riddaway launches himself at David. The academic bludgeons him with a poker. Cawsey bursts in wielding a knife, but David is unperturbed. Again wielding the poker, he beats the rat-catcher to death. In the meantime, Venner has found the shotgun. David tells him contemptuously that it's empty. 'It is now?' Venner counters.

'Why don't you pull it and show me?' David offers.

The standoff is broken when they are alerted by screams from upstairs: Scutt has gained entry and is attacking Amy, again with intent to rape. In a truly strange moment, the two antagonists – Amy's failure of a husband and violent rapist of an ex-boyfriend – jointly hurtle upstairs to her aid. Scutt pulls a knife. Venner shoots him – evidently he *had* reloaded – and David uses the confusion (Amy screaming, Venner stunned that he's killed one of his own) to knock the shotgun from his grasp. They go hand to hand. David finishes him off with the man-trap. 'Jesus Christ,' he mutters, surveying the bodies, 'I got them all.'

Not quite. Riddaway has regained consciousness. When he comes at David, his sheer size and strength put the academic at a disadvantage. Amy reluctantly avails herself of the shotgun and shoots him.

David leads Henry out to his car and drives him back to the village. The fog is still heavy, visibility minimal. Niles says apologetically that he doesn't know his way home. With a smile as inappropriate as it is humourless, David replies that he doesn't either.

The Siege of Trencher's Farm is a short novel whose self-contained setting, relatively small cast of characters and sustained climax give it the feel of a screenplay-in-waiting. The title was changed after a survey conducted by the producer indicated audience expectation of a western; Peckinpah settled on *Straw Dogs*, from a quote in Lao Tzu's philosophical work *The Book of 5,000 Characters*: 'Heaven and Earth are ruthless and treat the myriad of people as straw dogs.'

In a character trait absent from the film, David [2] is a fan of old movies, particularly westerns, and he perceives the assault on his house in terms of homesteaders on the prairie being set upon by marauding indians. Peckinpah doesn't need to have David slumped in front of the television, the black-and-white escapades of Roy Rogers or Audie Murphy flickering away, to draw the parallel. Western iconography is everywhere. The local pub, a spit 'n' sawdust joint, is the perfect stand-in for a saloon. When David pays his first visit, the labourers stand around in little cliques (like cowboys whose comradeship is dictated by the ranch they work on); a regular throws a mean arrow (dart board instead of card table); conversation stops when David asks for a packet of 'American cigarettes' (mistrust of someone who ain't from around these parts); things turn ugly when the landlord refuses Tom Hedden an after-hours drink (bar-room brawl/stand-off/go for your gun moment). During the hunt, Venner and the others carry their shotguns as unselfconsciously as western characters wear holsters. Major Scott, aloof in his status as the local magistrate, is an authority figure as resented as any sheriff.

Peckinpah co-wrote the screenplay with David Zelag Goodman, and they responded well to Gordon M Williams's genre references. Nonetheless, notable changes were made – changes that indicate a more cynical worldview on Peckinpah's part. Williams gives the couple a daughter, implying that protection of the family motivates David's recourse to violence. In the film, they are childless and their marriage is a sham; they owe nothing to Henry Niles, the man they are sheltering; David has no knowledge of Amy's ordeal at the hands of Charlie Venner. This makes his motivation dark and ambiguous. As the mob attempt forced entry, he declares that he will not permit violence against his house. But his actions against them go beyond defensive tactics – and way beyond reasonable force [3].

The daughter of the novel is pre-pubescent and makes friends with Janice Hedden, who is the same age. Janice's death results from being lost in the woods during a snowstorm – Henry plays no part in it even though the villagers automatically blame him. The film's Janice is older, on the cusp of womanhood and eager for the attention of men (in the opening scene, she walks behind Amy, copying her walk, obviously in envy of her more fully developed womanly charms); her death is equally accidental but Henry *is* the author of it, and the circumstances are sexual in nature. Hedden's lynch mob, therefore, are afforded a greater degree of empathy than Williams bestows. In the novel, they are more akin to torch-bearing peasants on a witch hunt – their assault on Trencher's Farm is based on a mistaken assumption; that they already harbour an imagined grudge against the 'bloody Yank' is just a fringe benefit.

The way Peckinpah sets it up, Hedden's extreme – but understandable – reaction to his daughter's death is the catalyst for Venner, having made a fool of David on the moors and raped Amy, to go all the way and inflict physical violence on the outsider (a man not just geographically, but intellectually and financially distanced from anyone else in the village) who married the girl who turned him down all those years ago, and for Scutt, who resents Venner as much as he does David, to get the chance to force himself on Amy again.

It is this element of the movie, established in the oft-criticised rape scene, which adds a dimension absent from the book.

There is no rape scene in Williams's novel.

Peckinpah's motives for putting one in the film have been called into question more often than any other directorial decision he made. Attempted rape features in *The Deadly Companions* and *Ride the High Country*, but is prevented in both cases. *Straw Dogs* made the act explicit, setting the tone for *Bring Me the Head of Alfredo Garcia* and *Cross of Iron*, and earned him the eternal wrath of feminists. It also resulted in a ban on the film's UK video release, which remains in force to this day. Non-availability only serves to enhance the hyperbolized perception of the scene, freighting the film even more heavily with a reputation it doesn't deserve.

Peckinpah includes the rape scene for a purpose. *Straw Dogs* is about two things: (a) the disintegration of a marriage, and (b) the question of whether a man's predisposition to violence is latent and deep-rooted, or something at which he must demonstrate his capability before he can call himself a man – in other words, a rite of passage. These two themes play out in counterpoint. David's evasion of conflict has dual consequences: escalation of the villagers' abuses against him, and increasing disharmony between him and Amy. The villagers can be seen as an externalization of the issues that the Sumners refuse to resolve. David's bookishness is challenged by their coarseness and physicality. His spectacles, woolly sweaters and loafers are the antithesis of their shotguns, donkey jackets and heavy boots. His mumbled, stuttering sentences are no match for their continual barrage of profane, loud-mouthed banter. In short, they represent the kind of man that Amy resents David for not being.

As spite against David, and perhaps in defiance of the lecherous glances she knows they are casting at her, Amy makes no attempt to downplay her physical attractiveness, even letting them catch a glimpse of her topless. It is David's ineffectuality that has allowed things to progress this far. The net result is his abandonment on the moors and Amy's rape by Venner and Scutt.

There's no avoiding it – the rape scene *is* disturbing. But then, it should be – any film-maker who presents such subject matter palatably is being hugely irresponsible. Peckinpah shows the act in all its awful sickening ugliness. Far from exploiting women, the director actually delivers a resounding guilty verdict against the darkest and most primal urges that inform the male psyche.

Nietzsche wrote, 'terrible experiences make one wonder whether he who experiences them is not something terrible'. Or, as *Straw Dogs* seems to suggest, whether they create these terrible experiences by their own actions.

Whether inadvertently, or driven by a subconscious urge to self-destruction, how often do we engineer circumstances detrimental to ourselves? Peckinpah would later say that there were any number of places in the film where David could have taken some form of action and put a stop to the escalation of events. Even before the opening credits, he could have made the decision to stay in the US (in an early scene, the locals rag him about the rioting they've seen on the news: 'Was you involved in it, sir?' they ask him; 'Did you take part?'). The entire first half of the film is stamped through with examples of his cowardice. Every challenge to his masculinity reinforces his head-in-the-sand attitude.

When Amy scrubs one of his equations from the blackboard, she is almost in tears. It's clear she hates herself for doing it, but she can see no other way to get his attention. David is too wrapped up in his work to realize this and spurns her further, accusing her of childishness; as a consequence she indulges this aspect of her personality, parading herself in front of the workmen in the hope of making him jealous and therefore more attentive. This is a huge mistake on her part, but symptomatic of their troubled relationship.

In a telling scene, David examines a piece of antique furniture. 'Is that your daddy's chair?' he asks Amy. 'Every chair is my daddy's chair,' she replies. Later, when he tells her 'You act like you're fourteen', she pouts and says 'I am.' The implication, while unlikely to earn Peckinpah praise from feminists, reveals the truth of their incompatibility: Amy wants a father figure and David – calm, reasonable and non-violent – just isn't manly enough. He exercises by skipping. In a rare scene of him and Amy making love, he prissily removes his glasses and watch and sets the alarm clock first.

Amy's tendencies to immature behaviour are equalled by his. Unwilling or unable to stand up to her, he vents his frustrations by throwing fruit at the cat. When Reverend Hood and Major Scott visit, he turns on a record of bagpipe music and beams delightedly at them. Quite why he does this – trying to be funny? A mistaken belief he's catering to their tastes? – is perplexing, and the bemused glances his guests exchange are matched by Amy's look of acute embarrassment. Or does he do it just to embarrass her? Whatever the answer, Peckinpah uses the scene to demonstrate that David's thought-processes are different from the other characters'.

By the end of the film, he has David play the record again – under different circumstances. Here we have Venner and co. staging their assault on Trencher's Farm as if it were some kind of demented playground battle. Cawsey and Riddaway liberate a couple of children's tricycles from an outbuilding (presumably the property of an earlier tenant) and peddle them around, deliberately bumping into each other. Cawsey is still wearing the red comedy nose he donned at the church social. David, however, has never been more serious: he is focused and fast thinking, his stutter replaced by a grim low-voiced monotone. When he plays the bagpipe music, turning the volume up to the max, Scutt and Cawsey start drunkenly dancing to it outside. 'He's playing music,' Riddaway gasps, his tone of voice suggesting that he thinks David has flipped.

Not so. David uses the music for a definite purpose: to spread confusion. Likewise, he instructs Amy to extinguish the downstairs lights and illuminate the property from upstairs. The result? Their visibility is reduced, his is improved. When Hedden tries to come in through a window, David uses an upended dining table to give him enough cover to get close. Hedden appears, feet first, shotgun at the ready. David uses a poker to knock the weapon from his hands. It discharges, blowing Hedden's foot off. Result: one attacker out of the game; acquisition of another weapon.

As these defensive strategies show, David's transformation into a one-man army (not only able to kill without hesitation, but a ruthless tactician as well) is as naturalistic as it is swift. What is genuinely chilling is not so much David's proficiency in the use of

violence, but that he approaches it with the emotionless logic that informs his academic research. While the mob waste time outside, their threatening behaviour punctuated by bouts of tomfoolery (when initial breaking and entering attempts fail, they seek solace in laying waste to the greenhouse), David is busy working out how best to put them at a disadvantage – and what he can use to kill with.

The reversal of David's role, from inactive to pro-active, is juxtaposed with the internal tensions that begin to fragment the mob. The lack of communication between David and Amy, which they so effectively exploited in the early scenes, now becomes *their* undoing: they enter Trencher's Farm separately, instead of functioning as a unit, thereby allowing David to deal with them one at a time. The rivalry between Venner and Scutt results in the latter's death – one less for David to worry about – as well as giving him his chance to take on Venner.

Peckinpah's intercutting between David alone on the moors (impotence/passivity) and the attack on Amy (rampant virility/brutality) shows us two negative aspects of how men behave towards women. Now, in comparing David's clinical use of weapons with the mob's dependence on heavy-handed thuggery, he presents an even bleaker view of how men interact with each other. Here there is no room for impotence or passivity; things between men have to be settled – by gun, knife or fist. Or poker. Or man-trap.

When Amy accuses him of running away in leaving the US, it is prescient of the understanding he comes to by the end of the film: you can't run; you can't hide; it doesn't go away; the more you try to avoid it, the worse it becomes. Conflict is inevitable – the only question is how long you leave it before you make your stand. When Amy lambasts him for not taking action over the death of her cat, David's evasiveness is just as questionable as his later espousal of violence.

> Amy: Scutt or Cawsey.
> David: Why?
> Amy: To prove to you they could get into your bedroom.
> David: I don't believe that.
> Amy: Well, who else is around all the time?
> David: We left all the doors unlocked. It could have been anybody passing.
> Amy: Anybody passing? David, a complete stranger comes into our house and decides to strangle our cat and hang her in the wardrobe? *Anybody passing?* Cawsey or Scutt!

Amy's right and he knows it. But it's not something he can intellectualize, so he looks the other way. He immerses himself in his research and pretends it didn't happen.

Straw Dogs is the first of the contemporary westerns; David Sumner is the first loner to appear in Peckinpah's work. There is no celebration of masculine codes of honour. As much as Venner, Scutt, Cawsey and Riddaway come across as a Cornish version of the Hammond brothers, as whiskery a stand-in as Hedden might be for Mapache (they're both drunkards who operate on a hair-trigger; Hedden's designs on Henry are in the same ballpark as Mapache's maltreatment of Angel), there is no central relationship that encapsulates the positive aspects of loyalty, fraternity and staying with a man once you side with him. There is no Judd and Westrum, no Pike and Dutch.

The westerns boast characters who are decent, whose tribulations are undeserved: put upon women such as Kit and Elsa, idealists such as Angel, old men such as Sykes and Don Jose who have a handle on life. This is not so in *Straw Dogs*. Everybody is guilty of something: Venner is a misogynist and rapist, likewise Scutt; Cawsey is a small-time thief who gets off on stealing Amy's underwear; Riddaway, who has no discernible reason for joining in the siege, is a hulking metaphor for mob violence, pitching in for the pure hell of it. Hedden, for all that the death of his daughter is a tragedy, is a vulgar dissipate who's always spoiling for trouble, an absent father for as long the pub remains open. As for Janice, she is sexually precocious; rather too close to her brother for comfort

Left: David arms himself in Straw Dogs.

(a scene where they huddle together, arms encircling each other as they spy on David and Amy making love, suggests that village life hinges on a certain degree of in-breeding); and perfectly willing to give David the come-on just to score points off Amy.

Amy, although the victim in many ways, is sullen and changeable at the best of times; at worst, she refuses to assist David in defending their home, tries to convince him to sacrifice Henry ('You don't care, do you?' David gasps; 'No,' she replies, 'I don't'), and threatens to betray him by admitting Venner. Yes, even Amy is guilty.

And David is perhaps the most guilty of them all: for letting things reach such a stage. Another line from Nietzsche applies: 'He who fights with monsters might take care lest he become a monster himself. And if you gaze for long into an abyss, the abyss gazes also into you.'

When David Sumner leaves Trencher's Farm, he and the abyss are pretty much on first name terms. With the last one of his enemies dead, David pauses barely long enough to enquire if Amy is all right. The question is perfunctory and the look that passes between them says they've come to the end of the line. He turns from her, hustles Henry out to the car and drives away.

The closing lines of the film – all the more devastating for being understated – spell out how far David has gone in the defence of his home; and how he will never be able to go back.

> Henry: I don't know my way home.
> David: That's okay. I don't either.

Unwarranted as it may be, the bad reputation that clings to *Straw Dogs* is dishearteningly understandable. It was strong stuff even in the 1970s, a decade heralded by the death of the hippie ideal at Altamont; a decade when cynicism and downbeat endings were the norm in mainstream film production, a tendency which has a direct sociological correlation to public disaffection with the war in Vietnam. But compared to other controversial 1970s' movies, such as *The Exocist*, *A Clockwork Orange*, *Driller Killer* and *The Texas Chainsaw Massacre* (all of which have had their video bans repealed), the continued denial of video release for *Straw Dogs* has only served to exacerbate public perception of it as a cinematic 'hot potato'.

Peckinpah's control over his material is masterful. The pace doesn't so much build as steadily gnaw away at the audience, a gradual erosion of possible resolutions until all that remains is the terrible inevitablity of bloodshed. Time is taken to get to the heart of David and Amy's ailing marriage, Peckinpah showing them in moments of frivolity even as the next row is brewing. The villagers are fleshed out beyond mere rent-a-mob yokels: their rough-edged camaraderie contrasts with David's isolationism, while the internal tensions that inform their interrelationships (Venner and Scutt's rivalry; class resentment against Major Scott; the landlord and Reverend Hood as marginal outsiders) remind us how closed off the village is from the outside world. From Hedden's petulant demands for an after-hours pint to Cawsey's soliloquy on how he feels closer to rats than people, Peckinpah gives us more and more cause to worry about what these people are capable of, all the while watching his nominal hero with almost clinical interest as he finds excuse after excuse not to face up to the steady escalation of events. And when Peckinpah sets the screen alight in the last twenty minutes, the effect is all the more devastating for the carefully developed emotionalism of what has gone before.

Technically, the film excels. The opening credits sequence establishes tone and location. A low-angled black-and-white shot of a headstone drifts out of focus as the main credits appear in stark black wording. Unique in his filmography, the director's name is above the title: *Sam Peckinpah's Straw Dogs*. As the secondary credits appear, the picture slowly begins to focus again – the same graveyard, but this time an overhead shot, the film in colour. Children thread their way through the headstones, playing ring-o'-roses. Within the walls of the churchyard, the children form a circle. One thinks of

David and a traumatised Amy at the church social in Straw Dogs.

wagons drawing together in a western, and the purpose here is similar: defence. Against the outside the world. Against anyone not of the village. At the centre of their circle is a headstone, symbolic of the age-old concern of keeping the affairs of the village within the village. When Peckinpah cuts to the next shot – of David and Amy's arrival in their sports car – we have already been told that this is the wrong place for them to settle.

The use of children to reflect the terrors of the adult world is classic Peckinpah. Indeed, most of his established directorial flourishes are present and correct: slow motion (sparingly used and the more effective for it: the first brick through the window, Hedden's shooting of Major Scott, Amy's of Riddaway); mirrors (when Janice and her brother spy on David and Amy, they see them in reflection); flashbacks (Amy's: to David during the rape, putting him in Venner's place; to the rape while at the church social); dissonant editing techniques (the church social is astoundingly well-edited, Amy's near-breakdown and Janice's overtures to Henry interwoven with observational vignettes that map out the power structure and unspoken tensions inherent in village life). All that is missing is the theme of men outliving their times (the closest the film comes is to suggest that David has outlived his social conditioning), and the use of freeze-frames. And Peckinpah omits these for a reason. The film is not about heroics, therefore it contains no mythic elements; no iconography.

For a film so reviled for violent content, *Straw Dogs* is arguably Peckinpah's most anti-violent work. The confrontations in his westerns have an heroic quality: Westrum riding back to stand with Judd against the Hammonds in *Ride the High Country*; Tyreen sacrificing himself in *Major Dundee*; the Bunch signing the pages of history with their own blood. The men, while flawed, have stature. Their deaths, while depicted realistically, are somehow magnificent. We are all afraid of dying – so when men like Peckinpah's protagonists meet death on their own terms, they are also acting on our behalf. Peckinpah understands, too, that it is human nature to confer martyrdom on anyone who dies young, dies fearlessly, or dies for a cause. People who die in such circumstances are exempt from aftermath: they will never recant, show remorse, or exhibit signs of trauma. The effects of their actions will never be weighed against them.

David Sumner does not die. Not physically, anyway. But something in him is killed. When the siege begins, David has reached a point where his marriage cannot be saved. By the time it ends, his home is in ruins. In the interim, his humanity goes the same way. When he drives into the village earlier in the film, after bickering with Amy, he is shocked to see John Niles bringing his brother back into line by striking him. During the siege, when Henry panics and attacks Amy, David subdues him by punching him in the face. This is where David crosses the line: he does something he was once appalled by. The blow he delivers is like the one we have already seen Venner inflict on Amy. The result? For the first time in the film, he is in control.

And this is the hard question that Peckinpah asks: how much does one have to lose in order to be thus empowered? The questions he backs it up with are equally thorny. What does it mean to be a man? How do men perceive, establish or defend their masculinity? And how often, by doing or not doing these things, do men destroy their own lives and the lives of others? Cumulatively, they are almost unanswerable.

Almost ... Because to come to an answer is to look into the darkest area of one's own psyche. This is perhaps why so many reviews of *Straw Dogs* latch onto the rape scene with such outraged zeal, using it to condemn the film entire so its psychological truths do not have to be confronted. It is easier to take a certain line, to use a neat all-encompassing tag such as 'political correctness'. And because such behaviour is self-defeating (hiding from bad things doesn't make them go away: ask David Sumner), it needs to be stated: for the record, *Straw Dogs* is a brilliant, disturbing work of cinema, and one of Sam Peckinpah's greatest achievements.

'SOME KINDA MOTEL COWBOY': *Junior Bonner*

Just as he had followed the intensity and controversy of *The Wild Bunch* with the non-violent, PG-rated *Ballad of Cable Hogue*, Peckinpah followed the intensity and controversy of *Straw Dogs* with the non-violent, PG-rated *Junior Bonner* [4]. However, this would not prove to be a continuing pattern.

Maybe it was the sheer weight of critical misunderstanding, the raised voices of the moral guardians questioning the corpuscle content of his output. Maybe Peckinpah felt that the only way he could convince his detractors of the artistic validity of his more violent work was to force them to confront their own demons by reflecting on screen the darkness that he knew festered somewhere in everyone; that only by inspiring exhilaration as well as revulsion (sometimes simultaneously) could he generate a truly cathartic response from his audience. Maybe it was the fact that his non-violent films disappeared at the box office. Whatever the reason, everything he made after *Junior Bonner* has about it a harshness, a blackness, that is unforgiving. Even the mainstream appeal of *The Getaway* is subverted by a despairing view of contemporary America as a soulless place where technology is a voyeuristic intrusion, the value of everything is reckoned in dollars and the emotional bonds of love and trust are tested at every turn.

The nostalgic side to Peckinpah, the part of him that said it was okay to get misty-eyed now and then, made its farewell performance with *Junior Bonner*. Likewise, the weaponry would be kept holstered, safety catches on, for the last time. There isn't a single shot fired in *Junior Bonner*. A bar-room brawl breaks out in the last half hour, but it's played for laughs. The long-anticipated dust-up between Junior (Steve McQueen) and his brother, Curly (Joe Don Baker), is all over in two blows: Junior hits Curly; forty minutes pass; Curly hits him back. And that's your lot!

*Right: Junior Bonner: a
cowboy ill-at-ease with
contemporary America.*

Nonetheless, Peckinpah communicates the passing of a way of life, the declining status of once great traditions, as powerfully as he did in *Ride the High Country* and *The Wild Bunch*. In the westerns, Steve Judd, Pike Bishop, Cable Hogue and Pat Garrett are overtaken by changing times – but enough remains of the old ways for them to cling to, even as they despair at the onset of modernity. For Junior Bonner, however, there isn't even the remembered glories of the recent past. He inhabits the America of 1971, but is perplexed by it; turn the clock back a century and he'd be in his element. Put simply, this is a man who outlived his times while his grandfather was still in the womb.

Nor does he have the bloodbath, blaze-of-glory, suicide-by-proxy ending of *The Wild Bunch* as an option. Near the start of the film, he swings by the old homestead on his way to a rodeo in Prescott, Arizona, the town of his birth. The land is being redeveloped and he watches in horror as a couple of bulldozers turn the house into so much matchwood. Trying to drive closer, his way is blocked by a churlish 'dozer driver who threatens to tip his load of gravel into Junior's open-top car if he doesn't back up. Junior backs up, turns round and drives away. Pike and co. die rather than change; Junior just has to live with it.

Which isn't to say that this scene doesn't bear any of the hallmarks of Peckinpah's more visceral work. Intercut with slow motion footage of the earthmoving behemoths (their tyres bigger than Junior's car) demolishing the property, are flashbacks of the house as it was and close-ups of a yellowing newspaper cutting, curled at the edges, pinned to a notice board inside. The cutting pertains to one of Junior's early rodeo victories. 'The past,' to quote L P Hartley, 'is a foreign country; they do things differently there.' A sentiment Peckinpah shared, and one he usually made visual with blood squibs and bad deaths. Here he visualizes it with industrial machinery and an empty house – and the result is just as effective.

The imagery also serves as a visualization of the recent downturn in Junior's fortunes. The film begins with him thrown from a Brahma bull of vicious temperament (the bull's name is Sunshine – its owner obviously has a sense of humour), the latest in a series of defeats that have seen him eclipsed in the rodeo community by his rival, the colourfully named Red Terwilliger. Returning for Prescott's annual rodeo, the heat is on for Junior to pull off a big win or lose face before a home crowd. He needs to be focused, his mind free of everything but staying in the saddle for the all-important eight seconds. But nothing is that straightforward in life – and certainly not in a Sam Peckinpah movie – and he finds himself side-tracked. In a wryly humorous vignette, which nonetheless stands as a metaphor for his complicated family life, Junior's preparations for the rodeo are delayed when his father, Ace, borrows (read steals) his horse.

When we first meet Ace Bonner (Robert Preston), he looks less like a domestic rustler than the Singing Detective without the skin condition. Laid up in hospital, he is content to harass the nurses and watch old black-and-white westerns on television. The box soon outlives its entertainment value, though. When the film is interrupted by a commercial for Curly's real estate business, Ace grabs the nearest thing to hand – the glass next to his jug of water – takes aim and puts the screen out [5].

Petulant, unrestrained, disrespectful of hospital property – guilty on all counts, but with good reason. Ace, an inveterate drinker, gambler and womanizer who is eternally short of the readies, has been forced to sell his land for redevelopment (hence the cheery little tableau that greets Junior). The agent for this redevelopment is Curly, whose lack of scruples in demolishing part of his heritage is matched by the callous way he beats down the price. It's like a warped version of a biblical parable: the good son going off a-wandering; the other, the one who is perceived as responsible and career-minded, staying at home and fleecing his father.

Junior learns of the circumstances from his mother. Elvira Bonner (Ida Lupino) is long estranged from her husband, but their lot in life is not dissimilar. Curly has designs on her house, too, and wants to set her up in a mobile home on his new trailer park.

That Junior calls on Elvira first makes Ace seem even more redundant. By the time he visits the hospital, a fifth of scotch hidden inside a bunch of flowers, Ace has discharged himself. It's a neat parallel. Ace and Junior, father and son, both go it alone.

Junior's untethered lifestyle is brought into contrast with Curly's *laissez faire* when, after a tense reunion dinner at Elvira's, the brothers stroll out onto the porch to take the evening air and have a little heart-to-heart. Visually, it could be a ranch house at any point during the last 150 years. There is even a hammock, a prop that Peckinpah goes on to use during a moment of dreadful hiatus in *Pat Garrett and Billy the Kid*.

> Junior: How much was it you paid for the old man's land, fifteen thousand?
> Curly: Which he proceeded to gamble and whore away in Nevada ... Now he's
>   got this scheme to go to Australia.
> Junior: Well, why don't you send him?
> Curly: Oh, come on, Junior! I put him on a weekly allowance and that's that. I
>   told him so.

For the moment, Junior is ruminative. He weighs up Curly's words, answering his excuses ('fifteen or thirty thousand, he still would have blown it all') with silence. His equilibrium is challenged when Curly goes on to offer him a job. And if offering a life of desk-bound ennui to a man such as Junior isn't insulting enough, his pitch is positively snide. When Junior makes a reference to the 'wide open spaces' that define his way of life, Curly responds, 'You know less about those wide open spaces than I do. I know that here's where it is. You're just some kinda motel cowboy.'

Despite Curly's provocative tone, Junior does not respond. He prowls the length of the porch, rolling a smoke and lighting it, holding himself in.

'Will you think on what I said?' Curly asks grouchily. 'I don't want you turning out like the old man.'

Which is the straw that breaks the bronco's back. Junior lands him a good one, connecting with such force that Curly is propelled backwards into the picture window, glass and the thin laths of the window frame disintegrating around him as he goes flying back into the dining room.

It is interesting that, for all the animosity, Curly is the only person who offers Junior anything concrete. Not counting Elvira's waiving of a loan he is unable to repay, Junior receives three fiscal propositions during the course of the film. The first is from Ace, to decamp with him to Australia and prospect for gold (another shared trait: they both live in the past). The second is from rodeo bigwig and owner of Sunshine, Buck Roan (Ben Johnson) to work for him (in what capacity he never says, although one gets the impression he is just out to belittle Junior). The last is from Curly, who not only specifies the position (salesman) but is honest enough to admit that he wants to exploit his brother's personality: 'Big cowboy like you,' Curly says, 'sincere, genuine as a sunrise.'

Needless to say, it's Curly's offer that Junior finds the easiest to turn down. The one that's hardest to decline is, of course, the one that's the least feasible – his father's.

In a rare moment of understanding between them, Elvira says to Ace, 'Dreams, sweet talk – that's all you are.' Very true. With his talent for loquacity and his inability to see the world in anything less than a rose-tinted haze, he is the film's romantic hero by default. Romantic in the sense of not being a realist, and by default because the film's actual hero (or rather protagonist, since Peckinpah, even at his blithest, doesn't deal in heroes) is far too laid back to aspire to such a pro-active role.

Junior comes alive when he has something of the bovine or equine ilk to deal with, preferably in front of a cheering audience. The rest of the time he's nonchalant to the point of blandness. Like Zhivago in the David Lean film, he is a character to whom events happen, not one who determines or shapes them. Nor is he emotionally charged; even when the centre of attention at his beloved rodeos, there is a lassitude about him that suggests he won't be doing the rounds at these events for too much longer. (In an early scene, Junior's convertible is overtaken by a carload of kids who call out 'How's the bull riding?' Junior's one-word answer: 'Lonesome.') As for the love of women, only

Elvira and Ace share a typically fractious moment in Junior Bonner.

once does Junior show any interest in female company. Even then, his motivation is more to get one over on a rodeo rival (he uses the chaos generated by a bar room brawl to steal the fellow's girl). After his one night stand, he parts from her at the airport; predictably, he has another rodeo to attend.

So it's left to Ace to wink at the nurses and rodeo groupies, make wisecracks, deliver homespun philosophy, and wax lyrical about his dream of Australia. The destruction of the hospital television is pretty much a statement of intent. Shortly afterwards, he discharges himself, much to the chagrin of Nurse Arlis, his carer and occasional consort. He plants a kiss on her lips even as she berates him, then heads off down the corridor. Her response is to summon the orderlies. As they converge on him, he hijacks a janitor's cart. He puts the mop to good use, wielding it like a javelin. 'I don't fight fair, boys,' he warns, grinning. They take him at his word. '*Adios*, sweet angel of mercy,' he adds, hastening outside to flag down a cab. 'Where to?' the driver asks. 'To the rodeo, partner,' he answers. 'Where else?'

This is Ace in his element, acting the goat and loving every minute of it. When Curly mentions putting his father on a weekly allowance, it says as much about Ace as it does Curly. The father-son relationships in *Junior Bonner* are inverted. It is the father who should give an allowance (or pocket money) to his son during childhood, not vice versa and with both parties of mature age. It is the father whose priority should be to earn a living, who should be pragmatic and worldly-wise. Here it is Curly who represents work and responsibility, while Junior speaks with the voice of experience.

Father and son: Ace and Junior in the grand parade in Junior Bonner.

Curly, who age-wise appears to be the youngest of the principles, is definitely the more mature (read boring) in terms of his outlook on life. Whereas fiscal considerations are incidental matters to Junior (who at one point tells Buck Roan 'money's nobody's favourite') and Ace (for whom a dollar earned is a dollar spent – usually in advance of him earning it), they are the be all and end all for Curly. His flourishing real estate business and trailer park development find their contrast in the ailing antiques shop Elvira runs, a going concern that just doesn't seem to be going anywhere (she takes in lodgers to make up the shortfall). How much of Curly's drive owes to his outspoken wife is left unsaid, but her acerbic evaluation of rodeos – 'never was a horse that couldn't be rode, never was a cowboy that couldn't be throwed [sic]' – speaks for itself. Certainly the remark, her one contribution to dinner table repartee, precedes Curly's job offer to Junior. Later in the film, Curly, still sniping at his brother, drops his guard. Accusation becomes self-revelation. 'I'm working on my first million,' he says. 'You're still working on eight seconds.'

By the end, though, it is Junior who reaches his objective first.

If the conflict between brothers gives *Junior Bonner* its drama, it is the affinity between father and son that gives the film its heart. With no love lost for his brother, no romantic entanglements to divert his attentions and no masculine friendships (Terwilliger is his out and out rival; Roan owns the bull that has come to symbolize all of his defeats), the stage is clear for a reaffirmation of the bond between Junior and Ace.

The key father-son episode comes during the grand parade through the centre of town. Ace steals Junior's horse so that he can participate. ('You fellas just sit around and let him take it, huh?' Junior says to a bunch of chuckling bystanders when he returns to an empty horse box.) Having registered for his rides in the rodeo ('I gotta go find my dad,' he tells the officials, 'he stole my horse'), Junior joins the procession, initially on foot, then hopping up onto Curly's float to ask if he's seen the old man. Again, Curly is shown in an unsympathetic light. He is towing his float behind a tractor decorated with bull horns, waving a cowboy hat in the air as he shouts out advertising slogans. (Later he will brag that the float 'came second in the commercial division'. Junior's response: 'Well, second's better than third.') There are plasters on his chin and forehead from the fist/dining room window incident. Peckinpah fleshes out the scene with crowd footage, capturing the carnival-like atmosphere as well as giving us plentiful of opportunity to observe that the real rodeo types ride horses not tractors and, no matter how often they're thrown, you never see them decorated with band-aids.

Curly answers that Ace is 'between the Indians and the flag', a literal description of his position in the parade and a wry comment on rodeo aficionados as anachronisms. (Two other drily amusing moments bear this out: a besuited wannabe with a saddle embroidered 'Wild Bunch', and the banner affixed to the deserted town hall, 'Prescott Frontier – Stay Cowboy'.) Before Junior can thank him (or otherwise), Curly adds 'I'm gonna whip your ass.' Unperturbed, Junior replies, 'Well, somebody is and it won't be the first time,' and so saying, climbs down from the tractor and goes to find Ace. Another pro-Junior touch: Curly has mechanized transport but Junior, on foot, still outpaces him.

Ace is cutting a fine figure at the forefront of the procession, even if Elvira, watching from the sidewalk, does call out to ask him where he stole his horse. Junior, though, makes no such accusation, nor does he remonstrate with his father.

> Ace: Hello, cowboy.
> Junior: Like your horse.
> Ace: So do I. Climb aboard.
> Junior: Are you sober?
> Ace: Sober as the day you met me.
> Junior: I've got a bottle. Want to drink it?

And so the two of them take off, cheered on by the crowd. Ace spurs the horse down an alleyway and through someone's backyard. They both plunge from the saddle as a washing line halts their progress. This comedic bit of business is intercut with crowd footage as the parade continues: Curly's float presents a dull spectacle, the name of his business spelled out in *faux* western lettering; elsewhere, horse riders are followed by a motorized cart, a small trailer hooked to the back of it, manned by two unfortunates whose job it is to shovel up the droppings. Peckinpah's camera faithfully records the pageantry – the formation riding of the police motorcyclists, a group of revellers in a mock-up of a stagecoach, the obligatory clowns – layers of detail from which he weaves a splendid tapestry of local colour.

Junior and Ace end up out front of the town hall, the horse tethered to one of the columns that forms its portico. 'Well,' Ace reflects, 'I hear you're doing very well.' The bottle is passed between them. 'Yeah?' Junior responds. 'Where did you hear that?'

A quiet interlude between men who were born too late: a quintessential Peckinpah moment. What is new is the generation gap. Judd and Westrum, Pike and Dutch, Cable Hogue and Joshua Sloane – all are more or less the same age. Nowhere else in Peckinpah's *oeuvre* is the father-son relationship portrayed. Most of his protagonists don't have families. Men such as Judd and Pike are in late middle-age as it is: their parents are either very old or dead – either way, fathers are absent. The same goes for younger characters: Kit's son in *The Deadly Companions* and Angel in *The Wild Bunch* both lose their fathers to untimely deaths; both, too, are doomed innocents themselves, their equally tragic deaths providing the impetus for other characters to act.

Ace and Junior on winning form in the milk race in Junior Bonner.

That Bonner Snr is still around, that he and his son can share a bottle of bourbon, hang out together and, in the film's rousing finale, participate jointly in the rodeo, explains why *Junior Bonner*, despite being coloured with the same 'changing times' ethos as so many other Peckinpah movies, has a more upbeat feel than is generally associated with its director. It also provokes the question of how much of the undeniable charm on display here, the 'feel-good factor', owes to wish-fulfilment on Peckinpah's part? It is tempting to interpret the easy-going scenes between Junior and Ace, their acceptance of each other for what they are – flaws, failures, and all – as the idealized relationship Peckinpah might have wanted with his father; certainly, it portrays one he never had.

The bar-room sequence that precedes the climactic rodeo can also be taken as an exercise in wish-fulfilment, given its emphasis on reconciliation. The penultimate round of rodeo events has seen Ace and Junior partner up for the milk race (a bizarre contest in which cows are lassoo'd, wrestled to the ground and forcibly milked). As much to their surprise as anyone else's, they win. The celebratory hoedown (obligatory Country and Western band twanging away) is eventful to say the least: in addition to an hilariously staged brawl, Junior and Curly are reconciled, Junior gets lucky with a rival's girlfriend, and Ace and Elvira get back together – temporarily, at least. From the tone of their conversation it's evident that, the impending act of conciliatory *l'amore* notwithstanding, Elvira isn't going to be fooled by him again.

> Elvira: As far as I'm concerned you can go to hell or Australia – but not with me.
> Ace: Well, they're both down under.
> Elvira: Dreams. Sweet talk. That's all you are.
> Ace: You stay with me, I'll sweeten the dreams too. Remember? [Elvira slaps him.] Well, sure as hell I had that coming.
> Elvira: You sure as hell did.
> Ace: But I'm leaving for good, Ellie, and I mean it this time.
> Elvira: Then all we've got left is today?
> Ace: Well anyway, Ellie, you seen one rodeo you've seen 'em all.

At which point they go off together, hand in hand. The sense of resolution in the scene, thanks to the interplay between Robert Preston and Ida Lupino, feels natural and unforced. Many Hollywood directors would have gone for out-and-out schmaltz, wringing every drop of sentiment from it (after all, the dysfunctional family has just got functional again, the big win at the rodeo is on the horizon and a happy ending seems assured). Not Peckinpah. He simply steps back and observes his characters, allowing whatever happens between them to do so in its own time.

This unwillingness to rush things is also evident during Junior's long awaited return to form at the final rodeo event. The editing is pure Peckinpah, an impressionistic layering of detail that captures the riders' preparation for (and the audience's anticipation of) their attempt to go the full eight seconds. The bulls lurch out of their pens in slow motion, every buck, kick and bone-juddering jolt accentuated. Falls are taken, men in western garb tumbling into the dust as if shot from their saddles by bounty hunters. Junior's ride seems the longest of all. Each protracted second of punishment he takes from Sunshine is marked by cutting to a close-up of the judge's stop-watch. That Junior stays on is through no want of trying by the bull.

But he makes it. Curly's still a-ways short of that first million, but Junior's got the eight seconds in the bag. He's reclaimed his crown – and done so in front of a home crowd. Plus, he's got the girl and things are a lot more stable family-wise than when he arrived. So what's next? Settle down with his new girlfriend? Stay around and spend his later years trading on former glories like the old man? Hell no.

He bids his inamorata adieu at the airport, then makes one trip back into town. He pays a brief visit to Elvira, already beginning to walk away when she doesn't immediately answer his knock on the porch door. 'Junior,' she calls, appearing at last. He stops and turns back. 'You had to win, didn't you?' she says accusingly.

'Yeah,' he replies. 'So long.'

She raises a hand as she watches him go.

He drives to the airline booking office, passing Ace en route. His father tries to flag him down – 'Junior,' he shouts, 'don't you hear me, boy?' – but he drives on.

Freeze-frames isolate each of these three moments of departure. Peckinpah uses the device once more when Junior, having used his prize money to buy Ace a one-way ticket to Australia ('deliver it to him in the Palace Bar'), pauses on his way out as the clerk asks him who she should say paid for it: 'Tell him Junior sent it,' he says. The freeze-frame not only emphasizes the sense of leave-taking in the foregoing scenes, but catches him, for the first time, playing a pro-active role in the lives of his family.

The last we see of him, he's driving away, alone, to wherever the next rodeo may be. Once again, the film invites comparison with *The Ballad of Cable Hogue*: just because it ain't heavy, don't mean there ain't depth.

'THAT'S THE TROUBLE WITH THIS GODDAMN WORLD' : *The Getaway*

At the risk of spoiling the ending, *The Getaway* concludes with its protagonists crossing safely into Mexico and driving off into a metaphorical sunset. This is the doing of Walter Hill, who adapted Jim Thompson's hard-boiled novel. His remoulding of Thompson's shadowy world into something slick and mainstream (another vehicle for McQueen in the style of *Bullitt*), meant the ending had to be changed – not least to cater for the involvement of Ali MacGraw, then McQueen's significant other. As Kim Newman has observed, 'the romantic teaming is so potent that Hill has to omit the novel's cynical last chapter, in which the characters are trapped in a Mexican hell-hole that swallows their personalities, though *Alfredo Garcia* might be seen as a feature length elaboration of the Thompson sketch' [6].

For the first and only time in his career, Peckinpah undertook to direct a formulaic action film in good heart, reminding his cast and crew that while they weren't creating a

TG.28.

work of art, they would still deliver a professional finished product. A few years later, reduced to helming perfunctory fare, Peckinpah's response was to draw attention to the banality of the material he was given to work with, a tendency most notable on *Convoy* where 'Peckinpah threw the script aside and encouraged his actors … to rewrite and even ad-lib their dialogue … Simple straightforward scenes in the script turned into amorphous, convoluted, and often incomprehensible improvizations on the set' [7]. He pulled the same stunt on *The Killer Elite*: again to quote Weddle, 'Sam had his actors ad-lib sophomoric asides that undercut the drama and encourage the audience to jeer at the movie they'd paid good money to see' [8]. This negativity, though pointed (emotionless words, emotionless images), ultimately weakened these films even further, and were self-destructive in the effect they had on Peckinpah's standing with the studios.

The Getaway stands taller than Peckinpah's other thrillers simply because he approached it with professionalism and not depressed resignation. Also, unlike the comic book shenanigans of *Convoy* and the convolutions of *The Killer Elite* and the Ludlum adaptation, Hill's *Getaway* script retains enough in the way of characterization, and enough of Thompson's edgy narrative, to give Peckinpah something definite to get his teeth into.

Steve McQueen and Ali MacGraw in The Getaway: *their offscreeen relationship was just as dramatic.*

His relish is most evident at the outset. In an eight-minute montage, Peckinpah uses harsh sounds and drab visuals to create an impressionistic portrait of prison life. Doc (Steve McQueen) attends a parole board hearing and learns his request has been denied. The officials' voices are underscored by the clatter of the industrial machinery which the inmates operate, working at textile production while they serve their time. The noise gets louder as Doc returns to work. Peckinpah freezes on Doc's machine running at full-tilt as he slams home the lever that regulates the speed. The image is frozen but the noise chatters on. Just as grating are the guards' voices as Doc participates on a work gang, clearing land and burning stubble. The continual haranguing resounds in his head like a mantra, intruding as Doc plays chess with an old-timer; he scatters the pieces angrily when he realizes he has lost. He showers communally, lathering himself quickly, not looking at the naked male bodies around him. He tries to push from his mind memories of love-making with his wife. Alone in his cell, he builds a model bridge out of matchsticks. The off-white of his cell walls is depressing. Two photographs of Carol (Ali MacGraw) remind him of what he's being denied. The repetition – the endlessness of it – presses in on him. He crushes the model, then cradles his head in despair. The editing gathers speed as Doc caves in under the pressure. The sequence of images reinforces a sense of circularity, of routines and regulation.

The minutiae of Doc's incarceration is absent from Thompson's novel, one of many significant differences. Only the basic structure remains: a corrupt prison official, Benyon [9] (Ben Johnson), arranges a parole for career criminal Doc McCoy; Doc pulls a robbery, part of the proceeds of which goes towards paying Benyon off. Doc's back-up, Rudy Butler (Al Lettieri), tries to pull a double-cross, but Doc is wise to him and shoots first. Leaving him for dead, Doc rendezvous with his wife Carol and together they go to Benyon's ranch to deliver the moolah. Benyon taunts Doc by implying that he organized his release not for the money but sexual favours from Carol. In order to silence him, Carol shoots him.

Meanwhile Rudy, injured but still alive thanks to a bullet-proof vest, swears vengeance. Needing medical attention, but unable to risk doctors or hospitals, he finds an out-of-the-way rural vetinerary practice and forces the vet, Harold Clinton, to patch him up, then to drive him in pursuit of Doc. Harold's wife, Fran (Sally Struthers), shows an even greater degree of complicity, tending to Rudy's libido as well as his wounds. The cuckolded Harold commits suicide.

Doc and Carol aim to cross the border into Mexico, but their progress is hampered when a con artist at a railway station manages to divest Carol of the bag containing their ill-gotten lucre. Doc's pursuit of the man and retrieval of the money alerts the authorities to their whereabouts and they are forced to go to even greater lengths to evade capture. This is where book and film part company.

Thompson describes in claustrophobic detail two days spent underground in a coffin-like cavern, an ordeal that drives Carol to the edge of a nervous breakdown. An equally lengthy spell in a hideout disguised as a dung heap on the farm of a family sympathetic to fugitives adds to their discomfort. When they eventually make it across the border, it is not freedom that awaits them but another sort of prison. They hole up in a colony of wanted criminals lorded over by the sinister El Rey (and Kim Newman is spot on – this guy is *Alfredo Garcia*'s El Jefe, Version One) where the remaining loot is bled away in payments to their host/jailer, death from any of their cohabitees is a constant threat, and a hideous form of slavery in the next village awaits once they run out of cash. Before you can say 'poetic justice', they are planning how best to rid themselves of each other.

It's a bleak, distorted view of human relationships. *Not* the stuff of which blockbusters are ordinarily made. Hence Hill's revisions. He omits the last quarter of the novel, amalgamates the claustrophobic elements of the cavern and the physical discomfort of the dung heap into a scene which has Doc and Carol hide in a dumpster only for it to be upended into a garbage truck, ups the ante on Doc's pursuers by giving Benyon a brother and a bunch of henchmen, all of whom grab automatic weapons and give chase, and

stages the climax at the Loughlin Hotel, a run-down establishment near the border, at which all parties converge and gunplay ensues. Also, the relationship between Doc and Carol is inverted. In the book, Carol's prostitution of herself to Benyon is implicit, stated nowhere other than by Benyon himself; she denies it to Doc after shooting her accuser and he gives every indication of believing her. The disintegration of their marriage occurs at the end and is brought about by financial hardship, not infidelity. For the most part, they hightail it across country, making eyes and whispering sweet nothings even as they blow anyone in their way to hell, coming across more like the couple in *Natural Born Killers* than McQueen and MacGraw's beleaguered bank-robbers.

In the film, Carol's infidelity is taken as fact. Doc slaps his wife around when he finds out, an act as thankless as it is brutal. 'You sent me to him,' she retorts. Later, she puts it to him rhetorically ('You'd do the same for me, wouldn't you Doc, if I got caught?') and he's even less able to confront himself. Tension exists between them even before the Benyon/Carol dalliance comes to light. Together on Doc's first night of freedom, they sit on the edge their bed, naked to the waist, backs to the camera. Their faces, their reactions to each other, are visible in a mirror. The reflection makes them look close, in actuality they are sitting noticeably apart. Doc can barely bring himself to touch his wife. He puts his head in his hands and tries to explain the psychological block he is under. 'It does something to you,' he says – and the words could be Deke Thornton's in explanation of his betrayal of Pike. 'It does something to you.'

Prison has eaten away at Doc. It has killed something inside him. McQueen's restrained characterization is excellent. There are instances where he struggles to be human, to connect, but always there is the icy soul of a hardened criminal dictating his behaviour. It is Doc's sense of distrust that makes him the faster draw, getting the drop on Rudy even though Rudy was waiting for him, pistol at the ready. And it is only Rudy's

Doc's thankless and brutal treatment of his wife in The Getaway.

earlier assertion that he has never had any use for a bulletproof vest that prevents Doc from shooting him in the face to make sure. A parallel is drawn when Doc removes his own bulletproof vest after dealing with Rudy. Regaining consciousness after Doc and Carol's departure, Rudy performs the same act. Rudy has already shot Frank Jackson, his partner, with just as little compunction. Doc's shooting of him simply reverses the roles. Doc and Rudy are both men for whom the double-cross is either a fringe benefit or an occupational hazard, depending which end of the gun they're on.

There are other parallels. Both men involve third parties in their schemes. Doc has already dragged Carol into a spiral of robbery and murder, instigating the whole chain of events from a prison visiting area when he implores her to approach Benyon. He is therefore indirectly responsible for her transition from accessory to the fact to murderer when Carol shoots Benyon at his ranch and later one of Benyon's hired guns at the Loughlin Hotel. Rudy plays a much more direct role in the fates of Harold and Fran Clinton. When Fran responds to Rudy flirtatiously, initially to safeguard against him 'stopping her clock', he exploits the situation in order to score points against Harold. Fran finds Rudy's dangerous lifestyle an increasing turn on; Rudy's leering domination of her leads to Harold's suicide. Finding him hanging from a light fitting in a motel bathroom, Rudy callously elbows in next to him and uses the john.

In the build-up to the gun battle at the Loughlin Hotel, Peckinpah again tars Doc and Rudy with the same brush. In the corridor outside Doc and Carol's room, Rudy silently mouths instructions to Fran to play the part of room service. Inside, suspecting that he's walked into a trap, Doc handles things in exactly the same way, wordlessly encouraging Carol to stall for time. The wall between them could be a mirror: two lawless men reduced to hiding behind their women as they desperately try to work out their next move.

There are differences between Doc and Rudy, of course, but these are matters of personality (Doc's shrewdness/Rudy's bullishness; Doc's pensive silences/Rudy's verbosity and bouts of temper) and outlook on life (Doc plans things, is pro-active – Rudy is re-active; Doc has a marriage, a commitment – Rudy uses, abuses and discards). In their *modus operandi* and capacity for violence, however, they are similar.

The difference between Carol and Fran is more palpable. Aside from one being a mature intelligent woman and the other a naive child trapped in the body of a sweater girl, the distinction is that Carol demonstrates an emotional reaction to the violence she encounters and the part she has played in it, while Fran clearly has no concept of accountability. During the final shootout, she behaves like a child, screaming for Rudy (one of Benyon's men dismisses her as a 'dumb broad'; Doc takes the more direct approach and punches her lights out) and eventually running away. It is her shrill, unappealing self-pity as much as her complicity in Rudy's depravity that makes Harold seem all the more a victim of circumstances: not only in the wrong place at the wrong time and practising the wrong profession (he'd have been no use to Rudy as a carpenter, say, or a car mechanic), but doomed – even before the gun-toting thug pulled into his driveway – for being married to the wrong woman.

This cynicism about relationships is, if anything, darker in Thompson's novel, particularly Fran's attraction to Rudy. In the film, her behaviour suggests complicity taken to the nth degree; in the book she's no more than a tart who takes the beatings Rudy dishes out with a passivity that borders on adoration. The tag 'misogynist' is often hung on Peckinpah. Those who incline to this line of thought would do well to check out Thompson's view of women.

With the real nastiness of the novel smothered for the screenplay, Peckinpah uses the material to comment on his favourite theme: men out of time – the onset (or onslaught) of modernity. In this respect, *The Getaway* is definitely a western brought into the second half of the twentieth century. The iconography spells it out for even the most subtextually-challenged viewer: Benyon's men, the con artist at the station, and the old-timer who helps Doc and Carol to cross the border all wear cowboy hats; Benyon's office is decorated with bull horns [10]; the guards supervising the prison work gang ride horses. When Benyon's men pile into a convertible and go roaring off to the Loughlin Hotel, clutching their hats against the wind (obviously none of them has thought of removing their headgear or raising the soft-top), it's as close as Peckinpah can come to having a group of bandidos saddle up.

Doc and Carol's flight to Mexico is the classic journey of innumerable desperados, posses, gunslingers and gringos in an equally countless number of westerns. But here the protagonists are challenged by more than any cowboy ever had to contend with. The first influxes of technology which send shockwaves through the lives of Judd and Westrum, Pike and his Bunch, and Cable Hogue, are now omnipresent. In prison, Doc cracks up to a soundtrack of machinery. Rows of cell doors close and lock as one at the touch of a button. Even as he leaves, a bank of security monitors mounted high on a wall behind him seem to leer over his shoulder, giving promise of what he'll soon be up against. Doc's release is signified by two seamlessly juxtaposed shots: one an extreme close-up of an electronically-activated bolt shooting back to open the prison's main gate; the other a long shot of the prison itself, Doc a tiny figure walking out. Technology is at the heart of everything, Peckinpah is saying, and it imprisons us.

Either that or it fails us. Or betrays us. Driving across country, Doc fiddles with the car radio, trying to get the news. He needs to know if Benyon's death has been discovered and if so, have they been linked to it? The radio malfunctions. 'Can't trust anything,' Doc grunts, earning a withering rebuke from Carol. Later, Doc's words are proved right when he stops at an electrical goods store to buy a portable radio. As the clerk rings up his change, a broadcast from a display model announces an update on the police hunt for the McCoys. Doc reaches over and snaps it off, but the clerk has already been alerted. Doc has been betrayed by the very thing he was relying on to stay one step ahead. As he hurries out of the shop, a row of televisions, their sound turned down, display his mug shot.

The greatest threat posed by machinery comes in the shape of a garbage truck. Fleeing on foot, the police close behind them, Doc and Carol head down an alleyway. They have few options left. In the end, it comes down to hiding and hoping the police officers overlook them. So they take the repulsive step of climbing into a dumpster and pulling handfuls of trash over themselves. Their pursuers close in. Then – and one can imagine his cynical belly-laugh – Peckinpah steps in with a device that turns all notions of a *deus ex machina* on its head. The truck's grab-arm takes their hiding place in its hold, tips it over the cab and empties them into the none-too-cosy confines of the compacting area. (Garbage trucks operate by hydraulically compacting each successive load of waste into a solid mass, thereby allowing room for the next load.) Peckinpah stages this claustrophobic set-piece with a panache worthy of Hitchcock, cranking up the tension by cutting between the hydraulic ram extending ever further, Doc and Carol scrambling into the murkiest recesses of the truck to avoid being crushed to death, and the driver operating levers in the cab. The red PTO (power turn off) button is kept in shot, within the driver's reach, but by God does he take a long time in reaching for it!

When the truck deposits them in a dumping ground (the wide open space of the freedom they seek replaced by a wasteland strewn with trash), they are still alive, but streaked with grime, cut and bruised, and itching from lice. While they wait for the truck to depart, they huddle in the shell of a burned out car. As a visual summary of the amount of cars that have been written off during the course of the film (crashed, blown up, abandoned, or peppered with shotgun fire) it's a nice touch. It also provides a pointer towards the ending.

Following the climactic bout of gunplay at Loughlin's establishment, Doc and Carol commandeer an old pick-up truck driven by an equally old guy (Slim Pickens), affectionately referred to in the credits as 'Cowboy'. He doesn't just co-operate – he enthuses. 'Been in trouble with the law mahself,' he drawls as he bounces over the curb,

Overleaf: Gunplay at the Loughlin Hotel in The Getaway.

cutting into traffic. All manner of junk clatters off the back as he hauls on the steering wheel. The scene is delightful as much for Pickens's good-ole-boy performance as for the seal it sets on the narrative. Fast cars and express trains having proved ineffectual, the final – successful – stage of the getaway is undertaken in a ramshackle old pick-up, all rust and bald tyres. It is also the only time that Doc and Carol receive any assistance.

The casting of Slim Pickens serves a dual function. Firstly, he is an older man, and can address Doc with the voice of experience, his advice tempered by gee-whizz avuncularity. Throughout, Doc and Carol contend with people who are either younger than them (the guitar-strumming hippies who clutter the park Doc strolls through on his first day out of prison, the sullen and immature Jackson, the con-artist, the annoying little kid on the train who squirts Doc with a water-pistol and later identifies him to the police, the barely-out-of-her-teens carhop who recognizes Doc and Carol at a drive-in and calls the cops) or of a similar age group (Rudy, Benyon, Benyon's brother, and the assorted gunmen). Cowboy is the only father figure in the film, and a link to the old times that have passed Doc by.

Secondly, as an actor (and particularly as an actor in a ten-gallon hat), Slim Pickens personifies the western. He had already carried over the iconography of the genre into Kubrick's chilling black comedy *Dr Strangelove*, and would go on to prove himself as adept at mourning its passing (in Peckinpah's next feature *Pat Garrett and Billy the Kid*) as he was at satirising its conventions (in Mel Brooks's *Blazing Saddles*). His laconic, self-deprecating characterizations are not dissimilar to Edmond O'Brien's turn as Sykes in *The Wild Bunch*. To stretch a point somewhat, O'Brien in the earlier film and Pickens in *The Getaway* essay the same sort of character: a wise fool, behind whose nickel-and-dime philosophizing lies a small nugget of truth.

The Sykes/Cowboy comparison gains credence in the light of other throwbacks to *The Wild Bunch*. The proliferation of hats speaks for itself, as does the basic story of outlaws fleeing to Mexico after a robbery. More specific are the appearances of *Wild Bunch* stalwarts Ben Johnson and Bo Hopkins. As Tector Gorch, Johnson shares a memorable speech with Warren Oates, the belligerent brothers sounding off about running whores in Hondo – 'in tandem!' – their object a cheap laugh at Pike's expense. In *The Getaway*, Benyon baits Doc with details of his liaison with Carol. Johnson brings the same licentiousness to the character, but the aim here is provocation, not amusement; the means is crueller, closer to the bone.

Hopkins's performance as Jackson provides the most explicit connection to *The Wild Bunch*. Preparatory to the heist, he is full of swagger: introduced to Doc, he acts all *blasé*; while Doc and Carol run through the plan, he dons his balaclava and strikes a macho pose instead of paying attention. During the robbery, however, he flips, shooting a guard then stupidly pulling his mask off in front of witnesses. Everything he does is of the moment, with no thought given to consequences. It hardly needs spelling out: Frank Jackson is 'Crazy' Lee dusted off and given a 1970s haircut. And his exit from the film is as much reprise as demise. Shot by Rudy to facilitate an easier getaway on his part, Jackson makes the transition from aggressor to victim as bloodily as 'Crazy' Lee did, a deliquent sacrificed so that older men – professionals – can get on with the business at hand.

An alternative take on this scene comes near the end of the film, just before Doc and Carol enlist Cowboy's services to get across the border. They leave the Loughlin Hotel, corpses littering the corridors and lobby, Rudy finally despatched, his body slumped on the fire escape. But one of Benyon's mob is still alive: a youth, fresh-faced and nervous. We are never told his name or offered any backstory – it's far too late in the proceedings for such things to be introduced – but there is a sense that he is just starting out, that this is his first big deal since entering Benyon's employ. That within a few years he could end up like Frank Jackson or the con-artist ... or end up dead. And damned if he doesn't come real close.

He tumbles out of a side door, gun in hand, straight into the path of Doc and Carol. Doc has just laid waste to all of his comrades, without hesitation, his every shot finding its target. He is now all that remains between the McCoys and the Mexican border. There is no reason for Doc not to shoot him. And besides, this is a Peckinpah film, right? Somebody read that kid the last rites.

But Doc McCoy, like so many other Peckinpah protagonists, resorts to unflinching violence only because he has been left with no other choice. When he gets the drop on Rudy in the hotel corridor, he knocks him unconscious with the butt of his gun. He then cocks the weapon, bends over Rudy and aims at his head. But he doesn't shoot. Never mind that he thought he'd taken Rudy out of the equation the first time around, that Rudy had demonstrated the strength of his obsession for revenge by travelling the length of the country after him; never mind that he now has an unrivalled opportunity to rid himself of someone who, if allowed to live, will just keep coming back till one of them is dead – *he doesn't shoot*. Likewise, on the train, he is content to immobilize the con-artist with a couple of elbows to the face when, with one good chop to the windpipe, he'd be one less witness (after all, it's the conman's plea to the water-pistol-toting kid to summon the conductor that leads to the youngster's identification of Doc from police mug-shots).

So now, with one gunman left, a nervous youngster blundering in front of him, barely able to hold his pistol steady, Doc assesses the situation and chooses not to add another body to those whose blood has redecorated the walls of the Loughlin Hotel. 'Don't do it,' he tells the youth, his own gun raised and held rock steady. 'Don't! Just run away. Now. Run away!' Sensibly, the youth obeys.

It is at this point that Doc and Carol hitch their ride with Cowboy. The two sides of Doc – the violent and the non-violent – are held in equilibrium. One hurdle is left: the border crossing. Cowboy, while never being anything less than deferential, opts to find out where he stands.

> Cowboy: Don't reckon you're goin' to shoot me, are you?
> Doc: I kinda doubt it.
> Cowboy: That's fine. I'll co-operate ... Can I ask you a personal question?
> Carol: Sure.
> Cowboy: Are you kids married?
> Carol: Yeah.
> Cowboy: Hey, I'm glad. That's the trouble with this goddamn world: ain't no morals.

The crossing into Mexico made without hitch, he continues his discourse: 'If I was you kids, you know what I'd do? I'd quit this runnin' around the country. You know, get a little bit of money together and buy a place, settle down and raise a family. I've been married for thirty-five years. Same old gal ... Everything I am I owe to her.' The looks that pass between Doc and Carol indicate that, now the Benyon business is behind them, they might just give him a run for his money.

Doc requests that Cowboy pull over and 'step out a spell'. There is a comparative scene in the novel where Doc hijacks a car and sweet-talks its driver into believing he won't kill him if he co-operates – then kills him anyway. Thankfully, there is nothing so gratuitous here [11].

Doc asks Cowboy how much money he made last year. 'Oh, I reckon about five thousand.' Doc offers him double that for the pick-up. Cowboy fills in the blanks himself: 'And I keep my mouth shut, and I don't say nothin' about the truck, and I never seen either of the two of you.' Doc nods. Cowboy thinks it over: 'How about twenty thousand?' Carol, watching from the cab, magnanimously offers thirty. 'Goddamn, ma'am,' Cowboy chuckles, 'you got yourself a deal.' There are handshakes all round, then Cowboy starts back for the border on foot.

So, an avuncular old-timer as the instrument of their salvation, reminding them of what they stand to lose emotionally even though they have secured their freedom, a romantic reconciliation, and an open road stretching out before them. You can dismiss the ending as cornball, or take it with the pinch of salt that Peckinpah intended (Slim Pickens must surely have been cast for his ability to walk the tightrope between pathos and send-up); either way, after the cynicism that has gone before, the feel-good factor is indisputable.

'NOBODY LOSES ALL THE TIME': *Bring Me the Head of Alfredo Garcia*

After *The Getaway*, Peckinpah stopped renewing his visa to the Mainstream Moviegoer's Republic Of Happy Endings. The film he made two years later shares some of the geographical and thematic concerns of *The Getaway* – a couple locked into a less-than-legitimate enterprise; a journey fraught with danger; Mexico as a haven for criminality – but is so far removed from Steve and Ali's box office clean-up that it's amazing it was made by the same man, let alone within such a short space of time.

It is a common misconception that *Bring Me the Head of Alfredo Garcia* is about a man who breaks one of the big taboos – grave-robbery – because of the lure of a million dollar bounty on the head of a man who is already dead. Actually, it's not till late in the film that he learns the true worth of the head, by which time he's sealed the fate of an innocent and damned his own soul. All for a few thousand.

When the real bounty is made known to him, he no longer has use for money. He has within his grasp a sum that still stands, twenty-five years after the film was made, as the ultimate measure of success, unattainable to the majority of us but dreamed of every time we buy a lottery ticket or watch a game show. But in acquiring it, he has lost everything.

Not that he had anything worth a damn to begin with.

Like a waking nightmare that has somehow been peppered with moments of inspired black comedy, this is how *Alfredo Garcia* unfolds:

Mexican crimelord El Jefe (Emilio Fernandez) has his daughter tortured until she reveals the identity of the man who has made her pregnant. No prizes for guessing his name. El Jefe calls for … his head.

A contingent of El Jefe's thugs, including the effeminate Sappensley and Quill (Robert Webber and Gig Young), scour Mexico looking for him. Every hombre to whom they show his picture responds with a shrug or a shake of the head. They get their first break from another American, a down-at-a-heel pianist named Bennie (Warren Oates) who just about scrapes a living banging out 'Guantanamera' for the tourists who frequent his seedy bar. Initially, they purport to being old friends of Alfredo's, but all pretence is soon abandoned. Bennie, sensing a quick buck is in the offing, promises to ask around. One of his regulars tells him that Alfredo was last seen consorting with Elita (Isela Vega), a lounge singer, hooker and occasional girlfriend of Bennie's who has recently been avoiding him.

When he confronts her, she admits that her excuses not to see him lately were just that – excuses. She had actually been saying goodbye to Alfredo. (Evidently, they parted on very good terms.) She goes on to tell Bennie that shortly afterwards Alfredo died in a car accident. When Bennie takes his leave of her to report to El Jefe's men, he is in a pensive mood. Not wanting to tell them that their quarry is dead (information that will doubtlessly devalue itself), he suggests that he undertake to track Alfredo down. They agree, stipulating that the head be brought back as proof of his demise. Bennie is given four days – after which they will come looking for him. So far, the pecuniary arrangement is merely for a couple of thousand dollars.

Bennie avails himself of a machete, gets Elita to tell him where her former squeeze is buried, and the two of them set off. They are oblivious to the fact that two bounty hunters, who more fully realize the value of Alfredo's head, are shadowing them. Bennie, keen to avoid telling Elita of his ulterior motive in visiting the grave, treats their trip as something of a macabre picnic. As they sit under a tree by the roadside, Bennie playing his guitar as they talk, Elita forces him to confront the pretences and fragilities of their relationship. The discussion ends with Bennie asking Elita to marry him.

Any notion of romantic fulfilment is scotched a few miles down the road when a blowout forces them to stop. They opt to spend the evening beneath the stars. Bad move. A couple of passing bikers exploit the situation: one holds Bennie at gunpoint while the other leads Elita off forcibly. Only by the time Bennie has got the better of his captor and hurried to Elita's aid, he finds her in a clinch with the second biker that doesn't look so forcible.

Bennie shows no hesitation in shooting both of the bikers, and when he and Elita get back on the road, there is a definite friction between them. Matters aren't helped when he tells her of his plans for Alfredo. She is horrified, but guilt compels her to go along with his scheme. They conclude their journey. Still the bounty hunters dog their tracks.

Arriving at the cemetery, Bennie finds members of Alfredo's family keeping vigil by the grave. He waits till they have left and returns under the cover of darkness to do the deed. Elita participates but exhibits a mounting sense of terror. She is right to. The bounty hunters ambush them. A shovel to the head lays Bennie out.

When he regains conciousness, Bennie finds himself lying in the now completely excavated grave, next to the headless corpse of Alfredo Garcia and the lifeless body of Elita. To put it mildly, he flips. After a demented monologue in which he alternately mourns Elita and curses her, he stumbles back to his car and sets off in search of (a) the bounty hunters, (b) the head, and (c) a hefty slice of revenge.

He soon finds his aggressors. They are pulled over with a flat tyre. One of them even begins to flag him down before recognizing the car. He kills them, retrieves the head, and goes on his way. Meanwhile, Alfredo's relatives discover the desecration at the cemetery, arm themselves to the teeth and follow his trail, also with vengeance uppermost in their minds. They catch up with Bennie as quickly as he caught up with the bounty hunters, and force him off the road.

Warren Oates as the down-at-heel Bennie in Bring Me the Head of Alfredo Garcia.

While Bennie rants that they may as well kill him there and then because he has every intention of delivering the head, Quill and Sappensley (who have come looking for him now the four days are up) happen upon them. Posing as tourists, they conduct an oblique conversation with Bennie, ascertaining that he has the head. Then the shooting starts. The Garcia clan are massacred, but not before they fatally wound Quill. Bennie finishes the job and shoots Sappensley.

Driving back to the hotel where the rest of El Jefe's mob are billeted, Bennie's behaviour grows even more volatile. He conducts embittered conversations with the head *en route*. At the hotel, he demands to know why the head is so valuable, how much it's really worth and to whom. He uses the tried and trusted shoot-first-ask-questions-later technique. When he leaves, the room is shag-pile deep in bodies and he has the name he wants.

Arriving at El Jefe's heavily guarded hacienda, he is searched and escorted at gunpoint to meet the man himself. The guards are complacent, however, and pay little attention to the burlap sack except to note that there's a disembodied head inside it. Bennie has packed it in ice to preserve it for the last stage of the journey. Beneath the head and the chunks of ice is hidden his gun.

El Jefe is happily celebrating the christening of his new grandchild and is in a magnanimous mood as he leads Bennie into his study. His daughter, gaunt and pale, watches in horror as Bennie places the sack on his desk. Bennie can barely keep his voice steady as he tells El Jefe that sixteen men have died since he posted the bounty. The Mexican shows no emotion, simply passes Bennie a suitcase stuffed with cash – one million dollars. Bennie opens the sack and takes out his gun. He ventilates the bodyguards, then turns on El Jefe. 'Kill him,' his daughter advocates. Bennie obliges.

Retrieving the head and the suitcase, he takes off at speed, ramming the gate at the perimeter of El Jefe's property. Mounted riders pursue him. A burst of machine gun fire from the guard-hut rakes his car and he swerves into a ditch. Gunmen converge on him, firing point blank.

If *The Getaway* has parallels with *The Wild Bunch*, then it is an earlier and much less satisfactory western that is revisited here. Odyssey-with-corpse was the basic premise of *The Deadly Companions*, but FitzSimons's interference meant that Peckinpah was lumbered with a phoney love story and a hat-ful of genre clichés. Here, Peckinpah has fun with his material, sending up the contrivances of the plot as outrageously as he might have done on *The Deadly Companions* had it not been for the producer's draconian presence on set.

Excuse me? *Fun*? In a film about grave-robbery and decapitation, where the only sympathetic character gets assaulted by rapists then killed by bounty hunters, a film that winds up knee-deep in bodies?

Well, yes. Whereas the narrative development in most of Peckinpah's films is determined by his characters' motivation, *Alfredo Garcia* hinges on coincidence and occurrences that are so arbitrary as to be absurd. Like *The Deadly Companions*, the script calls for things to happen in order to advance the plot. In order that Bennie and Elita are alone in the wilds when the two bikers pass by, it's a blown-out tyre that (in)conveniently strands them miles from a motel as twilight sets in. Later, in order that Bennie can catch up with Elita's killers, it's a blown-out tyre that (in)conveniently strands them by the side of the road.

Bennie's standoff with the Garcia bunch is likewise lampooned. On the surface, it's standard Hollywood melodrama: the lone hero, outnumbered, outgunned, out-every-thinged. Tension is cranked to the max. Then suddenly, just at the proverbial last moment, a new element enters the scene and the odds are tipped in our hero's favour. Here, it's Quill and Sappensley who provide the *deus ex machina*. Their arrival is totally outrageous – they spent the early stages of the film combing Mexico for Alfredo without getting a single lead, yet now they appear out of nowhere and stumble upon the entire Garcia family. Peckinpah acknowledges the contrivance by preceding it with an inspired comedic vignette: at the most tense moment in the stand-off – two cars sideways on across the road, every rifle cocked and levelled at Bennie, and things looking very bad indeed – along comes a bus. The Garcia family lower their guns, helpfully move their car out of the way and politely doff their hats as they wave the Greyhound past. As with so many of the weird little touches in the film, it's the incongruity that makes it funny.

In other places, though, dark humour subsides to just darkness. Unlike *The Deadly Companions*, the tribulations of long-haul corpse-bearing are demonstrated in detail – the omnipresence of flies, the acquisition of ice, the improper use of motel room showers for overnight storage – and not detracted from by a romantic subplot. Since Bennie doesn't have anyone to fall in love with *en route* (his romantic idyll has been destroyed by his greed as surely as Cable Hogue's is by his desire for revenge) it is left to the decapitated Alfredo to provide the only semblance of companionship he has during the final stages of his grim journey; indeed, for the rest of his soon-to-be-foreshortened life. In this sense, Alfredo is the deadliest companion, unable to exert any influence over Bennie, talk sense into him or make him turn back. Wrapped in a burlap bag, flies buzzing around, Alfredo's head becomes a symbol of Bennie's humanity: something wasted and degraded.

Alfredo's misfortune is to impregnate a crime lord's daughter, resulting in a price tag being attached to his head, then a dismayingly arbitrary accident costs him his life even as bounty hunters comb Mexico for him – and to top it all, his eternal rest is disturbed and his body mutilated. Like Bennie, Alfredo is a man whose losing streak is hopelessly irreversible and ultimately terminal.

How big a loser is Bennie? When we first meet him, he has only two things: a lousy job, and an on-off relationship with a fellow loser (Elita is as talentless a lounge singer as Bennie is a pianist) that's more off than on. The job is so bad that Bennie is given to reminiscing fondly about working in Tijuana – *Tijuana*, for God's sake! He's at a stage in his life where he'll do anything as long as it'll net him enough ready cash to move on. (Although it begs the question – to paraphrase Dutch – move on to what?)

Like anyone who struggles to make ends meet, Bennie thinks of money – or, more immediately, the acquisition thereof – as a sort of holy grail. From Quill and Sappensley's arrival at Bennie's bar, *Alfredo Garcia* establishes itself as a study in greed. When Quill tips him generously (more generously than his heavy-handed tinkling of the ivories deserves), Bennie's immediate response is 'Take me to your leader'. Inviting Bennie to drop by their hotel when he has more information on Alfredo's whereabouts, Quill gives him a gambling chip (a proof of identity which will gain him admission) – the metaphor is all too apparent. The scene pays off with an in-joke that tells us everything we need to know about the characters' amorality and the value they place on cold hard cash: when Bennie asks Quill's name, he gives the alias Fred C Dobbs. This is the name of the ruthless, paranoid prospector played by Humphrey Bogart in John Huston's *Treasure of the Sierra Madre*, whose mercenary behaviour is a case study in avarice [12].

Through greed, Bennie begins to lose his humanity. From the outset, Quill and Sappensley are up front about their reasons for finding Alfredo:

> Bennie: If he's alive, I'll find him.
> Sappensley: Alive is not a problem.
> Bennie: Well, how about dead or alive?
> Quill: Dead. Just dead.

Knowing this, Bennie sells his soul when he keeps his appointment at the hotel. Fitting, then, that another one of the deadly sins – pride – spurs him on to make his deal with the devil – or rather with Max and Frank, El Jefe's paymasters.

> Max: You're interested in money, aren't you? Money you can spend.
> Bennie: Yes, sir. Indirectly. I mean, there are other things, like I'd like to stay alive.
> Frank: A loser.
> Bennie: Nobody loses all the time!

A vengeful shoot-out in
Bring Me the Head of
Alfredo Garcia.

Bennie's frustration at anyone else having the same opinion of him that he has of himself resurfaces when he returns to the hotel towards the end of the film. By this time, he has lost Elita, gained Alfredo's head and is wrathful. He goes in wanting a name – El Jefe's. Max and Frank are quick to mock, calling him 'bartender'. For a man who has nothing to be proud of, the sting of pride acts on Bennie like histamine. By the time he leaves, nobody is left alive.

For the moment, though, Bennie is happy to go along with them. He asks for five thousand in advance – 'operating cash'. Quill mockingly asks if he intends to kill Alfredo with kindness. Max, ever the dour businessman, tells Frank to give him two hundred. And God have mercy on his soul, Bennie takes it.

No less disturbing is the way he justifies himself to Elita: 'The church cuts off the feet, fingers, any other goddamn thing from the saints, don't they? Well, what the hell? Alfredo's a saint. He's the saint of our money.' Desecration of a grave is a big religious no-no whatever the circumstances. Doing it for money – and then using a religious metaphor as justification – puts Bennie beyond redemption. A grim omen which plays on the idea of religion profaned comes when Bennie and Elita arrive at the cemetery. A group of children walk slowly along, a small coffin carried on their shoulders. It is too small for another child, a favourite pet probably. Later, stopping at a cantina for ice to pack around Alfredo's head, a young boy notices the fetid, fly-swarmed burlap sack on the passenger seat and asks Bennie what's in it. 'Cat,' Bennie replies. 'Dead cat. Belonged to a friend of mine.'

This implication of affinity between Bennie and Alfredo is at the heart of the film. Although Bennie expresses to Elita his contempt for Alfredo (understandable since the two of them were slipping around behind Bennie's back), he reveals more of himself than perhaps he realizes when he says, 'Nobody's going to miss him ... Alfredo's been trying to beat this rap all his life. So have I. So have you.'

Alfredo doesn't beat the rap. Nor does Elita. But that doesn't stop Bennie from trying. And as Bennie stumbles from one vengeful shoot-out to the next, the silent companionship of Alfredo's head mocks his odyssey as pointless and inevitably doomed. Nonetheless, an ersatz relationship develops between them, albeit one based on greed and sexual jealousy. 'You've got jewels in your ears, diamonds up your nose,' he tells the head. 'You son of a bitch ... I'll be damned if she's not keeping the best part of you company.'

Which says it all, really. The key to the Bennie/Alfredo relationship is that Alfredo is dead. Bennie, too, can be seen as a dead man – or at least, one who's rushing headlong towards death. He retrieves the head after gunning two men down; thereafter, every stage of his journey is marked by gunfire. This new-found talent for killing without compunction strips away all but the last vestiges of Bennie's humanity. At one point, in a scene that seems like a direct challenge to Peckinpah's critics, Bennie pumps a superfluous bullet into a man who's already dead. 'Why?' he growls, asking the question for us. 'Because it feels so goddamn good.'

Excepting Elsa's line to Billy Hammond in *Ride the High Country* ('I brought my mother's wedding dress – that is, if you still want to'), *Alfredo Garcia* is the only Peckinpah film to contain an onscreen proposal of marriage. It comes at a point when Bennie has not yet travelled so far into his own heart of darkness that he cannot turn back. And yet he has already set out along the road to grave robbing, madness and murder. It would seem he has to travel a certain way down the wrong path in order to gain some perspective on his relationship with Elita. There is certainly precious little affection between them in earlier scenes: his first line to her is 'You're a lyin', cheatin', no-good, two-bit bitch'; later he awakens her after a night of rather perfunctory sex by snapping a towel at her.

Until she forces his hand over the marriage proposal, Bennie never treats Elita as anything less than a whore. And yet when a motel owner refuses them admittance because of her profession, Bennie's reaction borders on moral outrage. This sense of ambivalence about Elita – not just as a person, but about her role in the film – is at the heart of the film's most uncomfortable scene: the bit of business between Elita and the biker. On the surface, it seems almost deliberately ambivalent. Rape? Seduction? As the biker leads Elita off, Bennie swears that he'll make him pay with his life. Elita tries to placate him, saying 'I've been here before – you don't know the way.' Bearing in mind an earlier scene when Sappensley elbows a hooker in the face and no one does a thing about it, this could be taken as implication either of a lawlessness in Mexico that the indigenous population take for granted, or resignation on Elita's part that all men are ultimately abusive. It is also worth considering that, since sexual congress with unappealing men is an occupational hazard for Elita, her conduct during the almost-rape is indicative of someone who is once again playing her part, trying to get the whole unpleasant business over and done with as quickly as possible.

On a thematic level, the scene is metaphorical, not literal: although the victim is Elita, what we are witnessing is the first part of Bennie's punishment. Like Raskolnikov in Dostoyevsky's *Crime and Punishment*, stricken with guilt even before he commits his crime, Bennie finds there is a price to be paid just for entertaining the notion of wrongdoing, let alone carrying it out. In Elita being taken away from Bennie, in the abuses she suffers (the biker slapping her around) and in her almost consensual response, the implication is that Bennie stands to lose her if he persists in going through with his plan, either through outside forces or an act of rejection on her part. In the shape of two boorish unshaven louts, Fate has chosen to fire a warning shot across Bennie's bows.

He ignores it, and the full implications of the scene are borne out. He loses Elita permanently. And he alone is to blame.

Elita, tragically, comes closest to redemption – but not quite close enough. Her apparent complicity in the almost-rape is an externalization of her complicity in Bennie's scheme. Afterwards, when she expresses revulsion and outrage at Bennie's stated intentions towards Alfredo, she becomes the voice of his moral conscience, just as Dutch is Pike's in *The Wild Bunch*. Again, Bennie doesn't listen; worse, he turns against her, using her perceived complicity as a means of emotional/moral blackmail to ensure that she sees the enterprise through with him. As a result, she dies.

Peckinpah's detractors latch on to such material as proof of misogyny. But as with *Straw Dogs*, Peckinpah paints all the male characters with a brush dipped in guilt and hatred. Elita, like Amy Sumner, is complex and changeable. In both cases, their sufferings are less a result of their own choices or behaviour, than the distorted way that men perceive them. A director who can be honest about this – particularly at the expense of members of his own sex – is not a misogynist.

David Weddle gives a glum account of the filming of *Alfredo Garcia*: 'Shooting began in the fall of 1973 and the production proceeded smoothly, but a blanket of melancholy settled over the company. It wasn't like the old days. Something had happened to Sam; the flame in those hazel eyes had flickered out' [13].

What had happened was the soul-destroying battle with James Aubrey over *Pat Garrett and Billy the Kid* (see introduction). The experience left Peckinpah with a weariness about film-making. When Bennie confronts himself in a grimy motel room mirror, alone in the world except for Alfredo's head, he is every inch Peckinpah's alter ego: beaten-down, close to broken, wondering why he's still trying to beat the rap.

Weariness and doubt are part of the fabric of the film. And the final shot tells us that the critics have played as big a part as producers and executives. Saddled with a reputation he doesn't want, Peckinpah rounds on those who have persistently misread his work. *All right then,* he seems to be saying, *if this is all you'll give me credit for, then here it is* .... Freeze-frame, close-up: the barrel of a smoking gun, 'directed by Sam Peckinpah' stamped across it.

CHAPTER FOUR
PAT GARRETT AND BILLY THE KID

On the evening of 14 July 1881, Patrick Floyd Garrett shot and killed William H Bonney, aka Billy the Kid. The place was Fort Sumner, New Mexico. Bonney was an infamous gunfighter, believed to have dispatched twenty-seven men during his reprobate career. Garrett's bullet brought that career to an end – and made a folk hero of a felon.

In the autumn of 1972, Sam Peckinpah and his friend Jim Silke met at the MGM studios to discuss the script, by Rudy Wurlitzer, for his next project, *Pat Garrett and Billy the Kid*. Three years had passed since *The Wild Bunch* spelled out the death of the west (and, it seemed to some, the western). *The Ballad of Cable Hogue*, bloodlessly and using humour instead of bullets, had further mourned the passing, not just of a genre, but of a period of time and a way of life. Three non-westerns (which, as we have seen, still managed to preserve the aesthetic) had followed: *Straw Dogs, Junior Bonner* and *The Getaway*. Now Peckinpah was preparing to make the film that truly would be his valediction to the Old West.

Wurlitzer had already received high acclaim for writing *Two-Lane Blacktop*, and his *Pat Garrett* screenplay was hot property: classy, elegiac, beautifully written. It effortlessly placed its central characters – as well as a whole supporting cast of memorable eccentrics – into a well-researched and factually-based re-imagination of the Kid's final days. What concerned Peckinpah, though, was its inertia, its lack of an internal dynamic. The purpose of his meeting with Silke was to discuss how to approach the material. It was Silke who posed the sixty-four thousand dollar question: the real story or the legend? It is said that the director mulled it over in silence for nearly half an hour. 'The legend,' he said finally.

Of course, this being Sam Peckinpah, it didn't turn out to be as simple as that. With typical iconoclasm he managed to do both, and delivered [1] a film that was as unromantic as it was mythical. This dichotomy serves the narrative well – the structure is contrapuntal, with parallels being drawn continually between Garrett and the Kid.

In keeping with the best of Peckinpah's work, the credits sequence acts as a self-contained movie, establishing tone, structure, themes and imagery. It is the calling card of a virtuoso. Opening to the strummed chords of Bob Dylan's guitar, the establishing credit 'near Las Cruces, New Mexico, 1909' is overlaid in red across a long shot of a horse and cart riding across hilly land, a second rider, horse-mounted, by its side. This is filmed in washed out black-and-white. Pat Garrett (James Coburn) is slouched in the cart, old and grouchy. The man riding beside him is John Poe (John Beck). The man driving the cart is one of Poe's henchmen. If their relationship is unclear – it's not till halfway through the film that we are told who Poe is – their dispute is evident:

Garrett: Thought I told you not to run them sheep on my land.

Poe: It's my land, Garrett. It became mine when we signed that lease.

Poe's henchman: He's right, Mr Garrett.

Garrett: I'm paying you off when we get back. And I'm breakin' that goddamn lease.

Poe: I don't allow as the law'll agree to that.

Garrett: What law's that, the Santa Fe Ring law? *Shit!* Goddamn laws are ruinin' the country.

And if all this seems unduly vehement, the following gives us some indication that there's more involved here than a few sheep:

Poe: Ain't you still a part of that law? I believe they elected you and paid you good wages for killin' the Kid.

Garrett: You rotten son of a bitch!

In the meantime, Poe's henchman has dismounted on the pretext of checking the saddle; he reaches for his weapon. From nearby undergrowth, a man clutching a rifle crawls out into the open and draws a bead on Garrett. Two minutes into the film and already the promise of gunplay, the sense of expectation heightened as colour seeps into the frame. Then we cut, not just to a different scene, but another location and events twenty-eight years in the past. 'Old Fort Sumner, 1881' reads the credit, an overhead shot confirming the location. A group of young men lounge against a wall, watching as Billy the Kid (Kris Kristofferson) takes aim at a chicken. The unfortunate fowl is quite literally a sitting target, buried up to its neck in sand, one of a number lined up in a row. Billy cocks his pistol, a carefree grin on his face.

The subsequent series of shots intercut target practice and assassination, the soundtrack overlapping so that shots fired playfully by young guys precede Garrett's grim and unceremonious demise, while the careful aim of embittered old men acting with cold premeditation is rewarded with images of the chicken's head exploding. The indignity of death has seldom been writ larger anywhere in cinema: it's bad enough buying it after an argument about sheep, falling from a rickety old wagon and landing painfully in the dirt like a drunkard, but to share the screen with a headless chicken....

The pathos is upped by the overlapping, also, of dialogue. 'Damn near perfect,' one of Billy's hangers-on remarks, the words sounding as Garrett takes another bullet.

The effect cannot be replicated merely by describing it in words – it has to be seen for the full emotional power of Peckinpah's artistry to be appreciated, as well as his fearlessness. As with *The Wild Bunch*, the opening credits make effective use of freeze-frames. The film is called *Pat Garrett and Billy the Kid*; its star – his name above the title – is James Coburn. Coburn's name appears on screen over a freeze-frame of him falling from the wagon after the first round of shots; the title appears as he hits the ground in an undignified sprawl, struggling to get up then sinking back, dead. In terms of today's mainstream fare, this type of daring is almost unthinkable. And even allowing for the pronounced pessimism of cinema in the Vietnam era and the reputation that proceeded Peckinpah courtesy of the bloodbath finales of *The Wild Bunch* and *Straw Dogs*, it's still a hell of a gamble having your protagonist die at the start of the film ... and die unheroically, to boot.

But there's more to come. Ol' Sam hasn't even got to *his* credit yet.

The death throes of the old Garrett are immediately replaced by his younger (although alarmingly middle-aged) self riding into Fort Sumner. The Kid and his entourage don't notice his arrival, and he grins as he hefts his rifle and proves himself the faster shot, blowing away a chicken Billy is still taking aim at. The laughter and banter that follows (credits inserted to make the most of pauses in dialogue) has the effect of setting reunion in counterpoint to betrayal. We have been shown the inevitable – Garrett's death – in

Reunion and betrayal: Pat Garrett and Billy the Kid, sheriff and outlaw.

explicit terms. The reunion, commencing with Garrett in effect sneaking up on the Kid, does the same thing, implicitly. One will die, then the other – cause and effect, and never mind the twenty-eight years in between.

Oh, and we still haven't had *that* credit.

Garrett and the Kid repair to a bar. It's an appropriate venue, what with all the drinking that gets done in the movie – along with whoring and talking about the old days, it's what the characters seem to do the most. (The true genius of Wurlitzer's script is not just that he manages to attach huge amounts of back-story to each character, but that he makes their soliloquies so memorably poetic.) There is some more idle conversation, harking back to their previous exploits. Then, reluctantly, they confront the issue.

> Billy: We did have some times, didn't we? It's got to be pretty hard to turn your back on all that, ain't it?
> Garrett: Times are changin', Billy. You want it straight?
> Billy: If that's what you're here for.
> Garrett: The electorate want you gone. Out of the country.
> Billy: Well, are they tellin' me or are they askin' me?
> Garrett: I'm askin' you. But in five days I'm makin' you, when I take over as sheriff of the county.

It's during this last sentence that the final freeze-frame occurs and Peckinpah's credit appears. The line might not be as tersely quotable as 'If they move, kill 'em', but using the credit as an enforced pause between 'I'm makin' you' and 'when I take over as sheriff' gives it the proper weight. The rest of the exchange leaves us in no doubt that we are firmly in Peckinpah territory:

> Billy (raising his glass): Sheriff Pat Garrett! Sold out to the Santa Fe Ring. How does it feel?
> Garrett: It feels like times have changed.
> Billy: Times maybe, but not me.

Ten minutes into the film, and strong echoes of *The Wild Bunch*: freeze-frames and black-and-white (redolent of *The Wild Bunch*'s sepia tinged credits); changing times and men unable to change with them; political machinations and mercenary landowners in place of impending war and officers of the Imperial German Army. A sense of sadness about the characters. A tendency to cling to the past, to obsess about what used to be. It's all in place.

Let's start the ball.

It goes without saying that the Kid doesn't leave within the alloted five days. The very next scene sees him and some of his gang members holed up in a derelict bunkhouse, readying themselves for a bit of rustling. The earlier derogatory remarks about the Santa Fe Ring are thrown into perspective as a casual line of dialogue – 'Chisum's cattle's waitin' on us' – clarifies who 'the electorate' (they who want him gone) actually are.

Garrett, now wearing his badge of office, watches from a promontory as his men surround the place. He is aloof, only speaking to his subordinates to give them orders. We feel he would rather be holed up with the Kid, taking his chances against the hired and deputised gunslingers of Chisum [2] and his like. This is Deke Thornton revisited, his soul in hock to authority, dealing with men and wishing to God he was with 'em.

Garrett's brooding silence is mirrored by Billy when one of his gang, a bespectacled young lad whose chin is barely dusted with his first growth of stubble, insists 'I ain't afraid of Pat Garrett.' Billy and Tom O'Folliard (Wurlitzer) regard him with unblinking impassivity. 'Well maybe a li'l bit,' he admits. They continue to stare him out. 'Bastards!' he says miserably. The exchange provides a nice comedic vignette before the shooting starts, but it also tells us that, sell-out or not, Garrett is still a force to be reckoned with.

The boy is the first casualty, wounded by one of Garrett's crew as he emerges to saddle the horses. Progressively, Garrett will gun down the Kid's followers [3]. Some he kills in an attempt to get information as he tracks down their leader after his escape; others he summarily executes, as if he could kill a part of his own past with each bullet he fires. For the moment, though, he is in control, able to tell his men to hold their fire when the Kid's surrender is imminent.

Billy strings it out for as long as he can, finishing a game of cards as warning shots ricochet around the bunkhouse. The boy's life ebbs away. 'I can't see the cards no more,' he says. 'Maybe it's time you took a walk,' Billy suggests.

'Hell, yes,' says the boy. 'Why not? I can still hold a gun.'

His complicity in the act notwithstanding, he is as sacrificial as 'Crazy' Lee: young, inexperienced and expendable. Bundled out of the door, taking the fusilade as Billy hurtles past him and dives for shelter, his death is pointless. Garrett orders a cessation of fire and calls for Billy to surrender.

The Kid obliges, arms raised to shoulder height, holster dangling from one hand. It is another *Wild Bunch* image revisited: the beaten and bloodied Angel, held in a crucifixion pose by Mapache. Here the effect is self-conscious, as if the Kid were striving to manufacture his own myth. His posturing elicits an offended reaction from one of the deputies, Bob Ollinger (R G Armstrong), who raises his rifle to shoot. J W Bell (Matt

Clark), a more sympathetic deputy, wrests it from him. (The dynamic here – religious imagery and conflict over Garrett's indulgent treatment of the Kid – sets up the next scene.) Garrett and Billy exchange smiles as the former walks slowly down to meet his captive.

Garrett and Billy play cards as the fanatical Ollinger looks on.

> Billy: You're poor company, Pat.
> Garrett: Yeah. I'm alive, though.
> Billy: So am I.

Though not for not much longer – not as far as the denizens of Lincoln County are concerned. We next see Billy sitting in the sheriff's office, shackled and under the watchful gaze of the shotgun-toting Ollinger, whiling away his time playing cards with Garrett and Bell as he waits on the noose. Incensed by the Kid's indifference to his own mortality, Ollinger starts preaching to him (that's preaching in the hellfire sense) and suddenly the R G Armstrong of *Ride the High Country* is back, as joylessly fanatical as before and this time wearing a badge. 'You'll learn to believe before I'm finished with you,' he promises. 'It's time you got close to God, boy.'

Garrett does nothing to diffuse the tension, taking the Kid's side:

> Garrett: Say, Bob, what else do you believe in apart from God?
> Ollinger: Me.
> Garrett: Just like old Ollinger. Always got to have a minority opinion on everything.

'Just move toward me':
Billy gets the drop on
Deputy J W Bell.

Garrett announces that he has to leave, and Ollinger seizes his chance, reminding Billy that he has eight days left in which to get on his knees and 'get acquainted with your lord and master'. The Kid isn't interested:

> Billy: Pat, keep that mule's asshole away from me before I have to break him.
> Ollinger: I surely wish you'd try, son. I got my shotgun full of sixteen cent dimes. Enough to spread you out like a crazy woman's quilt.
> Garrett: Bob! ... You mess around with him one more time, I'll have to send your ass back to Texas.
> Billy: Don't. I think I'd like to keep him around for awhile.

With Pat gone, and Bell throwing down his cards, the theological debate resumes:

> Ollinger: On your knees!
> Billy: Kiss my ass.

Ollinger broadsides him with his shotgun, dragging him up by his hair no sooner than he has knocked him to the floor. 'Repent, you son of bitch!' he yells, adding, 'I'll take you for a walk across Hell on a spiderweb.' Clearly, he is not the most well-adjusted individual in the county. Garrett's sympathies are reaffirmed by Bell, who draws on his colleague, urging Ollinger to desist. Ollinger grudgingly returns his shotgun to the rack and heads off across the street for a drink.

Billy seizes his chance. 'That last pop got my guts going,' he tells Bell, declaring that he needs to use the outhouse. Once there, he retrieves a gun hidden under a few sheets of newspaper and following Bell back to sheriff's office, regales him with the story of an antagonist whom he shot in the back. Reaching the top of the stairs, he turns and draws on Bell.

> Billy: I don't want to kill you, Bell.
> Bell: I sure hope you don't, Billy.
> Billy: Then just move toward me. [Bell starts to edge away.] Don't! Don't do it. Please.
> Bell (turning): You wouldn't shoot me in the back, Billy.

Billy would. And does. The bullet rips through Bell's body in trademark slow motion and he crashes through a window and out into the street. Ollinger, who moments before was happily watching a group of children at play (using the noose as a swing, a game even more macabre than the burning of ants and scorpions), is alerted by the noise and starts walking over. Billy, armed with the dime-loaded shotgun, appears on the upper storey verandah. Filmed from below, framed in truly iconic fashion, he calls to Ollinger: 'How's Jesus look to you now, Bob?'

'Bonney's killed Bell,' a disingenuous bystander tells the doomed deputy.

'Yeah,' Ollinger says philosophically, 'and he's killed me, too.'

There is another segue into slow motion as Billy discharges both barrels, the coinage ripping Ollinger apart. 'Keep the change, Bob,' he offers.

It would be convenient, particularly in the light of Peckinpah's decision to concentrate on the legend as opposed to the reality, to pause here and evaluate Billy's escape in suitably mythic style. Certainly, there is a whiff of traditional Hollywood myth-making in Billy's unhurried behaviour after the shootings – he lingers on the verandah as crowds gather beneath, then commands one of them to fetch him an axe (to free himself of the shackles) – as well as in the remunerative one-liner he delivers after relieving someone of their horse: 'I'll throw in about a dollar sixty worth of change if you can dig it out of old Bob there.' The crowds look on in silent awe as he rides away, Bob Dylan's balladry filling the soundtrack.

However: he is shown limping from the outhouse after recovering the planted gun, still doing up his pants as he rejoins Bell. He shoots Bell in the back. And as for the horse, it's a second choice. The first animal he picks proves too skittish and – for God's sake! – he falls off.

Mythic? Hardly. This is, in fact, a documented fact [4].

What Peckinpah demonstrates here is an understanding of how legends are created, and the circumstances they grow out of. In the same vein as his laconic, mocking surrender at the bunkhouse, the Kid knows he has an audience and plays up to them shamelessly. During the mêlée, we get our first glimpse of Alias (Dylan), a typesetter for the town's newspaper, and soon-to-be member of Billy's entourage. What we see in him isn't quite the awe-struck hero-worship the child at the telegraph office has for General Mapache, more the gleam of inspiration, the notion that a new and exhilarating way of life is possible. And, as with the child, it is an encounter that leads him to commit an act of killing. But Alias's role is greater than this: it is Alias, one feels, who will take the Kid's memory as his muse and create the myth [5]. Alias is the Bob Dylan of *John Wesley Harding*: the chronicler, the balladeer, the storyteller.

The presence of two folk-rock icons in the same film, their characters brought together narratively at this particular moment, one of them providing the music for the soundtrack, is crucial to Peckinpah's re-evaluation of the myth. Dylan's popularity and importance as a folk-rock singer-songwriter was already well-established when the film was released; Kristofferson's equally, *his* fanbase also straddling the Country and

Western market, an audience generically compatible with the western. Country music –
certainly in the 1970s, long before the arrival of pop-crossover acts such as Leann Rimes
and Shania Twain – was generally downbeat, enlivened only by desperado posturing and
novelty records [6]. Folk-rock was, at that time more than ever, the province of young
people, socially concerned and critical of politics and authority. The points of reference
provided by these two genres heighten the elegiac and valedictorial qualities of *Pat
Garrett and Billy the Kid*.

Kristofferson's physical appearance, long-haired and unselfconscious, is also an
important factor. His costume for the movie, while being generically congruous, is still
reminiscent of the jeans/open shirt combo you might expect him to wear at a gig. The
aesthetic also applies to the members of his gang: long-haired, unshaven, grungy. It may
be Old Fort Sumner, 1881, but they certainly fit the bill as hippies, liberals and draft-
dodgers. Their lifestyle – shared accommodation (for bunkhouse read commune) and
shared women (i.e. free love) – emphasizes the parallels. Their opposition to Chisum
mirrors that of the youth of America to Nixon and Vietnam.

The casting of Kristofferson as Billy necessitates that an older man play Garrett. In
1881, Pat Garrett was thirty-one and William Bonney ten years his junior. The age gap
between Coburn and Kristofferson is eight years, but otherwise the similarity ends. In
November 1972, when *Pat Garrett* went before the cameras, James Coburn was forty-
four and Kris Kristofferson thirty-six. Making the protagonists older allows Peckinpah
another *Wild Bunch* subtext: men growing old, outliving their times.

In fact, here he takes it one step further. Whereas the characters in *Ride the High
Country* and *The Wild Bunch*, never mind that they have ended up on opposing sides of
the law, would rather take a bullet than change with the times, Garrett and the Kid are
further divided by the fact that one of them has tried to change, while the other – the
younger – stubbornly refuses. What makes *Pat Garrett* a more pessimistic film than the
others is that both are doomed. When Judd and Westrum meet the Hammond brothers
head on (like it used to be) they are reconciled. When the Bunch take their long walk
through the streets of Agua Verde, they are functioning as a unit, all past conflicts
forgotten. Likewise, when Thornton renounces the company of T C and the rest of the
gutter trash, riding off instead with Sykes and the men from Angel's village, the slate has
been wiped clean and reconciliation effected.

Not so with Garrett and the Kid. The younger man tries to live it like he was still in
his heyday and Pat his partner, instead of a hired gun made legitimate by a sheriff's star
– and dies, shot by his erstwhile friend. Garrett tries to change with the times, side with
the politicians and landowners, and in general go straight – and dies, shot by the
paymasters to whom he has now become an outspoken embarrassment and a liability.
The tragedy, then, is that Garrett dies because, try as he might to change, he cannot
disguise the man he really is.

Examples abound of Pat as a man growing old. The hilarity which greets Billy's
retelling of a crude story about Garrett and a whore is brought into sharp contrast later
when Garrett arrives at Lamuel's bar. When Lamuel starts on his favourite subject
(recollections of whoring), his objectionable homily 'she got an ass on her like a forty
dollar cow and a tit, I'd like to see that thing filled full of tequila', is met with a look of
such distaste that we are left in no doubt that Garrett has moved on. (That Billy is still
laughing at such schoolyard humour indicates he hasn't.) [7]

Garrett's return to Old Fort Sumner in the aftermath of Billy's escape is also an
exercise in comparison. Billy's departure is on a fast steed (the first horse he chooses
is so feisty it throws him), his parting words a pithy one-liner, the crowd in awe of
him. Garrett's return is sedate: he rides into town in a buggy, holding the reins in a
manner that would seem effeminate in a less masculine actor than James Coburn. His
words are uppity – 'would some of you people get him up off the ground and into it'
– and the 'anything you say, *sheriff*' he gets in response falls considerably short of
respectful.

Two other scenes are crucial to the development of Garrett's character. Tracking down Black Harris (L Q Jones) to question him on the Kid's whereabouts, he enlists the help of Sheriff Baker (Slim Pickens). Baker is Garrett a few years down the road: he has no affinity for his job and doesn't bother with the trappings of authority (at one point he has to ask his wife where she's put his badge). He spends his time in his backyard building a boat. 'I'm going to drift out of this damn territory,' he says; 'this town's got no hat-size no how.' As it happens, he gets no further than the banks of the Rio Bravo. Gut-shot during a gunfight at Black's hideout, Baker stumbles down to the river and sits watching the silvery patterns of light on water, his breaths coming slow and painful, as 'Knockin' on Heaven's Door' plays softly on the soundtrack. The understatement and emotionalism are heartbreaking. It's one in the eye for Peckinpah critics who see him only as a director of violence.

Baker's death leaves scars on Garrett. The retributive shooting of Black offers no catharsis. The waste of Baker's life is summed up in the dying accusation Black makes to Garrett: 'Us old boys oughtn't be doing this to each other. Ain't that many of us left.'

The other scene – the one that *really* humanizes Garrett – is the most misunderstood in the whole film. During his post-production battles with a studio who wanted to cut the film ever shorter to resemble nothing more than a succession of bullet-riddled set-pieces, Peckinpah reputedly bartered other scenes, allowing them to be excised from the theatrical print, in order to retain it. Yet many critics, even as they praise its atmosphere and poetry, have deemed it superfluous; narratively redundant. Nonetheless, it is the single best scene in the film.

Garrett, following the Kid's trail, has camped for the night by the side of a river. Startled by gunfire, he looks around him. The source is an old-timer on a heavily-laden raft, taking pot shots at a bottle he has tossed into the water ahead of him, his family looking on. His aim is abysmal and Garrett takes it upon himself to reach for his pistol and test his own skills. He doesn't hit the bottle, either, nor is there time for a second try – the bargee swings his rifle in Garrett's direction and looses off a shot. Garrett scrambles for the shelter of a tree and assumes a retaliative position. For several elongated seconds, he and his antagonist have each other in their sights. Then – slowly – these two old men lower their guns. The raft passes on its away, out of the frame and out of the film.

Okay, it might not advance the story, but there is subtext here that runs as deep as the river. Firstly, it vindicates Baker. In lowering his rifle, Garrett accepts that 'old boys oughtn't be doing this to each other', which in turn means that he is coming to terms with growing old. Pike Bishop's assertion that 'the days are closing fast' applies; the only the difference is that Pike has his Bunch around him at all times and is able to communicate his thoughts. Pat Garrett is alone; there is no one to whom he can vocalize his sentiments. As with much of Coburn's screen work, it's all in the look.

Secondly, the image of a man, his loved ones in tow, floating away from a territory that has no hat-size no how, is the visualization of what Sheriff Baker doesn't live to achieve. Imagine what must be running through Garrett's mind when he takes that ill-advised shot at the bottle! What a life-changing moment when he lowers his gun!

Thirdly, the man on the boat becomes a stand-in for the Kid, someone Garrett doesn't *want* to kill. This time, he lowers his gun. Later, tragically, he doesn't.

Towards the end of the film, one final accusation is thrown in his face (by, as we shall see, a coffin-maker); during their exchange of words, the craftsman says 'you've finally figured it out, huh?' It's at this point, down by the river, that he figures it out; that it comes home to him as surely as it did to Baker.

In three key meetings with authority figures, Garrett – through his contempt and hostility – plants the seeds of the conspiracy that will destroy him.

Summoned to dine with Governor Wallace (Jason Robards) [8], Garrett is plainly uneasy amidst the opulence on display. The padded chairs and glasses of cognac are a world apart from a well-worn saddle and a shot of bourbon. By way of opening the conversation, Wallace waxes lyrical: 'I do hope you enjoy these rainy New Mexican evenings. They have a fabulous melancholy to them. They bring us closer to some greater design. At least, I hope so.' Poetic as this may be, it sounds decidedly insubstantial after the hard-edged exchanges that have come before. It adds another brick to the wall of class, money and political connections that forever separate men of their ilk from real men like Garrett.

Two men are already seated at the Governor's table. He introduces them as Holland and Norris. In their clean suits, and with their unsmiling countenances and shifty glances, they are clearly representative of the power behind Wallace's throne. An intriguing hint of their interrelationship is the introduction of Holland as 'Mister' while all Norris merits is his surname pronounced so curtly that you'd think Wallace could taste it in his mouth.

> Wallace: These gentlemen are very concerned about the escape of William Bonney, a concern I am sure you also share.
> Garrett: He escaped from my jail.
> Wallace: Exactly. This territory is vast and primitive. There's money here, growing investments, and political interests. We must protect these interests so that the area can continue to prosper and grow.

If Wallace assuages his conscience by verbosity (after all, 'vast and primitive' is a far more romantic phrase than the rape of the land that the 'growing investments and political interests' hint at), his associates reveal more mercenary tendencies.

> Holland: I believe you rode with the Kid ... You must be aware of his moves.
> Garrett: Well, I know Billy and he ain't exactly predictable.
> Holland: Oh come now, Sheriff. For a man's who's half outlaw himself and still smart enough to be elected sheriff by Chisum and the other big ranchers, I expect better than that. Now can you bring him in, or should we look elsewhere?
> Garrett: Oh, I'll bring him in – if the peckerheads don't mess things up by startin' another cattle war.
> Holland: I can assure you, Mr Garrett, that Chisum and the others have been advised to recognize their position. In this particular game there are only a few players left. I'd advise you to grab onto a winning hand while you have a chance.

Wallace remains quiet and contemplative throughout. Garrett, though subdued, is bristling against this pompous little man. But even Holland's arrogance is overshadowed by the blunt tactics of Norris. He pulls out a wad of banknotes and hands it across the table:

> Norris: We're offering a reward of one thousand dollars for the Kid's capture. You can have five hundred now.
> Garrett: Well, I aim to bring the Kid in. But until I do, you'd better take your five hundred dollars and shove it up your ass and set fire to it.

On which note, he puts his hat on and takes his leave, having handed the green folding stuff straight back. This repudiation of what amounts to little more than socially approved blood money not only strengthens Garrett's affinity with the Kid, but provides another example of Peckinpah's anti-establishment politics. If Billy and his gang represent hippies and war-protestors, then Wallace represents the government and Chisum big business. Holland and Norris are the faceless mediators. Poe, as we shall see, is the man who does the dirty work – the spy in Garrett's camp. Again, landownership becomes a metaphor for American involvement in Vietnam, and in this scene Peckinpah's hatred of the war machine (government + big business = the military-industrial complex) is writ large.

Back on the Kid's trail, bivouac'd down and staring into the embers of his campfire, Garrett is probably still brooding over this when he is approached by John Poe. Recognizable as one of the men pulling the trigger on him in 1909, and glimpsed during the scene just mentioned (present at the Governor's table but not introduced or given any dialogue), he loses no time in annoying Garrett.

> Poe: The Governor made me a deputy. I guess he probably told you.
> Garrett: I already got me a deputy.
> Poe: Two's better than one. I answer only to the Governor, Mr Norris and Mr Holland.

Which has to be the only example in the history of westerns of a deputy pulling rank on a sheriff. Poe reveals more of himself than he probably intends when he goes on to speak highly of Chisum, a standpoint that seems incompatible with Holland's attitude to the landowner.

> Poe: Chisum is a fine man. Country's got to make a choice. A man who goes with the drifters and the outlaws has got no backbone.
> Garrett: I'm going to tell you this once and I don't want to have to say it again. This country's gettin' old and I aim to get old with it. Now the Kid don't want it that way. He might be a better man for it, I ain't judgin' him. But I don't want you explainin' nothin' to me and I don't want you sayin' nothin' about the Kid and nobody else in my goddamn county.

Which is a pretty damn good example of an over-ambitious man being put firmly in his place.

With Poe in tow, Garrett pays a call on Chisum. Their encounter is brief and undramatic. Name-checked from the start, spoken of dismissively by Holland, idolized by Poe, it is fitting that Peckinpah introduce John Chisum (who, we realize by now, is the *real* villain of the piece) at the mid-point of the movie. The effect is to make the audience marvel at his blandness. *This* is Chisum? *This* is the man who, to quote the Kid, wants 'to put a fence around this country'? Who could, as Garrett feels, start a cattle war at the drop of a stetson? Whose men – as we shall see – shoot and rape their way across the plains in the name of land ownership and capitalism?

Frankly, he doesn't look like anything special.

He is mildly contemptuous of his acolyte-in-waiting, Poe. When he asks Garrett to stay for supper and Garrett refuses, Poe eagerly takes him up on the offer. 'Bunkhouse is right behind the lodge barn,' Chisum responds dismissively; 'the men usually eat when the cook lets 'em.'

He is also mildly suspicious:

> Chisum: Sheriff, tell me something. Why did you ride all the way out here? (9)
> Poe: We thought maybe you'd heard something.
> Chisum: Yeah, I'll tell you what I heard. Billy the Kid is in Tuscosa. Billy the Kid is in Tombstone. Billy the Kid is in Mexico … And Billy the Kid is at my table right at this moment, eating tacos and green chili peppers with my niece, just like old times. (10)

Add mildly sarcastic to the list, as well.

In fact, with his voice remaining neutral and his only remotely threat-like utterance being 'glad to be of service, but don't overuse it' (subtle, but nowhere near spine-chilling, particularly not to a man like Garrett), the only worrying thing about Chisum is his impassivity. Garrett is so underawed that when asked whether he'll bring the Kid in or not, he simply turns and rides away without bothering to respond.

Essentially, John Chisum is to capitalism what Holland and Norris are to politics, and is equally devoid of depth and persona. Like them, his place is in the background. It is easy to imagine Poe, snubbed or not, playing devil's advocate between all three, a Machiavelli with a six-gun and a handlebar moustache orchestrating the elaborate off-screen conspiracy.

Governor Wallace, Holland and Norris, Poe, and Chisum are all contrasted in scenes that follow the Kid's progress, first as he finds himself on the verge of taking Garrett's advice and leaving the territory, and later in the incident that makes him turn back.

The opulence of the Governor's dwelling throws the communal lifestyle of the Kid and his gang into an even more grungy perspective. Rejoining them after his escape, he finds his men holed up in cramped quarters, sleeping where they can find space. One of them, Luke (Harry Dean Stanton) is huddled up with a favourite whore of Billy's. Billy makes it his first priority to boot Luke out and get down to business with her himself. The scene says something about men together and their behaviour patterns – and does so without Peckinpah's usual moralistic take on the subject. It shows the disregard for convention in the outlaw lifestyle. And it deflates the myth a little more.

But as vulgar as Billy's Bunch might seem (and they aren't the kind of fellas who'd behave themselves at Governor Wallace's table), they are men of honour compared to the thugs who ride for Chisum. Their brutality is evident when they surprise the Kid and his followers, who are out chasing turkeys. Again, this is based on historical fact. The pursuit seems comic, not least for the use of lassos (traditionally used in westerns to rope cattle), but lends itself to darker undertones in recalling the chickens picked off in the credit sequence, as well as providing a metaphor for Garrett's systematic extermination of those associated with the Kid (i.e. a turkey-shoot). The situation turns nasty very quickly. Billy and Alias, having concluded the business of turkey-rustling while the others do the real thing and go after cattle, are busy wringing the bird's neck and conveniently out of sight when Chisum's men arrive. One of Billy's gang, interrupted before he can so much as rope a steer let alone make off with it, is issued a stern admonition – 'Them's Mr Chisum's cows. This is Mr Chisum's land' – and then his horse is shot from under him. No sooner has he picked himself up than six revolvers are emptied into him. A summary execution, carried out with cold indifference.

Billy and Alias respond immediately, springing from their cover, rifles blazing. A couple of riders go down; the others scatter in every direction. It's a marked contrast: the solidarity of the Kid and co. against the every-man-for-himself ethos of Chisum's boys (demonstrating that Chisum's men are cowards and have no character while Billy's are loyal to each other). The law might be on the side of the latter, but it's when Billy and Alias open up that justice is dispensed.

In a subsequent scene, the Kid bids farewell to a friend of his, a simple Mexican farmer named Paco (played, in a performance light years removed from Mapache or El Jefe, by Emilio Fernandez), warning him to stay clear of Chisum's land. Paco, however, is optimistic:

> Paco: I have no quarrel with Chisum. He's an old warrior whose war is over. Let him alone and he will let you alone.
> Billy: Don't you believe it, my friend.
> Paco: I must believe it. *Adios.*

The beautiful simplicity of the scene affords a contrast with the one that precedes it, the suspicious, undertone-laden encounter between Garrett and Chisum. And it becomes agonizingly poignant in retrospect when Billy, finally taking Paco's lead and Garrett's advice, sets out alone for Mexico. Like the Bunch in Agua Verde, their guns still smoking from the vengeful killing of Mapache, this is the point at which Billy still has a choice. He can keep riding, cross the border, and live. But he turns back.

Motivation is paramount in order that a scene of such dramatic import convinces. Sadly, this is the least impressive part of the film. On the surface, the situation is dynamite – Billy comes across Paco's ambushed and overturned wagon, the farmer dying as Chisum's men attempt to rape his daughter – and Billy's entrance, like a horseback angel of vengeance, is certainly impressive. What lets the scene down is the cornball speech Paco gives about the house he was intending to build, and fate-sealing moment where Billy decides to go back to Old Fort Sumner and damn the consequences. There is nothing here as brilliantly played and layered with meaning as the look that passes between Pike and Dutch, the tension stretched out till the screen almost vibrates with it, no heart-stopping moment where the avoidable tips over into the inevitable. There is just one borderline cliché – 'That tears it, I'm goin' back!' – then Billy drags his horse round and goes thundering off in the direction from which he has come, leaving Paco's daughter to weep over her father's body and fend for herself against whosoever else might happen along.

Billy deals out swift justice against Chisum's men.

It's a matter of regret that the scene couldn't have been rethought, Paco's speech replaced with something less lachrymose (or cut altogether), and Billy's decision communicated wordlessly, because the *image* on which it ends is absolutely vital: Billy the Kid, on the cusp of his transfiguration from outlaw to folk hero, riding back to a reckoning with the forces of change and commerce, personified in the man who, not so long along, would have ridden with him.

Billy the Kid, riding alone.

When Pat Garrett, having followed his quarry across half of New Mexico, also returns to Fort Sumner, he and Poe are joined by Sheriff McKinley. As the threesome converges on the town, the image is of Garrett flanked by two untrustworthy men. The meaning is obvious: he might as well be alone.

Dust blows off the plains behind them as they linger on the outskirts. All wear hats and long coats. It couldn't be more traditional save if tumbleweed came rolling through. But what follows is about as un-western as you can get.

Billy and his comrades have regrouped, but their behaviour is non-violent. In refusing to run after witnessing the atrocity against Paco, the Kid proves his integrity. In the ensuing scenes of camaraderie with his men and an evening of tender love-making with his girl, he proves his humanity. This quiet, intimate reappraisal of his character leaves the closing scenes of the film tinged not with adrenalin-laced excitement at seeing an outlaw gunned down, but a real feeling of loss at a man robbed of his life just when that life was beginning to resemble something good.

Billy's death at this point wipes the slate clean of his previous transgressions. In agonizing slow-motion – a good half minute elapses between Garrett's gun roaring and Billy's body, arms spread out, crumpling to the floor – Peckinpah shows us the finality of death, and the redemption/martyrdom of one of his protagonists. Crucifixion imagery is revisited in Billy's lifeless form. Earlier, when arrested, he was playing at it, striking a Christ-like pose out of mockery and self-aggrandizement. Now it is for real. This is calvary, but without resurrection. That his name will endure is hardly the point, at best just a fringe benefit. The man is dead.

But the film does not end here. That would be too easy, especially for Sam Peckinpah, who was always concerned with the *effect* of violence, not only on those who suffer it, but the men whose business it is.

The image of Garrett, Poe and McKinley waiting at the edge of town – one might say, at the gates – is portentous, doom-laden, almost Old Testament. On Garrett's instruction, they split up, agreeing to meet at Pete Maxwell's place on the other side of Fort Sumner. (Billy, in not the wisest choice of lodgings, has already been shown to take his girl there for a bit of privacy.) Garrett's slow introspective progress through the dark streets marks his lowest, loneliest point in the movie. But he still has one more demon to confront before he fulfils the job – the job for which he was paid and made sheriff.

Only one other townsperson is up and about: the coffin-maker Will, an old man, grizzled and white-haired. There is sadness in his eyes, weariness in his voice. This is a man the world has tried to crush but who is still standing.

The minute or two of screen time he shares with Garrett would be extraordinary if he were played by some ornery old character actor. But the role is taken by Peckinpah and the effect is astounding. There is a bitter humour to the way Garrett offers his hip flask and Will refuses (Peckinpah's drinking was public knowledge), but the humour is jettisoned just as quickly, and when Garrett takes his leave of the old-timer, there is only bitterness.

'You've finally figured it out, huh?' Will says, leaning on an almost-finished coffin. 'I thought you was pickin' shit with the chickens, cuttin' yourself a tin bill.'

Garrett, unresponsive, casts his eyes towards the Maxwell property.

'Go on, get it over with,' Will urges. Then, as if permitting Garrett a few more seconds of hesitation, he asks, 'You know what I'm gonna do? Put everything I own right here. I'm gonna bury it in this ground and leave the territory.'

At this, Garrett starts walking, and any sense of empathy on Will's part is negated by what he calls out after him. 'When are you gonna learn you can't trust anybody, not even yourself, Garrett? You chicken-shit, bad-brained son of a bitch!'

The purpose of a scene like this and the attribution of the dialogue quoted to a character such as Will (who enters the film for the first time, there having been no previous allusion to him, and disappears just as quickly when he's done) is to achieve a certain subtext. With Peckinpah himself in the role, the subtext breaks cover and becomes a living part of the film. When he speaks of everything he owns, the reference could be to his body of work as a film-maker – the burial of it could allude to the harm done to virtually every one of his pictures during filming or in post-production by studios who compromised his artistic vision for the sake of commercialism. Or it could be Peckinpah casting himself as cinema's answer to Prospero, drowning his book in the final act of *The Tempest*. The words 'bury it in this ground and leave the territory' echo with precognition watching the film now, three decades down the line. It hardly needs stating again that *Pat Garrett and Billy the Kid* was his last western.

Directors have placed themselves in their own movies before, but this is something more. Peckinpah is still directing, but he has moved from behind the camera, where he was directing the actor, in order to direct the character. And in abusing Garrett he passes comment on his own disaffection. But even playing a bit part, he is still Peckinpah. This placement of himself in his own film (aside from a non-vocal role as a cameraman in *Convoy*, he makes no other cameos) comes at a crucial moment: his instruction to Garrett to 'get it over with' precedes Garrett's shooting of the Kid. At the risk of supposition, one can easily imagine Peckinpah, anticipating the furore during editing, casting himself in a scene it would be virtually impossible to edit out, just to annoy his nemesis Aubrey that little bit more.

The Kid's death shows up Poe and McKinley as cowards. They have crept around the side of Pete Maxwell's house. Garrett's tactic is different – more direct. He simply walks up to the front gate, pauses in front of it, then throws it open. It is another hesitation, allowing for a fateful moment of stasis. And it prefigures a further hiatus when Garrett (in an act of common decency – never mind that granting it to a man you are about to shoot is decidedly uncommon) sits on a hammock on the porch and waits for Billy and his girl (played by Rita Coolidge) to finish their pleasures. The overlapping soundtrack of their orgasmic cries as Garrett sits alone (already conforming to the stereotype of an old man in a western, rockin' on the porch) emphasizes his isolation.

His passion spent, Billy emerges shirtless and dishevelled. He pads into Maxwell's kitchen looking for something to eat. Poe and McKinley, outside, see him framed in the doorway. 'That's the Kid, right there,' McKinley gasps; 'go on, shoot him.'

Both are carrying guns, both have a clear shot, both have taken hefty gulps from a bottle of bourbon in the name of courage. Neither has the guts. Neither is man enough.

Garrett has entered the house. Seeing the girl slumbering, he leaves her. He finds that Maxwell is still up, another old man sitting by himself, waiting out the passage of time. 'Hello, Pete,' he says, his voice subdued.

'What are you doing, Pat?' a startled Maxwell responds. The words are meant at face value, but it's easy to imagine Garrett, smarting from Will's send-off, taking them not as a question but an accusation.

In counterpoint to Garrett's progression from the porch to the interior of the house, Billy quits the (apparent) safety of the kitchen and walks outside to investigate the agitated whispering. He draws on Poe and McKinley and the cowards just stand there. 'Easy. We've come to see Pete Maxwell,' Poe announces, his hands nowhere near his gunbelt. Billy, not so convinced that they have stood down that he is willing to present them with an easy target, walks backward into the house.

'You chicken-shit bastard,' McKinley hisses at Poe. Hypocrisy isn't the word!

As Billy edges back inside, his naked back to the camera (and, by extension, to Garrett) he is caught alongside a full-length mirror. Turning, he now faces Garrett, but his back is still visible in reflection. So while there is nothing cowardly about the way Garrett does it (he neither shoots the Kid unarmed nor in the back), by God the image is there!

Garrett is seated, pistol at the ready. Billy's gun is still raised from challenging Poe and McKinley. He and Pat are equally matched. But the Kid just smiles. Whether he has decided to accept his fate, or whether he believes that Garrett will be unable to go through with it, the matter is purely academic. Garrett fires one shot. As the Kid falls, his reflection is replaced in the mirror by Garrett's.

Garrett's jaw slackens, his mouth a gaping 'O' of disbelief. This turns immediately to self-hatred and he fires into the mirror. As Billy finally hits the floor, Garrett approaches the mirror and stares at his own shattered image. The fragments of glass are the scars on Garrett's psyche; the face he sees is the man he will have to live with for the next twenty-eight years.

'I did it,' he says as he walks back out onto the porch, 'I killed the Kid.' One gunshot, one line of dialogue – a whole world of remorse.

Poe, his courage fully restored, comes strutting up. He is like Coffer in *The Wild Bunch*, saving his disparaging remarks about Pike Bishop until he is safely dead. Poe takes out his knife, announcing that he wants to cut off Billy's trigger finger and nail it to a fence post. With a scream of '*Noooooo!*', Garrett knocks him to the ground, adding (in another throwback to *The Wild Bunch* [11]), 'What you want and what you get are two different things.'

Having preserved at least some dignity, Garrett sits down once more on the hammock as a small knot of townsfolk, Alias among them, look on. He is still sitting there come daybreak. Poe and Alias are still hanging around. Accusing looks are still the order of the day. Bob Dylan's music kicks in, a reprisal of all that has gone before. Garrett rouses himself, walks slowly off the porch, and mounts his horse.

Peckinpah drives the final nail into the coffin of the traditional western, taking a motif from one of the best-known, best-loved examples of the genre, and thoroughly subverting it. George Stevens's *Shane* ends with Alan Ladd riding out of town after he has dispatched the murderous Jack Palance; the young boy from whose point of view the narrative has unfolded, and who has come to idolize Ladd, runs impetuously after him, calling his name over and over.

Pat Garrett and Billy the Kid ends with Garrett riding dismally away, the most despised man in the territory (not least by himself); a young Mexican boy goes running after him, hurls a stone disgustedly, then turns and walks back. Peckinpah then segues back into the prologue, and again we see Garrett caught in the crossfire of Poe and his cronies, taking bullets, falling from the wagon.

However he might have thought otherwise while discussing the script with Jim Silke, a simple choice between the legend and the reality was never an option for a man as complex as Sam Peckinpah.

There *are* mythic qualities on display: when Billy practises his sharp shooting before an audience of children, their expressions are awe-struck. They will go on to tell the folk tales to the generation that succeeds them, as surely as Alias will. Yet elsewhere, there is Billy's arrival at the trading post-cum-boarding house run by Mr and Mrs Horrell, the latter welcoming him as if he were a returning son, while the former grumbles at having to take down the door when Billy recognizes one of their guests as Alamosa Bill (Jack Elam), an old nemesis, and a duel ensues. (The door is taken down to use as coffin wood for the loser.) They agree on the usual procedure: ten paces, turn and fire. Billy turns and draws a bead on his opponent at two. Alamosa Bill turns and draws at eight. Billy fells him with one shot, then has the temerity to admonish him 'That wasn't ten.' Again he is watched by children, but one wonders if they will grow up to tell folk stories, or turn bad, run wild and live pointless lives terminated by early deaths, driven down this road by the abiding lesson that cheating works and a man's life is worth no more than a hypocritical wisecrack.

It is curious, too, that the scenes which *do* achieve an atmosphere – an otherworldiness – that hints at the mythic, are those which feature Garrett, not the Kid: most notably, Baker's death scene and the exchange of fire with the old man on the raft. But Garrett is not a mythic figure. In living on past the height of his fame (or infamy), and dying as ignobly as he does, he is more the subject of a cautionary tale.

Of course, that might have been the realization that Peckinpah came to somewhere between his conversation with Silke and calling 'Action!' on the first day of shooting: that – hell! – even legends ain't like they used to be.

CHAPTER FIVE
CROSS OF IRON

War films have always been problematic. Generally, mainstream American cinema has treated human conflict either by glorifying it (action spectaculars such as *Where Eagles Dare*) or by moralizing about it (*Saving Private Ryan* comes to mind). While opting for the former approach guarantees a certain degree of entertainment value, the resulting lack of psychological insight is such that film-makers run a risk of seeming to make light of their subject.

Opting for the latter can be equally worrisome. Trying to put a sheen of morality upon a set of global circumstances where moral concepts ceased to apply is an evasion of the true horrors of war. To quote a line from one of the few American films that have given us an insightful and non-judgemental view of men in the arena of conflict – Samuel Fuller's *The Big Red One* – 'the only glory in war is to survive'.

But as far as the other Sam is concerned, the truth of war is simpler, blunter, and far more bleak: in *Cross of Iron* there is no glory in survival.

There is no glory at all. Period.

In true Peckinpah style, the credits set the tone. His other films demonstrate his flair for editing and intercutting his own images; here he proves just as adept with stock footage. To the plaintive singing of German children, we see a black-and-white montage: Hitler at the Nuremburg Rally, small boys looking up at him adoringly; Hitler youth members planting the Nazi flag on a mountain; soldiers being decorated with the Iron Cross; the loading of shells into mortars and the resultant explosions; Hitler at the Eagle's Nest; internees and troops in surrender; tanks and half-tracks hurtling across bombed out landscapes; children, armed with nothing more than sticks, marching in solemn formation along a riverside; a firing squad executing a soldier. Flags and newsreel pictures of the Führer proliferate. We are assailed with the regalia of Nazi-ism, only for the Leni Riefenstahl-ish air of pomp and circumstance to be harshly juxtaposed with the pinched, hollow-eyed, anguished faces of men in the aftermath of battle.

With each credit, the image freezes and floods with red. Imposed upon a shot of weary evacuees trudging through a snowy wasteland, is the establishing credit 'Russia, the Taman Peninsula – 1943, the Retreat'. The pace of the editing quickens, the music having moved from children's voices to an orchestral march to simple military drumming (the kind of percussion to which the Bunch walk through Agua Verde). A frame of the film proper is inserted – in black-and-white, in keeping with the montage – of Sergeant Steiner (James Coburn) cautiously scanning his surroundings through a pair of binoculars. Then there is a reprisal of the dominant motif in this sequence, the Nazi flag, raised aloft on standards carried by troops who march like legionnaires. The flags fill with colour, black swastikas in white circles on a background of red. The film begins, Steiner's troops sheltering from mortar fire. An explosion rips a section of woodland

apart and the obligatory freeze-frame heralds the final credit, as effectively placed as in any of his other movies: 'directed by Sam Peckinpah'.

Such story as there is in *Cross of Iron* can be said to centre around the rivalry between Steiner and Captain Stransky (Maximillian Schell). The sequence of events unfolds like this:

Steiner and his platoon take a Russian trench during a reconnaisance mission, the only survivor being a young boy. Back at the German lines, an aristocratic Prussian officer named Stranksy arrives, having been transferred there at his own request. He meets the pragmatic Colonel Brandt (James Mason) and his disaffected sidekick Captain Kiesel (David Warner); in conversation, they warn him that Steiner is a dangerous man.

When Steiner's patrol returns with the boy, Stransky immediately pulls rank, reminding Steiner that no prisoners are to be taken. Steiner refuses the order to shoot the boy, telling Stranksy to do it himself. Stranksy reaches for his pistol. Steiner's right-hand-man Schnurrbart intercedes. He leads the boy off, ostensibly to his death, but hides him instead. Later, Steiner contrives to help him escape, only to see him mown down by machine gun fire as Russian troops advance.

In the ensuing battle, Stransky shows his true colours. And they're all shades of yellow. Steiner, meanwhile, is injured. He regains consciousness in a military hospital miles away from the line. Plagued by hallucinations, his recovery is slow, but he is comforted by the attentions of Eva (Senta Berger), a sympathetic nurse. However, when he is reunited with Schnurrbart (who has a minor leg injury) only to find that his friend is being returned to active duty, Steiner opts to accompany him back.

Things have worsened at the lines – the Russian bombardment is heavier, there is a new face in the platoon (Zoll – seconded from the SS), and Stransky is set on inveigling Steiner's corroboration of a falsified report suggesting he (Stransky) led an heroic counterattack. Steiner, knowing how desperately his superior wants the Iron Cross, refuses. Brandt, himself mistrustful of Stransky, offers Steiner the opportunity to get even with the Prussian by testifying against him before a court of honour. Steiner enrages Brandt by again refusing.

Events are curtailed as the Russians make a massive push, their tanks ploughing through the German outposts. Steiner and his platoon are driven deep into the Russian countryside. Keeping away from roads and doing their best to avoid patrols, they try to make it back to their unit. Coming across a farmhouse a group of Russian women soldiers are using as a billet, Steiner uses the opportunity to take their uniforms, a ploy that will make their progress through enemy territory easier. The animalism displayed by some of his men repulses him, particularly that of Zoll, who physically assaults one of the women before forcing her to administer fellatio. Alerted by the screams when she inflicts a bite wound during the process, Steiner leaves Zoll to the women, telling them 'Now we're even.' Their retribution is swift and bloody.

Using the uniforms to gain entry to a Russian trench, they open fire, capturing the position through the element of surprise. Salvaging a radio, they send a morse code message to Brandt's headquarters, advising him of their intent to cross no-man's-land at dawn. They signal the correct password and request a holding of fire until they are safely across.

The transmission is intercepted by Stransky, who orders his adjutant Trieberg to station himself in the machine gun post and personally oversee the obliteration of Steiner and his men. Trieberg, who is being blackmailed by Stransky over his homosexuality, dare not do otherwise.

Steiner's platoon make the hazardous crossing, many of them cut to shreds as the machine guns open fire. Only when one of the gunners realizes what is happening and defies Trieberg's orders, does Steiner have a chance to make it to safety. He gets Trieberg at gunpoint. Trieberg confesses. Steiner empties his gun into him, then goes looking for Stransky.

The film ends with the final, overwhelming stage of the Russian advance. The German encampment is systematically blow to pieces as Steiner tracks down his nemesis and forces him to walk out into the thick of the battle. Stransky is finally proved an incompetent coward, incapable even of reloading his weapon, and Steiner's derisive laughter rises above the din as annihilation closes in on them.

Is the film about rivalry? Rivalry is when two people want the same thing. Stransky wants the Iron Cross, but Steiner already has one. Nor does Steiner use it as a means of one-upmanship. In fact, he devalues it.

> Steiner: Why do you want it so badly? It's just a piece of worthless metal. Look.
> Stransky: It's not worthless to me.
> Steiner: Why is it so important to you? Tell me, Captain, why?
> Stransky: Sergeant, if I go back without the Iron Cross, I couldn't face my family.

Nonetheless, it is easy to see why Stransky is incensed, not only in making such a pathetic admission, but at Steiner's disrespectful tossing of the medal across the Captain's desk during the exchange. It is a virtual replay of an earlier scene where Stransky, newly arrived, puts on airs and graces for the benefit of Brandt.

> Brandt: Why did you ask to be relieved from duty in France?
> Stransky: I want to get the Iron Cross.
> Brandt: We can give you one of mine.

*Colonel Brandt and
Captain Kiesel.*

Stransky tries to laugh it off but *ach mein Gött*, does it upset him!

The key to Stransky's character is in the ambivalence in which he regards the titular medal – that something so sacrosanct, so yearned after for its own sake, should at the same time be so symbolic of nothing. As a German – moreover, a Nazi – emblem, what it represents is antithetical to Stransky's views on the Reich.

> Steiner: Didn't your Führer say that all class distinctions were to be abolished?
> Stranksy: I am an officer of the Wehrmacht! I have never been a Party member.
>   I'm a Prussian aristocrat and I don't want to be put into the same category.
> Steiner: We agree for once.

Steiner's use of '*your* Führer' indicates that he, too, doesn't care for the goose-steppers back in Berlin. In a speech he makes after first meeting Stransky, Kiesel refers sarcastically to 'the purity of the Great German Wehrmacht itself'. That Brandt, as his commanding officer, does not reprimand him speaks for itself. For all his omnipresence in the credits, no one gives a damn about old Adolf. In fact, the opposing sides come to look very similar in the mud and blood of battle: men in grey uniforms readying themselves for death.

No, what *Cross of Iron* is about – as Steiner proves when he quotes the party line that so infuriates Stranksy – is class. The dialogue leading up to Stransky's outburst centres round his attempt to coerce Steiner into supporting his bid for the Iron Cross. Newly returned from the hospital, he is wooed by Stransky, who tells him 'we are glad to have you back'. Steiner is unimpressed. Stransky offers wine – 'a Moscatel', he says airily, pouring a dainty thimbleful for himself. Steiner reacts by taking a hefty slug directly from the bottle as if he were downing a stein of beer. This is too much for the Captain's sensibilities and he feels obliged to put Steiner in his place.

> Stransky: But still remember that in civilian, as well as in military life, a distinction is made between people.
> Steiner: Is that what you meant when you said that all you are, and may become, is dependent upon this present company?
> Stransky: Well, the difference is a matter of ethical and intellectual superiority which is caused, whether you like it or not, by blood and by class differences.

Like a lawyer latching onto an inconsistency in a witness's testimony, Steiner delivers a well-timed riposte, reminding him of the humble origins of Immanuel Kant and Franz Schubert. 'They were exceptions,' Stransky snaps; 'we are talking about general concepts, not individuals.'

But I am one,' Steiner replies. 'And so are you. Didn't your Führer say that all class distinctions were to be abolished?'

This exchange moves *Cross of Iron* so far from the conventions and audience expectations of the war film as to strip away all the trappings of the genre. The concept of 'sides' – of who is fighting to establish tyranny and domination, and who to safeguard freedom and democracy – is lost. The 'us and them' attitude that separates enlisted men from officers, a potent theme in court martial dramas such as Stanley Kubrick's *Paths of Glory* and Joseph Losey's *King and Country*, is expanded beyond the military hierarchy to incorporate philosophy, aesthetics and individualism. And even though Kant and Schubert were German, the question of nationality is subverted to one of personal identity.

Another ground-breaking conversation, which not only sees Brandt in acceptance of Germany's defeat but looking past it in the hope of a more enlightened age, comes towards the end when he arranges for Kiesel's evacuation:

> Brandt: For many of us Germans, the exterminator is long overdue. But I have decided that you are worth saving.
> Kiesel: But I'm part of all this. There's better people than me.
> Brandt: There's nothing wrong with you, except that you smoke too much. You're a brave man, braver than you think. One day there will be a need for brave civilians. In the new Germany, if such a thing is allowed to exist, there will be a need for builders, for thinkers, for poets. I begin to see now what your job is to be ... You will seek out and contact these 'better people' ...

In the hands of many directors, a speech of this ilk would be made to a rousing score. There would be screen-filling close-ups of the two leads, hope and tears in their eyes. The effect would be sentimental, appalling. Not Peckinpah, though. He keeps the visuals grim throughout. Artillery pounds the encampment; explosions scatter chunks of masonry; even as Brandt speaks of poets, a line of men are cut down by tracer fire. We see Peckinpah at his most nakedly human, showing hope and world-weary cynicism melded into each other, struggling, trying to maintain a balance. There is no room here for anything watered-down, no shying away from reality. Peckinpah has the intellect and the emotional capacity to consider the nature of war in the way it should be considered: seriously.

The film is also a technical *tour de force*. Peckinpah's trademarks are all in place: slow motion (Steiner hurling a grenade at a Russian tank in purposeless defiance; his killing of Trieberg, spent casings ejecting from his machine gun in an arc that is strangely graceful); flashbacks (to key moments with now-dead platoon members as he pulls the trigger on Trieberg); mirrors (Stransky finds about out Trieberg's sexual predilections when, gazing lovingly at himself in the mirror, he catches sight of

Trieberg feeling up a young soldier); freeze-frames (during the credits and, as we shall see, in the closing scene); and blood squibs. Lots of blood squibs. *Cross of Iron* is easily Peckinpah's bloodiest film. Never mind that *The Wild Bunch, Straw Dogs* and *Bring Me the Head of Alfredo Garcia* are routinely berated for violent content, the violence in them occurs as isolated acts. There are calm, introspective – even nostalgic – moments between the roaring of guns. In *Cross of Iron*, violence is continual: every conversation, every briefing, every verbal stand off between Steiner and Stransky takes place to a backdrop of artillery fire. The characters cringe as shells drop ever closer, duck as the wooden posts that stanchion dugouts and bunkers are shook by the blast. The dead are everywhere: face down, heads still pumping blood into shell craters filled with muddy water; decomposing and rolled over by half-tracks; stretched out on barbed wire. With the exception of the hospital, every building in which the troops take shelter is derelict or bombed out, its walls (such as is left of them) pocked with bullet holes. During Steiner and his platoon's retreat, the abandoned industrial buildings through which they flee are destroyed completely as the pursuing tanks plough through them.

Even at the hospital, there is no relief from visceral imagery. Peckinpah here concentrates on the aftermath. In an unforgettable scene, a visiting officer of high rank walks from patient to patient, shaking hands, wishing them a speedy recovery (the better to be sent back to the lines). Thrusting out his hand to one wheelchair-bound individual, a stump is proferred in return. The officer extends his left hand instead. Another stump. A look of revulsion on his face, the officer draws back his hand. The patient brings his leg sharply and defiantly up, a gruesome parody of the Nazi salute as well as an indication of how much he'd like to kick the be-medalled bigwig in the balls.

Steiner's transition from battle to slow recovery is showcased in a display of editing techniques that goes one step further than anything on display in *The Wild Bunch* and *Pat Garrett and Billy the Kid*. Where the westerns utilize different film speeds and cross-cutting to emphasize and elongate the moment of death, showing us in human terms the terrible cost of pulling the trigger, the editing in *Cross of Iron* creates a dissonance which allows its director to move from the literal violence of the battlefield to a more disturbing landscape, and one that is considerably harder to capture on film. Peckinpah's concern here is psychological damage, the violence of a mind turning inwards on itself, rational perception fragmented by trauma.

A succession of images, delivered with the speed of a cardsharp dealing a hand, challenge the retina and seem to stamp themselves, almost subliminally, upon the mind. There are scenes of battle shot with documentary-style realism; surreal effects whereby the explosions resemble fireworks bursting across the sky; point of view shots (a close-up of muzzle flash is replaced by the pencil beam of a nurse's torch being shone into Steiner's eye); hallucinations (Steiner sees himself, his head bandaged, running alongside a lake – then throws himself in as the young Russian boy watches from the banks); flashbacks (an impromptu birthday celebration held for Lieutenant Meier earlier in the film). The clamour of battle ebbs to silence. 'Look at me,' the nurse instructs. 'Follow the light. Look at me.' These few words say everything about the nature of her brief relationship with Steiner. More subtext is added as she enters Steiner's hallucination, dragging him from the lake even as he struggles to his feet, revealing the water to be no deeper than a few inches.

Eva's importance is reinforced when the top brass come visiting, whipping up morale in order that they can have 'sixty-five per cent of these men returned to active duty in three days'. In between the ranking officer's encounter with the man whose arms are stumps, and a telling moment when he notices Steiner's Iron Cross and refrains from shaking hands with him (proving that class-related pettiness does not begin and end with Stransky), Steiner experiences more hallucinations. The crowded vista of patients assembled as if on parade, the officers reviewing them while an ensemble play light music more suited to a tea-room, is replaced, as Steiner rises from his wheelchair and

*Psychological
portraiture: Steiner
hospitalized.*

pushes his way forward, by a deserted terrace. He turns and sees himself, still in the
wheelchair, Eva behind him. At the height of his confusion, it is Eva who leads him back.
Shortly afterwards, as the officers congregrate around tables laid with immaculate white
clothes and stacked with food and wine in their honour, Steiner rises once more and goes
on a stumbling rampage, sweeping crockery to the ground and gathering bottles only to
let them drop. Again, it is Eva who placates him, Eva – and only she – who shows any
degree of care or humanity.

   Guilt at the boy's death; renewed hatred of officers; affront to his concept of
masculinity that he is reliant on the help of a woman; the realization that he is not in deep
water – for all that his life (or the last few days thereof) is flashing before his eyes, he is
not going to die – these notions might all contribute to the maelstrom in Steiner's mind.
Something has to give.

   That Steiner's hospital sojourn is psychological portraiture is obvious, but is it mental,
physical, or nervous breakdown? Take your pick. However one chooses to analyze the
sequence, it communicates the one truism of conflict that most film-makers brought
down to the level of cliché but which Peckinpah revitalized: war is hell.

Steiner's return to the front is another example of how far removed a Sam Peckinpah
film is from the mainstream. In an *über*-budgeted production, a tame director doing
what he's told by a strong-willed and marketing-obsessed producer, this would be a
hugely overwrought scene, with plenty of jaw-clenching from the sergeant and
trembling lower lip on the nurse's part. There would be a big speech about how he'd be
letting his men down if he stayed where it was nice and safe, miles from the fighting,
in the arms of an attractive woman ... The kind of scene, in short, that would have all
right-thinking members of the audience wondering what was wrong with him.
Peckinpah, however, stages it with restraint. Steiner has very little dialogue. It is his
silences which communicate.

Steiner: I'm going back.

Eva: I thought you were going back home.

Steiner: I have no home.

Eva: My home. Our home. [Steiner does not respond.] Do you love the war so much? [He starts to leave.] Is that what's wrong with you, Steiner? Why are you afraid of what you will do without it?

In essence, Peckinpah simply has Steiner walk out on a good thing (and let's face it, there were plenty of soldiers in wartime who resorted to self-inflicted wounds just to get away from the madness, let alone enjoy a dalliance with Senta Berger), and climb into a truck alongside Schnurrbart with only the briefest glance up at the window of the room he was, just minutes before, sharing with Eva.

But still, in the face of such self-denial, the question has to be asked: what manner of man is Sergeant Steiner? In a nutshell, a bloody contradictory one! Consider him in his own words:

'Nothing we haven't seen before.' (On discovering the bodies of Russian soldiers who are barely in their teens.)

'Just bring what you need to kill with.' (Instruction to one of his men before setting out on a reconnaisance.)

'Bullets, mortar fire, artillery salvoes, bad luck, syphilis. The usual things.' (Asked how some of his platoon were killed.)

'I believe God is a sadist but probably doesn't even know it.' (Replying to a question about his religious beliefs.)

'Do you think that because you and Colonel Brandt are more enlightened than many officers I hate you any less?' (To Kiesel and Brandt, in the face of everything they have done for him.)

Now weigh all that against his words to the young Russian boy, shortly before the latter is shot by his own countrymen: 'It's all an accident. An accident of hands – mine, others – all without mind. One extreme to another, and neither works, or will ever. Here we stand in the middle, in no-man's-land, you and I. Go! Go home.' And weigh it against his scream of agony, remorse and disbelief as he sees the child die in front of him.

Like Pike Bishop, he can be cold-hearted when he has to – yet take us by surprise with occasional glimpses of vulnerability, of humanity. Perhaps the real truth of Steiner – and this would explain why the film was so reviled upon its release and is still misunderstood by many today – is that he holds up a mirror to men and lets us see ourselves in all our contradictory, distorted and despairing glory.

And, as much as any other character in the director's filmography, he represents Peckinpah: iconoclastic, loyal only to those who work *with* him, fighting his own (almost indefinable) war even as the odds stockpile into something insurmountable. This is most evident in his dealings with officers and authority figures. He makes things harder for himself than they have to be in order to score points off Stranksy. Introduced to SS man Zoll, he acts in a deliberately provocative manner ('I hope you've memorized our serial numbers, our mothers' maiden names correctly,' he sneers; 'I wouldn't want the Gestapo to come and arrest the wrong man, woman and child.') And – in a scene that could almost be autobiographical (just substitute 'producer' for 'officer') – he turns down the opportunity to betray Stransky because it would mean beholding himself to another officer.

Self-denial or self-destructiveness? Nietzsche wrote, 'under conditions of peace, the warlike man attacks himself.' Peckinpah was a man who needed something to fight. And he understood that, deep inside, no matter how we try to deny it, most of us have this need. It is what makes us who we are. It is – paradoxically – the thing that keeps us alive ... and the thing that destroys us.

Peckinpah made films about men. All are honest, showing that weakness and the capacity for violence spring from the same place (David Sumner in *Straw Dogs* and

Bennie in *Bring Me the Head of Alfredo Garcia* are cases in point). Most suggest that, internal tensions notwithstanding, partnerships are preferable to going it alone. And even when former partners find themselves set apart, a certain code of honour still applies. *Cross of Iron* conforms to much of the Peckinpah aesthetic (Steiner's only loyalty is to his platoon and screw anybody wearing epaulettes), but differs in that the Steiner-Stransky opposition is not the reversal, brought about by a convergence of circumstances, of a former partnership. It is also – perhaps even more so than *Straw Dogs* – brutal, unflinching, and unforgiving in its depiction of masculinity.

The most contentious part of *Cross of Iron* is the encounter with the women at the farmhouse. Chickens peck the dirt outside, recalling images of *Ride the High Country* and *Pat Garrett and Billy the Kid*. But while the women in these films (with the exception of Mariette Hartley's reluctant bride) are whores, the women bivouac'd here are soldiers. That they are captured with such ease by Steiner's men (who have just secured a nearby river bridge with the same wordless efficiency that characterizes the Bunch's train robbery) is insult enough; that some of the men, demonstrating their most bestial tendencies, treat them like whores is an affront.

The situation starts to get out of hand even outside the farmhouse. One of the women is bathing in a wooden barrel, into which the leering Maag climbs. His unhealthy attentions are curtailed only when Steiner, checking on his whereabouts, drags him out by the hair. Steiner's instruction to 'pick up your weapon' has a double meaning which allows a brief touch of humour and a sigh of relief from audiences anticipating a sort of *Straw Dogski*.

Not that Peckinpah lets his characters or audience off the hook that easily. The pressure-cooker atmosphere inside the building is not helped by Steiner's command to the women that they surrender their uniforms. Their attempt to turn the indignity round by giving a jeering burst of applause to a teenage platoon member as he strips off his German uniform to don one of theirs further exacerbates things. When Kruger fires his machine gun into the rafters, yelling 'Stop your fuck-silly games!' it is a visualization of the control under which Steiner tries to rein them. But for all Steiner's loyalty to his men and theirs to him, for all the archetypal scenes of camaraderie, the group threatens to disintegrate at this point. It is comparable to Judd and Westrum falling out over the gold or the Bunch at stand off over a few bags of washers. Primal urges replace codes of loyalty and honour. They are in danger of no longer being a unit, a bunch; instead, they resemble David Sumner – the loner, the little man – reasserting their masculinity through brutality, and becoming dehumanized as a result.

Their loss of group identity is mirrored by the women in their brief, and ultimately unsuccessful, attempt to manipulate their captors. They share glances of wordless communication. There is a dynamic between them, an understanding. One puts herself in harm's way by distracting Zoll, knowing he will drag her off (an act not dissimilar to Angel 'playing his string out right to the end' so that Dutch can ride unharmed out of Mapache's camp); Zoll's absence makes it possible for the other women to overpower the teenager, seduction turning to stabbing. The woman who administers the knife blow sobs even as she takes his life. Amazingly, when Steiner returns and regains control of the situation, the youth's last words to him are 'Don't hurt the girl.'

Steiner finally re-establishes his authority after Zoll's victim responds, mid blow-job, with a DIY castration; he herds the Russians into the same room as Zoll and leaves him to them. As Steiner's troops move out, the women close in on Zoll. It is a fitting retribution – justice at its most basic – and there's no denying that Zoll deserves all he gets. But the question remains: does Steiner act out of expiation, or because it allows him to have rid of an SS man – someone, in other words, who represents the system?

Because, as previously noted, *Cross of Iron* is concerned with class. It could even be said to illustrate how class resentment is not just maintained during times of war, but brought perversely to the fore. Throughout, officers are shown in the worst possible light: the first thing Stransky does on arrival at the lines is to urinate openly on the ground; Trieberg's homosexuality is contrasted with Stransky's self-love; Stransky uses blackmail, flattery, deceit and rank-pulling to serve his ends instead of ever once acting like a man; when the bigwig at the hospital places himself at the head of the buffet table and gives an order to dig in, it is his staff who crowd forward, while the patients hold their positions; Trieberg, staring down the barrel of Steiner's semi-automatic, whimpers pitifully, blaming everything on Stransky and refusing to admit his own complicity; Stransky is seen to fall on his ass during the first battle and the last. Even Brandt and Kiesel are shown as a weary old man and a dissipated cynic respectively. (The louche manner in which Kiesel departs after Brandt's 'you are worth saving' speech makes one wonder about the Colonel's judgement.) A framed and mounted picture of the Führer – a visual symbol of the ultimate authority figure – is blown clean off a wall during shelling.

Peckinpah's most explicit indication of this theme is in the choice of code word as Steiner and company warily traverse the shelled-out, barbed-wire-draped no-man's-land.

'Demarcation!' they call as they draw within sight of their lines, most of them dressed in Russian uniforms, hands clasped behind their heads, their return as survivors recast in images of surrender and defeat. 'Demarcation! Steiner's coming in! Demarcation!'

Demarcation: a marking of the limits, a setting apart of things. Even Trieberg remarks upon the pertinence of the word. The awful, apocalyptic hail of bullets that follows seems all the more inevitable for the use of it.

The synthesis of *Cross of Iron*'s twin themes comes in the exchange of dialogue between Steiner and Stranksy at the end. Their confrontation comes when they are alone (literally and metaphorically – Stransky has fallen from grace with Brandt and his adjutant Trieberg is dead; Steiner has ordered the few who remain of his platoon to go on without him). Stransky tries to pull rank, but such trappings have ceased to apply.

> Stranksy: Where's the rest of your platoon? [Steiner does not respond.] I said where's the rest of your platoon, Sergeant Steiner?
> Steiner: You are, Captain Stransky. *You* are the rest of my platoon.

Their last two lines summarize and set the seal on the film's aesthetic as surely as the closing couplet of a sonnet. Steiner forces Stransky to arm himself while the *götterdämmerung* rages outside [1]. Stransky, although his ineptitude seconds later will give the lie to his bravado, accepts the inevitable.

> Stransky: I'll show you how a Prussian officer can fight.
> Steiner: And I will show you where the Iron Crosses grow. [2]

They go out into the thick of it. The Russian advance has been stepped up, aerial attacks supplementing the bombardment. Trucks pull away as buildings explode behind them; men clamber out of trenches (the certain death of going over the top indicating that nothing has changed from the First World War to the Second); others are blasted out from behind sandbags (no safety in shelter). Brandt, too, walks out into the fray, firing wildly, ready to get it over with. Freeze-frame. Children's voices join in song on the soundtrack as in the opening credits. Motion resumes, Steiner and Stransky make their way through a railway marshalling yard, wagons derailed and burning. Stranksy fires one round, then panics. 'How do I reload?' he wails, the final and absolute proof of his incompetence. Steiner's response is laughter. Like Sykes and Thornton, laughing even as they accept that things ain't the way they used to be, it is this sound that rises above the gunfire, and is still audible over the sombre black-and-white photographs of wartime indignity which punctuate the closing credits.

The most profound – and surreal – aspect of *Cross of Iron*'s conclusion (not so much a final act as a last stand, though even that makes it sound inappropriately heroic) comes when the young Russian boy reappears, armed with a machine gun, to fire off a few

Divided by class: Captain Stransky and Sergeant Steiner.

rounds at the cowering Stranksy. Steiner's last hallucination? A comment by Peckinpah on how the lessons learned by one generation are ridden over roughshod by the next, that for the countless young men who forfeited their lives in the Second World War, so many more would die a couple of decades down the line in Vietnam?

Both are valid interpretations, but there is also the subtext of innocence lost. The children in *The Wild Bunch* who prod scorpions into anthills then burn the lot; the children in *Pat Garrett and Billy the Kid* who lark around with a noose as if it were a swing and watch, impressed, as men practice with their guns and cheat at duels; the child in *The Getaway* who squirts Doc McCoy with a water pistol then shops him to the police ... all are on the verge of beginning their journey towards adulthood down a road of lessons wrongly learned.

The boy in *Cross of Iron* again embodies Peckinpah's concerns about the formative experiences of childhood, but also marks a fuller development of this theme, moving beyond being a figure that is merely cautionary to one that is genuinely tragic. When Steiner turns him loose and, in the hesitant speech he offers, tries to set him on the proper path ('go home' Steiner says emphatically), the lad turns and throws his harmonica to the sergeant. He is so close at this point – close to escape; close to a reaffirmation of his national and cultural identity (Steiner has already divested him of the German uniform Schnurrbart has dressed him in); and, in the giving of this gift, close to an understanding of the concepts of honour, friendship and reciprocation that Peckinpah's mature characters aspire to (even if they do fall short). Then – cruelly and needlessly – he is gunned down by his own countrymen.

Now, reappearing, he has a gun in his hands, not a harmonica. And it doesn't seem to matter anymore which uniform he is wearing. Childhood has been betrayed, innocence destroyed, the lesson gone unlearned. His reappearance is also a sort of rebirth. Still young, but too experienced to return to the things of childhood, he is a man-child. These are the most dangerous of Peckinpah's characters, ranging from the cherub-faced boy hoisting a rifle to shoot Pike (a man-*child* because he commits the darkest act of adulthood – taking a life – while still young in years) to 'Crazy' Lee (a *man*-child because his age belies his mentality), or Henry Niles (in whose adult actions and childlike incomprehensibility of their repercussions, both aspects find their volatile fusion). Each of these characters effects or incites a terrible event. The boy delivers the *coup de grace* to Pike; 'Crazy' Lee kills a group of hostages, alerting bounty hunters to his presence; Niles's accidental killing of Janice is the impetus for Venner and his cronies to lay siege to David Sumner's property, which in turn causes David to take up arms.

These considerations of birth, death (literal and in the sense of innocence lost) and gut-wrenching inevitability are brought together in *Cross of Iron*'s final credit, a quote from Brecht:

> Don't rejoice in his defeat, you men.
> For though the world stood up and stopped the bastard
> The bitch that bore him is in heat again.

Cross of Iron was Sam Peckinpah's last great film and is possibly his most despairing.

CHAPTER SIX
THE LATER FILMS

All directors have made underwhelming films. Sometimes it's due to youthful inexperience or budgetary constraints. Sometimes it's a case of burn out. With Peckinpah, he made a handful of substandard pictures rather than not make films at all. Towards the end of his life, an epic drug problem dragging him down, he found himself with fewer and fewer choices. He had fought running battles with studios, leaving a trail of inflated budgets, box office losses and disaffected producers scattered in his wake.

In his last nine years, he made only four films. *Cross of Iron* saw the maverick fire off his last brilliant salvo. The other three were made because they were the only jobs he could get.

Having said that, Peckinpah does seem a strange choice of director for *The Killer Elite* and *The Osterman Weekend*. Generally Peckinpah's films tell simple stories, made complex by subtext and characterization: they are about groups of men reaching the end of the line (outlaws in Mexico in *The Wild Bunch*; German troops at the Russian front in *Cross of Iron*), former partners on opposing sides of the law (*Ride the High Country, The Wild Bunch, Pat Garrett and Billy the Kid*), flawed men doing bad things for money (robbery in *Ride the High Country, The Wild Bunch* and *The Getaway*; licensed bounty-killing in *Pat Garrett and Billy the Kid*; grave-robbing in *Bring Me the Head of Alfredo Garcia*) and the need for escape (*The Wild Bunch, The Getaway*). They are about camaraderie (the westerns) and the dangers of being a loner (the contemporized westerns). Espionage tales are the antithesis: simple motivations fuel complex plots, the characters merely puppets in the hands of faceless governments. Suspicion, mistrust and duplicity are the watchwords of the spy, not loyalty, friendship and staying with a man once you've sided with him.

It is predominately for this reason – incompatibility with Sam Peckinpah's worldview – that *The Killer Elite* and *The Osterman Weekend* emerge as second-rate. Both are adaptations, and in neither case did Peckinpah have the opportunity to rewrite the script. Nonetheless, there are glimmers of Peckinpah's genius in both, occasional flourishes where the mark of a great director can still be seen – even if they are more like watermarks than hallmarks. These moments make one wonder whether, had the films been helmed by a more journeyman director, they would have garnered some degree of acclaim. Are they only weak because they were made by someone as talented as Sam Peckinpah?

Sadly, nothing as charitable can be said of *Convoy*. Although it would seem (superficially, at least) the more logical choice for a Peckinpah project, the outlaw anti-heroes of the westerns recast as truck drivers banding together in defiance of police persecution, the script is so awful and the finished product so uninspiring that it makes one appreciate how deeply Sam loved being on a film set that he agreed to direct it.

'IT'S NOT A GREAT SHOW' : *The Killer Elite*

If the officers in *Cross of Iron* can be said to represent Peckinpah's hatred of producers, Comteg (the shadowy organization at the heart of *The Killer Elite*) is comically symbolic of studios themselves: run by crotchety old men (i.e. executives, accountants, heads of production), riddled with internal politics (power games); a breeding ground for ill-made decisions, the outcome of which affect the success of men in the field (directors).

Comteg is a privately run secret service, undertaking the sort of black operations the CIA ('Circumcised Italian-Americas' as a Comteg operative mocking calls them) don't want to soil their hands with. Based in San Francisco, the outfit is run by Cap Collins (Arthur Hill) and Lawrence Weyburn (Gig Young). Their top men, friends as well as fellow agents, are Mike Locken (James Caan) and George Hansen (Robert Duvall). The friendship takes a downturn, however, when Hansen sells his services to a higher bidder and shoots a Russian informer he and Locken are supposed to be protecting [1]. This done, he disables Locken with shots to the elbow and knee. Thereafter, he's basically freelance.

Locken's recovery is slow and humiliating. Stairs are a nightmare. He embarrasses himself in a restaurant, falling over and taking half the menu with him. Despite the attentions of his doting girlfriend, who envisages a more domestic future, and the insistence of his bosses that his injuries mean he's out of the game, he perseveres. Physiotherapy gives way to karate training. He wants payback.

The opportunity comes when Weyburn, appearing to be operating independently of Collins, offers him an assignment to safeguard visiting Japanese statesman Yuen Chung (Mako). Chung and his precocious daughter have already survived one assassination attempt on their arrival at the airport. The attack, masterminded by eastern crime boss Negato Toku (whose reign of terror Chung is opposing), is co-ordinated by Hansen. Collins, to whom the CIA has passed on this information, wants nothing to do with it. Weyburn sees the vengeful Locken as the perfect frontman. Lured by the promise of a showdown with Hansen, the deal sweetened by Weyburn's by-your-leave to assemble his own team, Locken agrees.

He enlists the services of sociopath-for-hire Jerome Miller (Bo Hopkins) and retired agent Mac (Burt Young) and they set out to pick up Chung and his daughter. Hansen and a group of Uzi-packing bad boys are waiting for them.

Shoot-out; car chase; the usual.

Unaware that the Collins-Weyburn relationship is rapidly degenerating into mutual distrust, Locken contacts Collins and arranges to borrow his yacht, the quicker to ferry Chung to the arranged rendezvous the next day. They hole up in an abandoned waterfront building for the night, Locken and Mac staking out the yacht, Miller perched like a sniper atop a dockyard crane. Collins, meanwhile, informs Hansen as to Locken's whereabouts.

Chung's daughter, convinced she has the requisite martial arts skills to take care of herself, decides to check out the yacht, much to Locken's displeasure. Her reckless behaviour leads her right into Hansen's hands. Holding her at gunpoint, Hansen converses with Locken. He admits that Collins is party to Toku's plot, reiterates that he's only in it for the money, and suggests that he might be able to negotiate a better deal and cut Locken in. This isn't the showdown Locken was anticipating. He orders Miller and Mac to stand down and is prepared to walk away and leave the Chungs to Hansen. Miller, however, gets the drop on Hansen and shoots him in the back. He is rewarded by a punch in the face from Locken.

Next day, Locken and his little group (the aforementioned altercation seemingly forgotten) arrive at the rendezvous: a mooring area for decommissioned vessels. Rusting hulks of freighters and tankers tower above the yacht. They moor alongside a particularly unsafe-looking ship and climb aboard. Collins is waiting for them, backed up by Toku and an army of ninjas who look like they failed the audition for *You Only Live Twice*. Locken confronts Collins about his treachery. Collins, like Hansen, admits that top dollar is the bottom line – big bucks, highest bidder. Locken shoots the son of a bitch.

Mike Locken and sociopath-for-hire Jerome Miller.

The kung-fu crew stage their attack. Locken, Mac and Miller counter some fancy hand and foot moves with good old-fashioned hot lead. Guess who wins? Miller takes a bullet, but by now enough ninjas have plunged from the ship in slow motion for the battle to be over. Toku resorts to putting in an appearance himself, inviting Chung to settle things *mano-a-mano*. Locken and Mac offer to shoot him and have done with it, but Chung's sense of honour dictates otherwise.

Duel; swordplay; the usual.

Toku bites the dust (or at least the deck). Weyburn turns up. Locken accuses him of knowing Collins's motives from the outset, of setting up the whole violent escapade as a means of settling Comteg's internal power struggle. Weyburn responds by offering him Collins's now vacant position. Locken responds in turn by politely inviting him to shove it. Locken swipes the fifty grand in payoff money Collins had on him (as well as his yacht), and he and Mac sail off beneath the Golden Gate bridge like a nautical version of two old gunslingers riding off into the sunset.

If *The Killer Elite* can loosely be said to centre round a conspiracy (Collins, Hansen and Toku are conspiring against Locken and co., while Weyburn toys with the fate of them all), a similar degree of collusion seemed to occur during filming. The actors are in on it: Caan and Burt Young exchange as many sheepish looks as they do facetious comments, as if to say 'what are we doing here?' Hill and Gig Young mumble their way tiredly through a sequence of supposedly intense scenes, as if to say 'can we go home now?' Duvall punctures an early scene with manic laughter, as if to say 'have you seen the script?' The ninja hijinks seem to say 'enter the sad 'un' rather than *Enter the Dragon*. The composer's in on it, as well. Jerry Fielding underscores major plot points and acts of treachery with lounge jazz so relaxed it could be used as a cure for insomnia.

It hardly needs saying that the two groups who weren't in on it – critics and audiences – pulled off an unspoken *coup d'etat* of their own, ensuring the film flopped. True, it enjoyed the most profitable opening weekend for a Peckinpah film since *The Getaway* but afterwards audiences stayed away in record numbers. In retrospect, it still seems weak – there isn't even the insidious subtext that just about rescues *The Osterman Weekend* from mundanity – but what the critics seem to have missed is the one thing that makes the film watchable: the very disdain Peckinpah has for the material.

Movies about movies are a popular sub-genre. The quality is variable: *The Player* and *In the Soup* are terrific; *The Big Picture* has its moments; *S.O.B.* doesn't bear thinking about. The constant theme is that the internal movies (the cinematic equivalent of the threatrical play-within-a-play) are uniformly awful. With *The Killer Elite*, Peckinpah takes the concept to its logical extreme: instead of making a film about the making of a film that's so excoriatingly derivative that it perfectly encapsulates its producers' delusions, he simply makes the film itself.

The credits sequence is a calling card in parody. The music is overtly melodramatic, the cinematography shadowy and portentous. The setting seems to be a basement. A masonry drill bites into a wall; the hole is plugged with plastic explosive; detonating cord is spooled out from a cable drum; sticks of dynamite are strapped to some pipework; a timer is set; someone splashes petrol across a concrete floor; a torch clicks off. It's the kind of thing that's been done many times before, and is still being done (in increasingly frenetic style – consider the opening of Brian de Palma's 1996 big-screen *Mission: Impossible*). Peckinpah, rather than be derivative and take the pay-cheque, compiles a po-faced checklist of visual clichés, subtly insulting the audience for being undiscerning enough to watch such a dumb action picture. That the main credits are flashed up in absurdly small lettering implies that all involved should be equally ashamed of themselves.

And as the for the director's credit, it's hard to see how much further, short of having his name removed from the film entirely, Peckinpah could have distanced himself. The basement-based montage of booby-trapping ends with a strangely poetic shot of a bird's nest in a dim corner, the adult feeding its young. The words 'directed by' appear alongside. Just those words – no name. Peckinpah then makes seven cuts – to a car pulling up outside; to the fuse burning down; to the timer ticking away; to a long shot of the exterior of the soon-to-be-demolished building, the Comteg agents running out; to a close-up of these agents piling into the car; to the timer seconds away from detonation; to the car speeding away – before returning to the nest and his name appearing, on its own, on the screen. Then the building goes up in flames.

To split the most prestigious credit in a film is remarkable – to insert seven shots in between, and then to detract from it with a display of pyrotechnics, is an act of evasion. *Me?* Peckinpah seems to be saying. *Direct this?*

Marc Norman and Stirling Silliphant's script (from a novel by Robert Rostand) doesn't just serve up clichés at the beginning. They're omnipresent: Miller practices clay-pigeon shooting over the Golden Gate bridge without ever attracting the attention of local law enforcement; Mac, overweight and out of ammunition, beats up highly-trained ninjas; at one moment in the climactic battle, Locken has to steady himself on his cane to squeeze off a shot – the next, gun and cane divested of, he's throwing kung-fu moves like a good 'un. It's all hugely risible, and Peckinpah sends it up at every turn.

Take Locken's discussion with Mac *vis-à-vis* requirements for a car. Locken insists on something heavy and fast. The two men stand in the middle of a garage, Mac wiping grease and oil from his hands with a rag. This is the cue for action thriller aficionados with a penchant for classic cars to anticipate something cool, something that will burn up the road in the inevitable chase scene. Not so. They roll up for the rendezvous with Chung in a drab, utilitarian yellow cab; the only flash car to be seen is on the billboard under which Toku's gunmen crouch during the shoot-out, the image peppered with bullet holes as a burst of fire goes wild.

Deliberately ludicrous kung-fu in The Killer Elite.

Take O'Leary's account of Toku's attack on Chung and his entourage at the airport. Not only is the urgency of the scene deflated by O'Leary's hysterically pointless monologue about his houseplants ('I often read the love sonnets of Elizabeth Barrett Browning to them'), but his bland description of the incident is intercut with flashbacks in which Peckinpah deliberately stages the kung-fu to look as absurd as possible. Martial arts films are usually concerned with speed; editing emphasizes the swiftness of the moves, as does the proliferation on the soundtrack of monosyllabic grunts and cries. Peckinpah, however, uses the slow motion option. Result: the 'chop-socky' seems even more ridiculous.

The full contempt of the director for his material is reserved for the finale. There has been gunfire and hand-to-hand fighting; ninjas have been thrown off ships. Chung appears, ready to face his enemy. Locken berates him for not remaining below deck on the yacht as instructed. But Toku has seen him, and the time has come.

The dialogue speaks for itself:

> Toku: Chung – now!
> Chung: I hear.
> Locken: Now hold it. That's it. He's going to the SFPD. It's over. You got it?
> Chung: Some things you don't talk away. You don't push away. My country grows many like Toku.
> Mac: I'll shoot the guy, Mike.
> Chung: No, please don't. If I don't survive, I'm not the man that's needed.
> Locken: I've never heard so much bullshit in all my life.

Chung and Toku circle each other, swords glinting in the sun. This is the moment where the joking should stop, the dramatic music resume on the soundtrack, and the duel to the death be fought. But Peckinpah does not grant this material even an ounce of solemnity. Locken and Mac's banter undermines the scene.

> Locken: What's with those outfits, anyway?
> Mac: I dunno. Ritual gowns?
> Locken: Goofy lookin' things.

And finally, as Chung and Toku lock swords, Locken delivers the sort of line from which no dramatic scene can possibly recover: 'Lay me seven to five – I'll take the little guy.'

This is the best way to take *The Killer Elite*: purely as comedy. Much of the dialogue is flippant. There's Locken's exchange with Miller, for instance:

> Miller: I don't think your company'd hire me. They've got me tapped as a psycho.
> Locken: Well, they just don't understand you, Miller. You're not a psycho, you're the patron poet of the manic-depressives.

There's Hansen blaming himself for a screw-up: 'There's a credo at the company I forget to remember. Always operate on six key principles: proper planning prevents piss poor performance.'

There's the agent, stuck in front of a surveillance monitor all night, who's guarding the safe house Locken and Hansen take the Russian to: 'We watched some horny ducks on the late infra-red show. Did you ever see a duck making out? It's a good show. It's not a great show, but it's a good show.'

This is actually a reasonable epitaph for the film, if somewhat over-charitable. *The Killer Elite* is a decent show. It's not a good show, but it's a decent show.

'BREAKER ONE-NINE, THIS HERE'S THE DUCK': *Convoy*

Films based on novels are one thing, but a film based on a song? It's not unheard of – Sean Penn's dour but powerful directorial debut *The Indian Runner* is based on the Bruce Springsteen ballad 'Highway Patrolman' – but a song by C W McCall? 'Convoy' is a three and a half minute novelty record about a group of truck drivers led by Rubber Duck who suffer all manner of police harassment as they drive across the United States of America. The lyric doesn't cite any reason for the convoy, just that it keeps growing in size (a group of born-again Christians in a microbus join them at one stage); nor is there any good reason for the police action against them. But then again it's just a catchy tune, not epic narrative poetry, and McCall's only point is to indulge in some CB-speak (the device was at the height of its popularity in the late 1970s) and a bit of anti-establishment sloganeering.

An intelligent CB movie had already been made – Jonathan Demme's *Citizens Band*. The less cerebral crowd-pleasing smash-em-ups *Gumball Rally* and *Smokey and the Bandit* had made big bucks at the box office; *The Cannonball Run* was just around the corner. *Convoy* was inevitable, really: the only surprise was that Peckinpah directed it.

The basic plot, expanded from C W McCall's slice of vinyl, goes like this: Rubber Duck (Kris Kristofferson) and his fellow drivers are routinely harassed by a corrupt traffic cop, Dirty Lyle (Ernest Borgnine), who supplements his wages by taking bribes to waiver bogus speeding offences. The situation comes to a head when Lyle badgers them at a truckstop, his motives spilling over into racism in a tirade directed at black trucker Spider Mike. There is a fight and Lyle is left unconscious and bound with his own handcuffs. Rubber Duck and co. decide it's time to, ahem, haul ass.

Lyle's crusade against them, now a personal vendetta, it reflected in the truckers' solidarity; more and more wagons join the convoy. The Friends of Jesus tag along, as does poor little rich girl Melissa (Ali MacGraw), who is looking for meaning in her life; or for a little rough trade courtesy of a hairy trucker, or something.

Rubber Duck, who is hauling high explosives, heads up the convoy, figuring that his payload will prevent the undue erection of roadblocks. When the media becomes involved, he unwittingly finds himself spokesman for the drivers.

The Governor of New Mexico (Seymour Cassel), whose balliwick the truckers are about to roll on through, sees an opportunity for some valuable re-election publicity. He invites them to discuss their grievances with him, assuring them that facilities will be laid on and their stay in his judiciary will be free of police intervention. He even dreams up a harebrained scheme for a convoy to the White House.

Most of the drivers are in favour of his proposals and the trucks grind to a halt at the designated site. Spider Mike, however, continues on his way – his wife is due to give birth and he wants to tip his load and rejoin her. Of all of them, he is the one with the most to live for – ergo, everything to lose. And before you can say 'innocent victim', Dirty Lyle and some of his Texan law enforcement buddies have arrested young Spider, taken him to the cells, and given him the kind of seeing to that wouldn't be out of place in a James Ellroy novel.

When word of this outrage reaches Rubber Duck, he leaves his second-in-command, the just as ludicrously monickered Pig Pen (Burt Young), to continue the discussions and heads for Texas, intent on freeing Spider Mike, kicking smokey's butt, and writing off as many cars and crashing through as many outbuildings as possible.

This done, and the Governor's political solutions forgotten, the convoy gets back on the road. Dirty Lyle, having somehow insinuated himself into the chain of command, calls in the military; when Rubber Duck thunders towards a toll bridge with no intention of paying the toll, he orders them to open fire. Rubber Duck's rig gets blown into the raging waters below. Cue shocked reactions from his pedal-pumping compatriots and much quivering of the lower lip from Melissa.

Dirty Lyle's racial harrassment of Spider Mike in Convoy.

Cut to Rubber Duck's funeral service, a three-ring circus stage-managed by the Governor. The coffin is driven around an arena on a low-loader. The Friends of Jesus are saying their 'dearly beloved' eulogy. Melissa, still blubbing, climbs up into their microbus only to find a heavily disguised Rubber Duck gloating at having put one over on Lyle. The truckers thumb their noses at the Governor, roaring off with the coffin. Even Lyle sees the funny side, laughing as his former sworn enemies drive away.

If, with *The Killer Elite*, Peckinpah had accepted a more commercial assignment than usual through fear of being offered nothing else to direct if he declined, he must have approached *Convoy* with an even greater sense of desperation. Not only had his previous film, *Cross of Iron*, flopped but he had injected large amounts of his own money into the budget. *Convoy* wasn't just about remaining doggedly behind the camera: this time, Peckinpah needed the money.

It is easy to imagine him beginning work on the project – a director for hire – under a cloud of resentment. Certainly, his drinking and drug abuse escalated on set to such a degree that he was frequently incapacitated. For this reason, *Convoy* is a frustrating film to assess. As a movie, it is recognizable as an example of studio product, designed to cash in on the success of *Smokey and the Bandit* and its ilk (and, as such, achieved its ends – it was a box office smash). But as a Sam Peckinpah movie … well how much of it is his? Between James Coburn's impromptu directing while Peckinpah was unable to and EMI's in-house editing after Sam had walked, it is difficult to divine anything 'Peckinpahesque' about it. True, the camera lingers on some impressive vistas (the highways of the US as a modern wilderness), and there are some effective scenes of trucks framed in long shot against darkening skies. But a true Peckinpah film is about more than just nice visuals.

Media coverage of the convoy.

The characterization and subtext which lift the best of his work into the realms of art are absent here. Rubber Duck and co. are never fleshed out beyond being a bunch of macho guys in T-shirts driving big rigs. For all Peckinpah's indifference to the project, blame for this must be directed towards B W L Norton's screenplay. No less a luminary than Alfred Hitchcock once said that to make a good film you need three things: a great script, a great script, and a great script. Give even the most masterful film-maker something second rate to shoot from, and the result is a severely compromised movie.

The deficiencies of Norton's script echo in every scene. There is no character motivation. Rubber Duck is a bland hero, his position at the head of the convoy seeming accidental (while other drivers use the media coverage to air their complaints about pay and police harassment, the best he can do is shrug and say that they only purpose for the convoy is to keep moving). There are holes in the plot you could (pardon the pun) drive a truck through. Rubber Duck's explosive payroll negates roadblocks and barriers, but doesn't stop him from ramming a jailhouse; Lyle, a humble traffic cop, somehow wields enough authority to lead a platoon of the National Guard; none of the drivers ever stops for diesel.

Quite who we are meant to sympathize with is a mystery. The truckers are cyphers. Their 'handles' (the names by which they refer to one another over the airwaves) are absurd. Their conversation is indecipherable: dialogue such as 'all green and clean', 'what's your twenty?' and 'back 'em down, we got a bear in a plain brown wrapper' leaves one thinking that the video ought to come complete with a Gibberish-to-English dictionary. The Governor, though he acts in accordance with his own political agenda, is the only character who shows any sympathy towards the drivers; nonetheless, he is ridiculed in the finale. Lyle, up to this point, the villain of the piece, joins the truckers in laughing at him.

At best, a slender case can be made for *Convoy* as a modern western. Truck drivers are comparable to cowboys in that theirs is an essentially solitary existence; they take valuable goods across untold miles (trunk routes as opposed to cattle drives) for the benefit of anonymous businessmen; the job is low-paid and the conditions poor. These are not generalizations. Read Graham Coster's *A Thousand Miles From Nowhere*. The lot of the long-distance truck driver has potential for a serious existential movie.

Sadly, *Convoy* is not that movie.

'JUST ANOTHER EPISODE IN THIS WHOLE SNUFF SOAP OPERA':
The Osterman Weekend

Robert Ludlum's tales of manipulation and double-crossing, while entertaining, are formulaic. Ludlum's recipe for a best seller, undeviated from in novel after novel, begins with the title: definite article, name, noun. As in *The Bourne Identity, The Scarlatti Inheritance, The Prometheus Deception*. His plotting is akin to a conspiracy, the typical Ludlum hero peeling away one lie after another until he is faced with a truth that threatens his very existence. The complexities are overlaid with enough action to keep the reader's eye off the ball. The denouements are fast-paced and bloody.

Kudos to Peckinpah that, with a constrictive budget and a script (by Alan Sharp – from a separately credited adaptation by Ian Masters) that reworks the novel until the convolutions are even more befuddled, he could still emerge with a film that turns the paraphernalia of spies – surveillance equipment – upon the spies themselves; a film that portrays as equally guilty the politicians who licence these men, the media vultures who latch on to the tawdry secrets that are uncovered, and – ultimately – the audiences who gorge on such fare. Moreover, he achieves this in just over an hour and a half, and throws in a couple of decent action scenes, too.

The Osterman Weekend doesn't lend itself easily to synopsis, but here goes. Ambitious politician Maxwell Danforth (Burt Lancaster) is determined to smash the Russian spy ring Omega. To this end, he enlists the help of secret agent Lawrence Fassett (John Hurt). An unorthodox operator, driven by his need to avenge the death of his wife at the hands of KGB hit men, Fassett doesn't need asking twice. He compiles surveillance footage that implicates Bernard Osterman (Craig T Nelson), Richard Tremayne (Dennis Hopper) and Joseph Cardone (Chris Sarandon), a TV writer, plastic surgeon, and banker respectively. The three men share a friendship dating back to their college years with John Tanner (Rutger Hauer), host of the controversial TV show 'Face to Face'. Tanner probes current affairs and political scandals, subjecting his guests to harsh questioning live on air. The foursome and their wives meet up once a year for a weekend of drinking and reminiscing: the Osterman weekends of the title (Osterman being the one who instigated the tradition). Tanner is due to host this year's reunion.

Fassett arranges a meeting with Tanner and shows him the evidence he's amassed. Tanner is dubious, but Fassett's allegations are backed up by Danforth. Tanner hesitantly pledges his co-operation, allowing Fassett to rig up surveillance cameras all over his house. Fassett also wants him to help 'turn' one of them (i.e. recruit them as a double agent). Tanner is even less enthusiastic about this, but agrees – on the condition that Danforth appear on his show.

As Fassett and his team install the cameras, Tanner gets cold feet about the involvement of his wife Ali (Meg Foster) and their son Steve. Against Fassett's advice, he drives them to the airport, determined to send them away for the weekend. Agents intercept them and stage a kidnap attempt on Ali and the boy. The timely intervention of Fassett sees the family reunited. Tanner assures Fassett he'll play it his way from now on.

The weekend arrives and Tanner finds it difficult to maintain an act in front of Osterman, Tremayne and Cardone. Old wounds are reopened; bitchiness prevails amongst the womenfolk; and from his command centre, a surveillance vehicle parked at the perimeter of Tanner's property, Fassett gleefully watches the group's gradual disintegration. He manipulates a video of the previous year's celebrations so that the Omega symbol appears on screen. Tanner is out of the room at the time and has no idea that Fassett has just pulled this stunt. When the others confront him, his incomprehension is naturally convincing. Osterman persuades Tremayne and Cardone to let the matter lie.

Next day, however, tempers flare up again. A game of handball in Tanner's swimming pool turns into a bout of macho one-upmanship. Things come to blows when Cardone kicks Tanner's dog. The evening meal is a silent and morose affair. Fassett livens up the proceedings by triggering the television to switch on automatically to a documentary about Switzerland. The innocuous voiceover drones on about international banking. Another verbal stand-off ensues. Tremayne's drug-addict wife Virginia (Helen Shaver) drops a few barbed comments of her own – and is promptly decked by a right-hook from Ali.

The fraught friends all retire to their rooms. A scene looks set to develop between Tanner and Ali, but they are interrupted by Steve's screams. Raiding the fridge for a midnight snack, he has discovered the dog's head on a plate (bring me the head of Fido, anyone?). The others, also perturbed by the commotion, hurry into the kitchen to see what the cause is. Tanner accuses Cardone of perpetrating the atrocity and another bout of fists looks set. Osterman, taking a closer look at the head, realizes that it's only a mock-up. Nonetheless, it's the last straw for Tanner, who tells them he wants all of them gone by the morning.

Leaving Ali to comfort Steve, Tanner heads off to Fassett's surveillance vehicle. Osterman follows. When Fassett admits him, Tanner is shocked by the offhanded way he orders his field agents, who are posted around the property, to terminate Osterman. Tanner tells him he wants out, but Fassett is having none of it. Sinisterly, he tells Tanner to be careful on his way back to the house – he could easily be mistaken for Osterman.

Osterman, however, has proved himself adept at dealing with one of the field agents, using his karate skills to disable the gunman. Tanner makes it back more through luck than judgement.

Meanwhile, threatened with the unwelcome attentions of Tremayne and Cardone, Ali and the boy have fled the house. Ali arms herself with a crossbow stored at the pool house and takes to the woodland surrounding the property.

Tanner confronts Osterman and they fight. Osterman overpowers Tanner, but instead of killing him forces him to listen to his side of the story. Osterman, Tremayne and Cardone are guilty of little more than tax evasion and undeclared income. Fassett, still in control of all the cameras, video and televisual equipment in the house, treats Tanner and Osterman to some footage of Tremayne and Cardone and their wives trying to escape in Tanner's mobile home. Fassett sets off an explosive device, which destroys the vehicle.

Field agents enter the house, intent on terminating Tanner and Osterman. They fight them off and flee to the pool house, unaware that Ali has already taken the crossbow. The two men are unable to arm themselves. Forced to dive into the pool as bullets explode around them, Fassett orders his men to pour gasoline on the water and light it. From the cover of the woods, Ali kills two agents with the crossbow, but Fassett takes Steve hostage and forces her to surrender the weapon. Still, her actions save Tanner and Osterman.

Again using the video link-up, Fassett finally reveals his hidden agenda: he wants to be patched in from his own makeshift studio when Tanner interviews Danforth live on air. Fassett has discovered that it was Danforth who ordered the assassination of his wife and intends to take his revenge by publicly charging him with her murder.

Tanner enlists fellow TV professional Osterman to engineer the show. With Danforth also appearing via video link-up, Tanner is able to pre-record his segment of the programme. When Fassett goes on air, he is under the impression that Tanner's questions are part of the live broadcast. What he does not know is that a helicopter outfitted with a tracking device is circling over the city. As he and Danforth bicker on air, Tanner touches down at his dockside hideout, bursts in and confronts him. Fassett raises his gun but is too slow – Tanner has no compunction about shooting him dead.

Tanner and Osterman go hand to hand in The Osterman Weekend.

Danforth, broadcasting live from his office, can only gape in wordless horror as his political ambitions go down in flames.

There is only one innocent in *The Osterman Weekend*: Fassett's wife. Her murder is shown in the form of a surveillance tape in the opening scene. The editing, however, and the multiplicity of camera angles are far removed from your average CCTV footage. It has, instead, the look of a 'mini-movie'. The murder is preceded by an act of love-making between Mr and Mrs Fassett. Already Peckinpah is giving the unnecessarily complicated narrative short shrift and concentrating instead on questions of perception, the manipulation of visual images, and the complicity of an audience in the acts they see on screen.

Quite why Danforth has Fassett's wife taken out is never explained. There is a reference to her being employed at the Polish embassy, but even at the height of the Cold War, when the Red Menace was the faceless villain of every espionage thriller produced, surely even the least discerning movie-goer would have found such motivation flimsy. The only other explanation is that a contented, romantically requited Fassett would be of no use to the Red-bashing Danforth, so he had his best agent's beloved bumped off just to keep him on his toes. Although no less hackneyed and melodramatic, this interpretation does at least reveal another subtextual theme: obsession.

Danforth is so obsessed with hunting the 'goddamn pinkos' that he's willing to destroy the lives of his own men. Fassett is so obsessed with getting revenge that he's willing to set up four strangers. Osterman, Tremayne and Cardone are so obsessed with money that they play right into Fassett's hands by holding 'secret' meetings and behaving suspiciously. Tanner is so obsessed with the truth (or at least a version of it conducive to high ratings) that he can be easily manipulated.

With Mrs Fassett cruelly terminated in the opening frames, there is no one to sympathize with. Tanner is nominally the hero because he has a family to protect. Tremayne and Cardone are married, but their wives are junkies and sex objects respectively. Osterman turns up for the reunion alone, his predilection for close-contact physical sports and his Village People moustache inviting none-too-subtle questions about his preferences.

Not that Tanner is much of a hero. He can barely hold his own against Cardone in the pool fight. Osterman proves to be superior when they go one on one. When he and Osterman are trapped in the pool, they only manage to tackle one gunman between them. It's left to Ali, ghosting through the trees like an avenging angel, crossbow at the ready, to even the odds. Not that she is allowed to become too heroic. Fassett soon forces her hand; her and Steve's incarceration sets up the vengeful finale.

Of course, close analysis of espionage films is anathema. The characters emerge as cardboard cut outs. The plot twists, unravelled and ironed out, reveal more holes than a lump of gruyère. A first viewing of *The Osterman Weekend* induces head-scratching at just how much the script leaves implicit. A second induces even more befuddlement at the discrepancies arising from these implications. Consider the following:

(1) Who is behind the kidnap attempt on Tanner's family? Not Omega, surely – if they were aware of Tanner's alliance with Fassett, all they'd have to do is warn Osterman, Tremayne and Cardone against attending the reunion. (This would save on manpower and not leave them open to counteraction by Fassett.) The implication is that it's Fassett's doing, to persuade Tanner to go along with the original plan. But Tanner announces he's sending his family away at the last minute, literally mentioning it to Fassett as they drive off to the airport. The staged kidnapping is remarkably elaborate, involving several vehicles, the intervention of Fassett's helicopter and the 'gunning down' of an agent – something that could hardly have been organized at a moment's notice.

(2) Who plants the mock-up of the dog's head in the fridge? Not Cardone, no matter how angry he is at Tanner – where would he get such a convincing prop at short notice? Again, the implication is that Fassett has done it. (The dog is later revealed to be alive and well inside Fassett's surveillance truck.) But the question remains, why does he do it? At this point, Tanner is still under the impression that Fassett is kosher. Surely such blatant provocation would make him question Fassett's role in the operation?

(3) Why does Fassett order Tanner's termination along with Osterman when the purpose of the whole elaborate set-up is to strong-arm Tanner into giving over his TV show as a platform for Fassett to make his accusation against Danforth? With Tanner dead, he'd be back to square one.

(4) What is all this Omega business anyway? When Fassett's motive is revealed at the end of the film, one of Danforth's aides asks 'Why did he try to make us believe Omega existed?' 'The existence of Omega,' Danforth quixotically replies, 'has never been disproved. Omega is as real as we need it to be.' So if Omega is the invention of Fassett, why do Osterman, Tremayne and Cardone freak out when they see an Omega logo on a video, and why does Tremayne receive a communication written on Omega letterhead stationery? Or is Omega just the name of a Swiss bank – and if so, why has no one in the entire intelligence agency brought the fact to Danforth's attention and saved him the trouble of investigating a spy ring that doesn't exist?

Had Peckinpah been able to rewrite the script, maybe these questions would have been answered – or, more likely (and better still), the plot streamlined and all peripheral distractions excised. But the producers, Peter S Davies and William N Panzer, hired him for one reason only: his proficiency with action scenes.

On completion of *The Osterman Weekend*, Peckinpah would grumble that he had just made his first exploitation movie. Harsh self-criticism, but his state of mind is understandable. (Watch *The Osterman Weekend* back to back with *The Wild Bunch*, multiply the sour feeling by a thousand and throw in a decade-long hangover to boot ...

Burt Lancaster as the quixotic Danforth with Sam Peckinpah on the set of The Osterman Weekend.

you get the picture?) The truth is, *The Osterman Weekend* is too well-crafted to be just another exploitation thriller; but still, there are elements of the film that would, had it been made today, mark it out as a direct-to-video quickie. The locations are strictly bargain-basement: Danforth's office (desk, three chairs, some panelling, American flag) is straight out of the Ed Wood Guide To Set Design; Fassett and Tanner hold their first meeting at premises so gloomy and rundown it's doubtful the most glib estate agent could sell it for warehouse space; even Tanner's complete-with-swimming-pool pad in the country looks like it's been loaned out from a daytime soap opera. The violence is designed to incorporate as much weaponry as possible: from hands (Osterman's kung-fu skills – a throwback to *The Killer Elite*), to what's-to-hand (baseball bat), to actual hardware (crossbows, pistols, semi-automatic rifles). And there's plenty of gratuitous nudity.

This last is perhaps the most unfortunate aspect of *The Osterman Weekend*, lending credence to those who seek to label Peckinpah a misogynist. The female characters actually serve definite, if peripheral, functions: Cardone's gum-chewing wife (Cassie Yates) exudes an impassivity that provides a laconic counterpoint to all the macho posturing (symbolizing Peckinpah's attitude to the source material); Ali, cutting loose with the crossbow, gives the film its one genuine iconic moment; and Virginia Tremayne brings a belated degree of humanity to the proceedings. Easily the most pathetic character, scantily clad or coked to the gills throughout, it is her child-like docility in Tanner's mobile home (just before she, her husband and the Cardones are blown to pieces) that elevates the scene above a special effects set-piece. Stoned, frightened and confused, her face streaked with the residue of cocaine, she begins to sing a child's song: 'Jesus loves me, this I know / For the Bible tells me so.' There is such a naive simplicity to it, her voice faltering but sweet, that the scene no longer plays as an exciting escape attempt, but is instead overshadowed by an awful inevitability. When, seconds later, the explosion tears through the vehicle, Virginia's song continues on the soundtrack.

Her addiction (also a staple of exploitation cinema where such character traits are a shortcut to characterization) is subverted by Peckinpah into a metaphor for an audience's addiction to the visual image. Made at the end of his career, *The Osterman Weekend* found its largest audience through home video. Three decades earlier, the content of *The Rifleman* and *The Westerner* had been modulated by producers to attract family audiences. Now video was offering viewers undiluted slices of sex and violence in the comfort of their own homes. More strident regulations had yet to be applied to the medium. In Britain, the Video Recordings Act, the legislation at the centre of the infamous 'video nasties' tabloid hysteria, was still a year away. Peckinpah's meditation on video and televisual technology as a means of manipulation was incredibly timely.

Television is Tanner's whole life: he has achieved fame and financial rewards by using it to belittle the public figures who appear on his show. When he isn't watching playback of his latest victim, he's busy casting his eye over other shows, assessing the competition. No matter the unconscionable things Fassett does, there is a grim pleasure to be had in watching him use the medium against Tanner, the mass of hidden cameras turning Tanner's house into an ersatz studio. Tanner's favourite trick of cutting to close-ups of sweating politicos, caught out by his devious questioning, is mirrored in Fassett's manipulation of video screens to taunt him with images of things that are beyond his control or intervention: the death of the Tremaynes and Cardones, the hostage-taking of his wife and son.

And in this grim pleasure lies Peckinpah's final sneaky achievement, one that comes across even more effectively if the film is watched on video. Where *The Wild Bunch* and *Straw Dogs* are calculated to incite self-questioning of one's emotional response to what one sees on screen, *The Osterman Weekend* accuses its audience of complicity in exploitation purely because they have chosen to watch. 'Just another episode in this whole snuff soap opera we're all in' is how Fassett puts it. Tanner, who has more in common with the renegade agent than he would probably care to admit, airs a similar sentiment in his pre-recorded broadcast: 'As you know, television programmes are just a filler between attempts to steal your life. So if you want to save some [of it], switch off. It's simple. It's done with the hand and what's left of your own free will.'

In 1959, Michael Powell's controversial masterpiece *Peeping Tom* turned the movie camera on cinema-goers and found them as guilty as hell. *The Osterman Weekend*, for all its narrative incoherence and bargain-basement production values, points the television screen at the video generation and shows them the reflection of their own blank faces.

CHAPTER SEVEN
'DON'T PUT ME DOWN TOO DEEP'

It happens all too often – the critical reputation and public perception of an artist's work is dictated by misconceptions. It usually happens one of two ways: (a) a small section of the *oeuvre* is assumed to be typical of the whole, or (b) the artist's public persona is allowed to cloud their creative achievements. As an example of the former, take D H Lawrence, remembered principally for his frank depiction of sexuality (a reputation that rests almost solely on *Lady Chatterley's Lover*[1]), but who was also a poet, travel writer and essayist. As an example of the latter, take Ernest Hemingway, whose espousal of an unrepentantly macho lifestyle (drinking, womanising, bull fighting) masked his intelligence and sensitivity.

Sam Peckinpah is the victim of both types of this reverse-hagiography. Two criticisms in particular continue to be levelled at him by those unprepared to consider his films in the depth they demand: (a) that he was a director of violence, and (b) that he was a misogynist. Both accusations are trotted out with such predictable regularity that it is worth taking a few moments to address them.

VIOLENCE FOR VIOLENCE'S SAKE?

The Wild Bunch, Straw Dogs, The Getaway, Pat Garrett and Billy the Kid, Bring Me the Head of Alfredo Garcia, The Killer Elite, Cross of Iron and *The Osterman Weekend* all feature scenes of violence – or at least, scenes of violence deemed strong enough to merit an 18 certificate. That's eight films out of fourteen. *The Getaway* and *The Osterman Weekend* can easily be discounted. What they trade in is the kind of action scenes that are a staple of Hollywood product, certainly no more gory than anything you'd find in your average Jerry Bruckheimer production. *The Killer Elite*, too is action movie fare, and more comic-book in style.

This leaves five films – approximately a third of his output. Let's consider them individually.

The Wild Bunch's reputation as a violent film owes to its opening and closing sequences. The Starbuck shoot-out is between two groups of bad people: hardened criminals (the Bunch have yet to be humanized courtesy of their sojourn in Angel's village) and bounty hunters (licensed killers). By the end, all except Thornton and Sykes have come to a bad end, and even they are forced to accept that the codes they have lived by are outdated. In this respect, *The Wild Bunch* emerges as a very moral film. They who live by the gun (thieves, bounty hunters, revolutionaries) die by it. The anguished detail in which violence and the effects of violence are depicted also has to be considered in context of the film's geographical subtext. The incursion of American forces (both

Violent imagery in The Wild Bunch.

mercenary and military) into Mexico is a metaphor for Peckinpah's opposition to US involvement in Vietnam.

As mentioned in an earlier chapter, the Vietnam War cast its shadow over a decade of film production. *Straw Dogs* mirrors the social upheaval and public unrest engendered both in America and Europe. When the Cornish locals challenge David Sumner's masculinity, they make reference to footage of riots in America which they have seen on TV: 'Was you involved in it, sir? Did you take part?' In the climactic attack on Trencher's Farm, violence is used to demonstrate mistrust of America (David is routinely referred to as a 'bloody Yank') and as a metaphor for social division (in hounding Niles and killing Major Scott, Venner and co. are seen to turn on their own).

The staging of violent scenes as a statement of anti-violence has its most poignant exegesis in *Pat Garrett and Billy the Kid*. In Sheriff Baker's pointless and agonisingly protracted demise, in Billy dying just after an act of love, and in Garrett's assassination by the very forces he has sold himself out to, Peckinpah communicates an overwhelming sense of waste, of lives manipulated and destroyed by the combined efforts of politicians and businessmen. Of all Peckinpah's films, *Pat Garrett* offers his most nakedly emotional response to Vietnam.

Bring Me the Head of Alfredo Garcia treats violence as the end product of avarice. Like *The Wild Bunch*, a moral point is being made (the pattern here is Faust: sell your soul, you pay the price) but the morality is darker, more ambiguous. The geography is also concurrent with the other films – American incursion into a foreign territory – but the Mexico of *Alfredo Garcia* is a psychological landscape, a visualization of the protagonist's corrupted soul. Which isn't to say that Vietnam doesn't apply. Peckinpah, who sent numerous telegrams to the President in vociferous denunciation of the conflict, includes a satirical moment where Max, trousers round his ankles and attended to by a couple of hookers, studiously reads an issue of *Time* magazine with a craggy picture of Nixon on the cover.

If these films, however allegorically, are a reaction to Vietnam in particular, then *Cross of Iron* enunciates Peckinpah's hatred of war in general. As already stated, the violence is continual: inescapable. There is nothing metaphorical here. *Cross of Iron* is realistic and unflinching. It does not cop out or trade in heroics the way most war films do. Peckinpah strives for verisimilitude – and succeeds. And where war is concerned, the truth is ugly.

It is clear, then, that when Peckinpah uses violence in his films, he does so for a reason. Political and social issues motivated him, as they did most directors of that era. Narratively, violence occurs in his films when all other options have been exhausted by the characters. Nowhere is violence depicted without its aftermath – the suffering it causes, the dehumanizing effects on those who inflict it – being demonstrated in equally visceral terms. As Paul Seydor puts it, 'Peckinpah ruthlessly scorned the fatuous certainties and the pious hypocrisies rampant in our official culture, and he undermined every absolute he came across. When he cursed the human race, he was sweeping about it, but he always included himself. He did these things with an obsessiveness so wanton in its disregard for his own well-being and a fearlessness so breathtaking that it was impossible not to recognize in him the wounded romantic, the tragic idealist, the agonized believer' [2].

WAS PECKINPAH A MISOGYNIST?

Superficially, the evidence seems to be against him. Whores abound in all the westerns; such is Elita's profession (when not moonlighting as a lounge singer) in *Alfredo Garcia*. There are scenes of rape, attempted (*The Deadly Companions, Ride the High Country, Pat Garrett and Billy the Kid*) or actual (*Straw Dogs, Cross of Iron*). Women die ugly deaths (Teresa and Aurora in *The Wild Bunch*, Elita in *Alfredo Garcia*, Fassett's wife, Virginia Tremayne and Betty Cardone in *The Osterman Weekend*).

Again, let's consider the list point by point.

Whores. Their omnipresence in the westerns is succinctly accounted for by Richard Luck: 'The problem is that there weren't too many care workers or recruitment consultants operating on the American prairie in the 1880s, so Sam can only show women in their two principle frontier functions as housewives and as prostitutes' [3]. Not that Peckinpah ever gets judgmental. Quite the opposite: Kate in *Ride the High Country* is a successful businesswomen, running her establishment on her own terms; her girls are easily the most sympathetic characters in Coarsegold; Hildy in *The Ballad of Cable Hogue* is the romantic heroine and makes good by the end; the whores that Amos Dundee and Pike Bishop dally with are not so much emblematic of Peckinpah's attitude to women as the personification of his characters' psychological state of being. And let us not forget the female characters in the westerns who aren't whores: Elsa in *Ride the High Country*, Teresa and Linda in *Major Dundee*, Teresa and Aurora in *The Wild Bunch*.

Rape. Prevented or not, it's a repulsive subject and any director who chooses to depict it walks a tightrope. An argument exists as to whether it's *ever* necessary to depict rape on screen. Certainly, there are many films where its inclusion is needless. Any number of seedy exploitation directors use the rape/murder of the hero's wife, sister, daughter or girlfriend to kick-start a bout of gunplay-fuelled revenge. Michael Winner's objectionable opus *Death Wish* comes to mind.

Hildy, the romantic heroine of The Ballad of Cable Hogue: *a more lyrical side to Peckinpah.*

How one responds to the depiction of rape in Peckinpah's films depends upon one's politics and/or aesthetics. All this author can offer is the observation that when Peckinpah includes such scenes, it is for a genuine narrative purpose, or (as with Elita's almost-rape in *Alfredo Garcia*) a metaphorical reason. Similarly, the unwholesome designs Chisum's men have on Paco's daughter in *Pat Garrett* are indicative of their employer raping the land. The rape scene in *Cross of Iron* is in keeping with Peckinpah's aforementioned concern with showing the brutal reality of war. The high incidence of rape by invading or occupying forces in time of war – such as the atrocities inflicted on female civilians by the Russian troops who captured Berlin at the end of World War II – is a matter of historical fact.

The on-screen death of female characters. Given the amount of *male* characters who suffer painful and undignified deaths in Peckinpah's work, the point is hardly worth debating. Virginia and Betty's demise in *The Osterman Weekend* is in the explosion that also kills their husbands, and therefore does not indicate a singling out of women. The murder of Fassett's wife is a different matter, and frankly it *does* come across as gratuitous; nonetheless, it is the visual and visceral hook by which Peckinpah, from the outset, organizes an otherwise redundant espionage thriller into a meditation on perception, manipulation and audience complicity.

In *The Wild Bunch*, Teresa and Aurora are both shot by jealous men; likewise, Elita dies because of a set of circumstances engendered by a man (Bennie). As with Venner

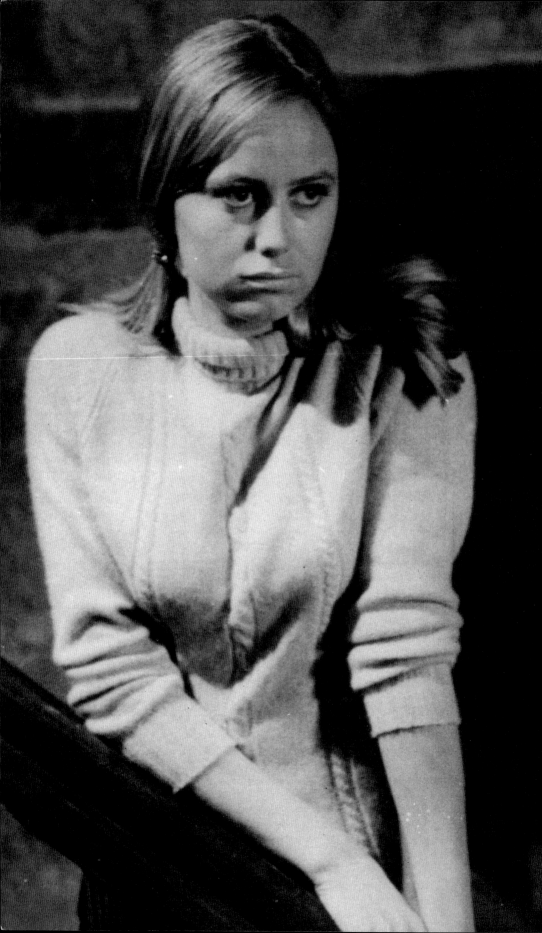

and Scutt's attack on Amy in *Straw Dogs*, these incidents owe to male dysfunctionalism. As previously stated, it is proof against the accusation of misogyny that Peckinpah can be honest about the wrongful way in which men can perceive women, and that he points the finger of guilt at members of his own sex.

It is true that he had troubled relationships with the women in his life, but this should not necessarily be carried over into an analysis of his achievements as an artist, nor can it be taken as evidence of misogynistic tendencies. With Peckinpah, as with many creative people, the fractiousness of his personal relationships owed to an artistic temperament.

Perhaps the best way to answer the critics of Peckinpah's work is by making reference to the work itself.

Consider the director in his romantic, humane and lyrical moments – in other words, the moments his critics persistently overlook:

Heck and Elsa reconciled at the end of *Ride the High Country*. Ryan and Linda reunited in *Major Dundee*. Hogue and Hildy's romance in *The Ballad of Cable Hogue* (the 'Butterfly Mornings' sequence is the very definition of heart-warming). The brief but tender reconciliation between Ace and Elvira in *Junior Bonner*. Doc and Carol's escape and romantic reaffirmation in *The Getaway*. Steiner's interlude with Eva in *Cross of Iron*. The positive aspects of friendship and honour between men can be found in virtually every film Peckinpah made.

And as we have seen – in the Bunch's last stand, in Sykes and Thornton's reluctant admission of change, in the deaths of Garrett, Billy and Sheriff Baker, in the death of the young Russian boy in *Cross of Iron* – even the darkest aspects of Peckinpah's vision elicit no less an emotional response.

It is Paul Seydor who deserves the last word: 'Peckinpah was certainly an artist who practised what he preached. Whatever else can be said of his films, they are a remarkable extension of the man. In them he transmuted the most important things he knew and felt and believed into some of the most beautiful works of film art ever made' [4].

Susan George as the beleagured Amy in Straw Dogs.

NOTES

Introduction: *Bloody Sam*

(1) Michael Reeves is the greatest 'what if...' story in cinema. After the low-budget features *The She-Beast* and *The Sorcerors*, he did for horror films with *Witchfinder General* (1968) what Peckinpah would do for the western with *The Wild Bunch*, wiping the board of genré cliches in order to present an intelligent examination of the motivation behind, and effects of, violence. Also like Peckinpah, he drew performances from his stars (Vincent Price and Ian Ogilvy) that are miles away from the lackadaisical, self-deprecating turns they tendered for other directors. Reeves died young, in 1969, and one can only wonder what he would have gone on to had he lived.

(2) Don Siegel is one of the unsung heroes of American cinema. His association with Peckinpah aside, he played a hugely important role in Clint Eastwood's formative years, casting him in *Coogan's Bluff, The Beguiled, Two Mules for Sister Sara, Dirty Harry* and *Escape from Alcatraz*. When Eastwood made his directorial debut with *Play Misty for Me*, he cast Siegel as a bartender so that he could have his mentor on set. Eastwood's finest film, *Unforgiven*, closes with the dedication 'to Sergio [Leone] and Don'.
Other notable Siegel films include John Wayne's swansong *The Shootist*, and the brilliant *Charley Varrick*.

(3) Richard Luck, *The Pocket Essential Sam Peckinpah* (Pocket Essentials, 2000), p.29.

(4) *The Hi-Lo Country* finally made it before the cameras in 1999, with Stephen Frears at the helm.

(5) The potential for *Hendry Jones* was huge. Had Brando's ego been kept in check, the world would have had a film by Stanley Kubrick from a script by Sam Peckinpah with one of the world's foremost method actors in the lead role. Sadly, with Kubrick dropped from the project as ignominiously as Peckinpah, Brando opted to direct himself. The result, retitled *One-Eyed Jacks*, was a mess: overblown and self-indulgent.

(6) *The Pocket Essential Sam Peckinpah*, p.10.

(7) The USC screening was instrumental in heightening public awareness of the film in an unmolested (or at least a *less* molested) version, and paved the way for its restoration for home video, undertaken by Roger Spottiswoode.

(8) Probably the right move as far as *King Kong* was concerned. Directed by John Guillerman (the man behind such average fare as *The Blue Max* and *The Bridge at Remagen*), *King Kong* was a flop of *Ishtar*-proportions. *Superman*, however, was the very definition of a blockbuster. Its director, Richard Donner, already a hot property thanks to *The Omen*, went on to helm the *Lethal Weapon* series.

Chapter One: *Redefining the Western*

(1) In collaboration as well as content. Lucien Ballard's peerless cinematography emboldens Peckinpah's vision. He had worked for Peckinpah in television and would go on to photograph *The Wild Bunch, The Ballad of Cable Hogue, Junior Bonner* and *The Getaway*.
L Q Jones, Warren Oates and John Davis Chandler (playing the less aesthetically pleasing Hammond brothers) all make their first appearance in a Peckinpah film, as does R G Armstrong. Oates and Armstrong had already worked with Peckinpah on episodes of *The Rifleman*. All would go on to star in *Major Dundee*.

(2) It says something about Peckinpah's contrariness that this dynamic (crucial to his later films) receives its first exposition in the form of such a motley bunch.

(3) This sense of equilibrium is also manifest when they rescue Elsa from the Hammonds, but is presented in a way that subtly emphasizes the difference between them. In working to the same end, Judd does it by the book (trusting to the decision of a miner's court) while Westrum takes the law into his own hands.

(4) The images of a broken mirror and a defeated, agonized figure on horseback having stones thrown at him are revisited, with an awesome clarity of vision, in *Pat Garrett and Billy the Kid*.

(5) David Weddle, *Sam Peckinpah: 'If They Move ... Kill 'Em'* (Faber & Faber, 1996), p.380.

(6) Earlier, when Potts leaves Dundee at the hospital, he worries that Dundee's identity will be discovered. 'You make an unlikely looking Mexican,' he says, in a wonderful in-joke. (Heston had played a Mexican seven years earlier in Orson Welles's *Touch of Evil*.)

(7) A more subtle comedic touch comes in the form of an in-joke. The town of Gila (namechecked but never visited) recalls the setting of *The Deadly Companions* – that Hogue, given a choice of walking out of the desert in either direction, opts for the less appealingly-named Dead Dog, is a nice thumbing of the nose to Charles FitzSimons. That most of the characters in *Cable Hogue* refer to Gila thereafter as 'Lizard' speaks for itself.

(8) The snakes serve two purposes: allegorical (garden of Eden/serpents that poison Man's paradise) and gastronomical. Cable's recipe for 'desert stew' calls for 'rattlesnake, ground squirrel, black gophers, horny toad, grasshoppers for seasoning, and pack rats and prairie dogs to fill in'.

(9) The contrapuntal note that this assertion introduces, because it does not become manifest until the closing scenes, achieves a measure of poignancy without detracting from the comedy.

(10) The technique was at the height of its popularity at the time. While certain films – Norman Jewison's *The Thomas Crown Affair* (1968) for example – are remembered for their split-screen sequences, it soon fell from grace with audiences, most directors using it in a heavy-handed fashion that showed it up for the gimmick it was.
Peckinpah, for whom the spatial and textural world of the film was sacrosanct, puts it to proper use to demonstrate the ardour of Hogue's plight, the passage of time and the endless, unchanging vistas of a desert that threatens to swallow him.

(11) Again, the presence of the word 'ballad' in the title is highly appropriate. Nowhere else in Peckinpah's cinema is music so keyed into the imagery, the soundtrack becoming an almost organic part of the narrative. Bowen and Taggart sing ditties of their own composition, firstly when they leave Hogue in the desert, and then when they stage their ill-advised burglary; Hogue and Joshua join in a chorus of 'I Can't Go Back to Memphis Anymore' as they make a trip into town together, riding in at nightfall on the same horse and singing away like a couple of good 'uns; 'Tomorrow is the song I sing', is reprised when Joshua leaves Hogue to run the way station by himself; Hogue and

Hildy's love duet, 'Butterfly Mornings', resurfaces after Hogue orders Bowen to inter Taggart, his desire for revenge supplanted by a yearning for the love he's lost.

(12) Hildy's re-entrance is *very* theatrical. Just check out the staging of it (as well as the use of costume) next time you watch the film.

Chapter Two: *The Wild Bunch*

(1) Quoted in Paul Seydor, *Peckinpah: the Western Films – A Reconsideration* (University of Illinois Press, 1980, new edition 1997), p.136.

(2) Pike's defence of Thornton is mirrored in an earlier scene where Thornton declares an affinity with the Bunch. Rounding on the posse he is forced to ride with, he sneers at them: 'You egg-suckin', chicken-stealin' gutter trash ... We're after *men* – and I wish to God I was with 'em!'

(3) Which is not to say Dutch's morality is inspired solely by Angel's capture: earlier, when Dutch describes Mapache as 'just another bandit grabbing all he can' and Pike quips, 'Like some others I could mention,' Dutch retorts, 'We ain't nothin' like him. We don't hang nobody. I hope some day these people here kick him and the rest of that scum like him into their graves.'
'We will,' Angel promises.

(4) *Peckinpah: the Western Films – A Reconsideration*, p.170.

(5) The scene in question is one whose narrative purpose – Mapache receiving confirmation of the train robbery from a telegraph office at a nearby town – is transformed by Peckinpah into a sweeping political set-piece. Mapache and his forces have comandeered their own train and, as they wait at the station for a young boy – perhaps only six or seven years old – to bring them the telegraph, they are shelled by Villa's forces. Villa is mentioned only in dialogue prior this, and only in the context of Mapache being compared to him: now, for the first and only time, Villa's might is made manifest and the reality of revolution comes home to Mapache. In a moment that is truly disturbing, Mapache's waning sense of conviction is reinstated as the boy, dressed in a soldier's uniform (a motif that will recur in *Cross of Iron*), gamely salutes, smiling up at him in adoration.
It should also be noted, in the interests of accuracy, that when the boy reappears as Pike's nemesis, he is not actually played by the same child actor. Peckinpah *had* intended him to be (and for this reason it is critically acceptable – as well as dramatically and structurally obligatory – to assume that the director's wishes had prevailed), but following the telegraph scene, the lad was inadvertently packed off home and therefore unavailable when the massacre at Agua Verde was filmed.

Chapter Three: *Relocating the Western*

(1) The tag-line on the poster – The Knock at the Door Meant the Birth of One Man and the Death of Seven Others – is not only the kind of hyperbole that plays right into the hands of Peckinpah's critics, but is patently wrong. Hedden, Venner, Scutt, Cawsey and Riddaway number five men. Hedden, although he sustains a cringe-inducing shotgun wound, is not seen to die. So even allowing for the killing of Major Scott, only five people buy it during the siege.

(2) The character is called George Magruder in the novel, his wife Louise. The film being the main consideration, the couple are referred to as David and Amy throughout the chapter.

(3) The order and manner in which David dispatches his antagonists is for the most part replicated faithfully from the novel. There are two exceptions. The boiling water specified by Williams is replaced, in a witty touch, by boiling whisky – presumably unable to reach a tap, David draws on the contents of his drinks cabinet. The bear trap (Venner's death in it easily the most stomach-churning part of the film) doesn't feature in the novel at all.

(4) *Junior Bonner* is also comparable with *The Ballad of Cable Hogue* for its use of split screen in the opening credits. Again, Peckinpah uses the process intelligently, creating a montage of juxtaposed images, the minutiae of rodeo riding set off against the transience of the lifestyle.

(5) For a man who made his name in television, and returned to the medium to make the splendid *Noon Wine* when he fell from grace with the movie moguls, this speaks volumes about his bloody-mindedness and obsession with the big screen.

(6) *Empire*, issue 62, August 1994.

(7) David Weddle, *Sam Peckinpah: 'If They Move ... Kill 'Em'*, p.515.

(8) David Weddle, *Sam Peckinpah: 'If They Move ... Kill 'Em'*, p.499.

(9) The character is called by Beynon in the novel. For the same reasons cited in note 2, he is referred to as Benyon throughout.

(10) Check out Joe Cabot's similar decor in Tarantino's *Reservoir Dogs*.

(11) Okay, so there's plenty of pump-action mayhem in the film, but Benyon and co. are hardly innocent bystanders. The victims in Thompson's novel *are*, and his descriptions of violence, while brief, are often thoroughly unnecessary.

(12) The influence of *Treasure of the Sierra Madre* can also be seen in *The Wild Bunch*. Walter Huston's character is a prototype for Sykes, whiskey and given to laughing in the face of adversity. The bandit chief declaring 'we don't have to show no stinking badges' is amusingly restaged in Herrera's 'you damned gringos' speech.

(13) David Weddle, *Sam Peckinpah: 'If They Move ... Kill 'Em'*, p.494.

Chapter Four: *Pat Garrett and Billy the Kid*

(1) Given that the studios pulled their usual stunt of removing the film from Peckinpah's hands and re-editing it, maybe 'delivered' is the wrong word. 'Was robbed of' is perhaps closer to the truth.
Pat Garrett and Billy the Kid exists in at least three versions. For the purposes of this book, reference is to the Warner Home Video release S050159, which is optimistically packaged as 'the director's cut'. It isn't really – it's a re-edit by Roger Spottiswoode, who was one of the original editing team, but is still missing a good many scenes. (Even the most fair weather Sam fan will have cause to wonder at the presence of Aurora Clavel's name in the credits, as Ida Garrett, when the lady in question is conspicuous by her absence.) The video is also panned-and-scanned, a format which denies the full glory of the director's compositions.

(2) John Chisum is a name probably most familiar from Andrew V McLaglen's eponymous 1970 film starring John Wayne. Its revisionist slant is predictably in keeping with Wayne's notorious right wing politics, sanctifying its subject and omitting any reference to him hiring Garrett to kill the Kid.

(3) Billy's bunch are introduced in their entirety in the credits sequence. Just as the chickens provide them with a shooting range, they will meet a similar fate at Garrett's hands.

(4) Robert M Utley's *Billy the Kid: A Short and Violent Life* (Touris Parke Paperbacks, 2000) provides an excellent frame of reference. It is interesting to note that Billy's smashing of the stock of Ollinger's shotgun after gunning him down with it is also a recorded fact; when Kristofferson does it in the movie, the act resembles a rock star smashing his guitar at the end of a gig.

(5) Compared to the Kid – whose motivations are self-evident, whose leisure interests (drinking and whoring) are commonplace and vulgar, and whose continual discourses about the old days deny himself the image of a man whose past is shrouded in mystery – Alias emerges as the more enigmatic character. Later, arriving at Billy's hideout (along with three others, who turn out to be bounty hunters), he gives his name and is promptly asked 'Alias what?' 'Alias anything you please,' he replies. He gives no account of himself, nor any reason why he wants to ride with the Kid. When the bounty hunters make their move, he is quick to demonstrate deadly accuracy with a knife; a skill surely not learned in a newspaper office.

(6) Such as – oh, dear – C W McCall's 'Convoy'.

(7) Curiously, this does not stop Garrett, towards the end of the film, from frolicking with no less than five prostitutes at the last saloon he visits before he catches up with the Kid. This comes after Rupert, the proprietor of said establishment, taunts him that last time

the Kid was there 'he had four – to get it up. And five to get it down.' (Garrett keeping up as well as catching up with him?)
If the scene comes across as gratuitous (and it does), the shot that follows – of Garrett walking downstairs next morning, rifle in one hand and saddle in the other, moving slowly and looking, frankly, shagged out – confirms that he is indeed past his prime.

(8) Lew Wallace (1827–1905) is prinicpally remembered as the author of *Ben Hur* (filmed in 1959 by William Wyler); the novel was published in 1880 while he was still governor of New Mexico.

(9) The topography of the search is confusing. It is often difficult to tell where Garrett is in relation to the Kid at any point in the film. Whether or not this owes to a structural flaw in the script, the resultant aimlessness of Garrett's odyssey comes across powerfully. He seems to do all he can to postpone the inevitable. His visit to Chisum's ranch is just another delaying tactic.

(10) Sallie Chisum and Billy the Kid were known to have had a brief relationship.

(11) The scene is Deke Thornton's argument with Harrigan after the massacre at Starbuck. The railroad boss asks why he should let Thornton go after Pike and Bunch. 'You might join them,' he says. 'You'd like that, wouldn't you?'
Thornton, guilt-ridden but not enamoured with the idea of going back to prison, replies, 'What I want and what I need are two different things.'

Chapter Five: *Cross of Iron*

(1) Another parallel with *Straw Dogs*, but whereas Sumner uses weaponry effectively but loses his humanity in the process, Stransky just shows himself up as an even more useless bastard than before.

(2) There is an odd but typically Peckinpah moment just prior to this: Stransky, racking his gun, realizes he has the drop on Steiner, but desists. It recalls Billy the Kid deliberately hesitating when he has a chance against Garrett; Doc McCoy lowering his gun when he could easily pump a round into the unconcious Rudy Butler; the bounty hunters who interrupt Bennie's impromptu exhumation of Alfredo Garcia knocking him out when they could kill him as effortlessly as they do Elita. All are instances where the opportunity of offing an antagonist is there for the taking. Spurning them gives an indication that Peckinpah's characters live for the fight as obsessively as their creator did.

Chapter Six: *The Later Films*

(1) The Russian is played by Helmut Dantine, one of the film's producers. He gets shot in the head, slow motion lovingly protracting the moment. Tells you something, doesn't it?

Chapter Seven: *'Don't put me down too deep'*

(1) The controversy surrounding the novel uses the sexual aspects as something of a smokescreen. Like Peckinpah's *Cross of Iron*, what it's really about is class.

(2) Paul Seydor, *Peckinpah: the Western Films – A Reconsideration* (introduction).

(3) Richard Luck, *The Pocket Essential Sam Peckinpah*, p.14.

(4) *Peckinpah: the Western Films – A Reconsideration*, p.367–368.

SELECTED BIBLIOGRAPHY

The author is indebted to the following
publications.

Sam Peckinpah: 'If they Move ... Kill 'em' by
David Weddle, Faber & Faber, 1996.

*Peckinpah: The Western Films – A
Reconsideration* by Paul Seydor, University of
Illinois Press, 1980, new edition 1997.

The Pocket Essential Sam Peckinpah by
Richard Luck, Pocket Essentials, 2000.

Billy the Kid: A Short and Violent Life by
Robert M Utley, Touris Parkes Paperbacks,
2000.

A Thousand Miles From Nowhere by Graham
Coster, Penguin, 1995.

'The Wild Man', an article by Kim Newman,
Empire issue 62, August 1994.

ACKNOWLEDGEMENTS

My thanks to the following for permission to
quote from copyright material: Faber and
Faber for *Sam Peckinpah: 'If They Move ...
Kill 'Em'* by David Weddle. The University of
Illinois Press for *Peckinpah: the Western Films
– A Reconsideration* by Paul Seydor. Pocket
Essentials for *The Pocket Essential Sam
Peckinpah* by Richard Luck. *Empire* for an
excerpt from the article 'The Wild Man' by
Kim Newman.

Thanks to Tina Persaud at B T Batsford for
giving me the go-ahead, and to Joel Finler for
providing illustrative material.

On a personal note, a mention in dispatches to
the following: my Mother and Father, Andy
Addison, Viv and Dennis Apple, Sue Challand,
Alison Davies, Sarah Evans, Martin and
Glenda Holroyd, Marie Horry, Mandy Morrell,
Carole Parnell, Liz Richards, Paul Rowe, Alex
Thompson and Tony Wass. Thanks to Patience
Davenport and Chris Wells for the loan of
research materials.

INDEX

Italics denote picture/illustration